Mythic Texas
Essays on the State and Its People

Bryan Woolley

Republic of Texas Press

Library of Congress Cataloging-in-Publication Data

Woolley, Bryan.
   Mythic Texas: essays on the state and its people / Bryan Woolley.
      p. cm.
   Includes bibliographical references and index.
   ISBN 1-55622-696-9 (pbk.)
   1. Texas—Description and travel. 2. Texas—History Anecdotes.
   3. Texas—Biography Anecdotes I. Title.
   F386.W86   1999
   976.4—dc21   99-39123
                                                                          CIP

© 2000, Bryan Woolley
All Rights Reserved

Republic of Texas Press is an imprint of Wordware Publishing, Inc.
No part of this book may be reproduced in any form or by
any means without permission in writing from
Wordware Publishing, Inc.

Printed in the United States of America

ISBN 1-55622-696-9
10 9 8 7 6 5 4 3 2 1
9908

Nearly all the pieces in this book appeared first in *The Dallas Morning News*, some of them in a slightly different form. They are reprinted here with permission.

All inquiries for volume purchases of this book should be addressed to Wordware Publishing, Inc., at 2320 Los Rios Boulevard, Plano, Texas 75074. Telephone inquiries may be made by calling:
(972) 423-0090

To the memory of
BARRY SCOBEE
who taught the joys of journalism
to a boy

Books by Bryan Woolley

Nonfiction
Mythic Texas
Generations
The Bride Wore Crimson
The Edge of the West
Where Texas Meets the Sea
The Time of My Life
We Be Here When the Morning Comes

Fiction
Sam Bass
November 22
Time and Place
Some Sweet Day

Contents

Introduction vii

Part I—Mythic Texas
A Legend Runs Through It 3
Cattle Proud 15
Serving the Lone Star 23
The Leather Throne 33
The Kingdom and the Fading Glory 39
The Tower of Dreams 48
Shooting Texas 53
A Whole Other Country 60

Part II—Texas Our Texas, Some People and Places
The Pavarotti of the Plains 69
Medicine Ball Man 77
Weeping Mary 82
A Postcard from the Past 89
The Pride of Cross Plains 93
The Star Party 99
In a League of His Own 104
The Sacred Harp 109
The Last of the Big Four 115
The Dog Woman 125
In All the Wrong Places 129
The Limpia Creek Hat Company 133
Clyde's Sister 137
Clyde's Sister: A Sequel 143

Contents

The Chicken Dance	147
Laos on the Prairie	152
Tumbleweed Smith	161
When Hollywood Came to Marfa	165
The Last Bell	170
Marker Man	176
FDHS Reunion	181
Country Cum Laude	184
The Death of the Burro	191
The Adventure of the Eccentric Sherlockians	196
Remembering the 761st	203
The Red Menace	211
Concordia	216
The High Frontier	221
Morris Neal's Handy Hamburgers	228
Getting It Wrong: A Memory	234
Preacher Men	237
Rattler Roundup	243
Three Little Towns	250
La Vida del Charro	261
Fort Davis Christmas	268
Index	275

Introduction

Longhorn cattle, ranchers, and cowboys. Rangers and outlaws. Oil wells and millionaires. The Alamo. All these symbols sprang from the history, culture, and geography of Texas. But some have evolved into stereotypes, often with the help of Hollywood and self-promoting "professional Texans" who distort the truth for their own purposes, which are usually commercial.

In the spring of 1998, I set out to re-examine some of the symbols that over the course of a century or more have come to represent Texas in the world's mind. I wanted to know whether they still stand for anything real, or are they relics of a bygone time, only shadows with no substance behind them anymore? Does the Texas that inspired its famous symbols still exist?

Halfway through the six months I spent traveling, interviewing, and writing these eight essays for *The Dallas Morning News*, I began to notice that an elegiac tone kept creeping into them. The Texas that inspired its symbols, I realized, is not only changing, it's disappearing faster than most of us can comprehend.

But while the landscape around them is being swallowed with breathtaking speed into the homogenized, mass-produced America of franchise food joints, shopping malls, pretentious-but-ugly suburban architecture, and bumper-to-bumper expressways, I found that Texas people somehow remain a uniquely colorful and eccentric tribe.

The second, and longer, section of this book is about them.

During my almost thirty years as a journalist in Texas, it has been my job and my joy to roam the state from top to bottom and from side to side and hear the stories of hundreds

Introduction

of Texans of all races, backgrounds, and regions. No matter what were the circumstances of their lives in the moments that I encountered them, nearly all possessed two qualities in greater abundance than I have found in the inhabitants of any other place: humor and hope.

They're the traits that have always made Texans the heroes and heroines of their own myth.

Bryan Woolley
Dallas

Part I
Mythic Texas

A Legend Runs Through It
The Pecos River

*I*n Zane Grey's classic novel *West of the Pecos,* young pioneer heroine Terrill Lambeth gets her first look at the river and cries: "Oh, Dad! Take me back! This dreadful Pecos can never be home!"

"The place was desolate, gray and lonely," Grey writes, "an utter solitude, uninhabited even by beasts of the hills or fowls of the air."

But, plucky lass that she is, Terrill stays. The desolate Pecos becomes her home, where she lives happily ever after with a heroic cowboy whose name is... Pecos.

Writers of Western novels and makers of Western movies have always liked the name. "Pecos" sounds cowboy. Texan. And geography and history have made the river a worthy setting for tales of frontier valor and desperation.

The Spanish conquistadors, who saw the Pecos and its blistering Chihuahuan Desert in the sixteenth century, named the region *el despoblado,* the uninhabited place. Three hundred years later, pioneer cattleman Charles Goodnight cursed it as "the graveyard of the cowman's hopes," and buffalo hunters claimed that when a bad man dies, his soul goes either to hell or the Pecos.

Despite its rigors, people have found reason to live along its banks. And the lives of its inhabitants—the Comanches,

Part II—Texas, Our Texas: Some People and Places

Kiowas, and Apaches, the Mexican bandits, Texas Rangers, soldiers and stagecoach drivers, the cattlemen and cowboys, rustlers and nesters, the holdup men and treasure hunters, the women driven insane by loneliness and the incessant wind—have matched the toughness of their land and made their terrible stream the mythic river of the mythic West.

You wouldn't think it from seeing the Pecos now. For several decades, dams and irrigation farming have reduced it to a vestige of its frontier self, a mere trickle in places, no longer a killer of men and destroyer of dreams. Truckers and travelers crossing its bridges barely notice it.

"It's hard to believe it's the same stream," says Patrick Dearen of Midland, who has written four books about the Pecos. "Now it's shallow, it's smothered in salt cedars, it's polluted with oil. It's hardly a river anymore. You have to look deep to find the sweat and blood of the cowhands and immigrants and pioneers who saw in it a challenging obstacle."

Living along the Pecos still requires a certain strength, stamina, and sense of humor. If, as they say, Texas ain't for amateurs, the Pecos is strictly for the hardiest professionals. Even for them, unless they were born there, life on the river is an acquired taste.

When Elgin "Punk" Jones, a cowboy turned oil-field worker, moved his wife, Mary Belle, and their babies to the east bank of the river forty-five years ago, she saw it as Terrill Lambeth did:

"I looked all around and said, 'My God, Punk, how long are we going to stay here?' And he said, 'Just till we get enough money to get somewhere else.' I cried for three years. The wind and the dust would blow, and I would mop, and I would cry.

"Well, we're still here. I got used to the quiet and the solitude. Now I couldn't imagine living anywhere else."

4

A Legend Runs Through It

The Pecos begins as a clear mountain stream in the Sangre del Cristo Mountains northeast of Santa Fe, N.M. Trout live in its cold waters there. As it flows southward toward its rendezvous with the Rio Grande 900 miles away, it nourishes the fields of Hispanic villages and Indian pueblos and the cattle of Anglo ranchers, good water in a thirsty land.

Then just above the Texas border it begins to change. Gradually it loses its rocky bottom and flows instead through a soft adobe soil laden with alkali. By the time it crosses into Texas for the second half of its journey, it has left behind all its mountains and coolness and sweetness and has entered a flat, hellish desert of mesquite and greasewood. Buzzards soar above the flat, torrid land. Dust devils dance across the plain like small, brown tornadoes. Oil well pump jacks dot the landscape, many of them leaking. Quicksand forms below the river's banks, and its water turns too salty for man or beast to drink.

A century and more ago, when the Anglos arrived to stay, the desolate Pecos was a place of cattle stampedes, Indian massacres, robberies, ghosts, lethal thirst, and madness. Its name became a verb: to "Pecos" a man was to murder him and throw his body into the river.

"In those days, the Pecos was a very swift, turbulent stream with extremely steep banks and lots of quicksand," says Mr. Dearen. "Between the New Mexico line and the Rio Grande there was only a handful of places where you could cross it safely."

The first to cross it regularly were the Comanches, on their journeys from the High Plains to plunder the ranches and villages of northern Mexico. In the early 1850s, immigrants crossed it to search for wealth in the California gold fields. So did Indian-fighting soldiers, marching to their West Texas forts, and stagecoaches carrying passengers and the mail from San Antonio to San Diego.

The river was a major hazard for them all. Along the seventy- nine-mile stretch of waterless desert between the Middle

Part II—Texas, Our Texas: Some People and Places

Concho River and the Pecos, many died before they even reached its banks. One immigrant party drank the blood of its livestock to survive.

In 1866 Charles Goodnight and Oliver Loving drove a herd of longhorns from near San Angelo, Texas, to Fort Sumner, N.M., opening the Goodnight-Loving Trail. They lost one hundred head to stampede and quicksand at Horsehead Crossing on the Pecos. But over the next decade they drove 250,000 cattle across the river, expanded the range of the longhorn as far north as Montana, and provided the inspiration for Larry McMurtry's epic *Lonesome Dove*.

"In their day, the river was 50 to 100 feet wide," says Mr. Dearen. "During floods it spread to a mile. When the water receded, it left lakes of alkali water, a brine that is deadly to cattle. One early traveler said that at Horsehead Crossing you could step from one steer carcass to another for a square mile without touching the ground."

Over time, stories of hardships on the Pecos got enlarged into legends and tall tales. Rumor had it that beleaguered Spaniards had buried treasure in the desert, and that ghosts of massacred immigrants roamed the sand dunes near Monahans. A bigger-than-life cowboy called Pecos Bill became a nationally popular hero. As an infant, it was said, Bill fell out of his family's wagon as it was crossing the Pecos. He was reared by coyotes, fed his horse barbed wire, rode tornadoes, and used a prickly pear pad for a napkin.

Those who popularized the tales claimed Bill was an authentic folk hero invented by cowboys swapping yarns around their campfires. But Paul Patterson, an eighty-nine-year-old cowboy, teacher, and poet who has lived along the river most of his life, doesn't think so.

"Cowboys never thought much of Pecos Bill, because he could do anything without putting a strain on himself," he says. "That doesn't ring true with people in this country. You can't do anything here without straining yourself. Pecos Bill was a fabrication. Some writer made him up."

A Legend Runs Through It

Yet libraries and bookstores still offer children's books, music CDs, and video cartoons, written by authors and songwriters in Connecticut and California, celebrating Bill's exploits.

Early in the twentieth century, as the frontier was fading, the inhabitants of the Pecos became models for the heroes and heroines of Zane Grey and other writers of Western pulp magazine stories and novels. A few years later Hollywood discovered the Pecos and cranked out such B movies as *The Pecos Kid* (Fred Kohler Jr., 1935), *King of the Pecos* (John Wayne, 1936), *The Stranger From Pecos* (Johnny Mack Brown, 1940), and *Robin Hood of the Pecos* (Roy Rogers, 1941).

Of course, none of them had anything to do with the real Pecos.

"The Pecos River holds a fascination for people," says Mr. Patterson, "unless they have to stop and camp and drink the water."

Skeet Jones, a son of Punk and Mary Belle, claims that after a coyote drinks Pecos River water, he immediately licks his behind to get the bad taste out of his mouth.

"It's just terrible," says Mr. Patterson. "It sears up your taste buds. One time when I was working on a ranch between where Rankin and Iraan are now, I broke the water jug. After a while, the fellow I was working with said, 'I just got to have some water. I can't do without it any longer.' He took two or three swigs of the Pecos, and he could do without water from then on."

Mr. Patterson now lives in the city of Pecos, a few miles west of the river. At some 12,000 population, it's the largest Texas town along the stream. Pecos was the site of the world's first rodeo in 1883, an event still repeated every Fourth of July. In the hot, fertile fields that surround the town grow the

Part II—Texas, Our Texas: Some People and Places

world's juiciest, sweetest cantaloupes. In a small park near the center of town, gunfighter Clay Allison (1840-87) lies buried.

Mr. Allison didn't die the Western gunman's traditional death. He was driving a wagonload of supplies from Pecos back to his ranch one day after lingering too long in a saloon. He fell off the wagon, and a wheel rolled over his head. "Gentleman and Gunfighter," his wooden grave marker says. "R.I.P."

To Mr. Patterson, such people are far more interesting than the superhuman characters that Hollywood and the novelists invented. "Take Gid Redding," he says. "When I was a young cowboy, I batched a winter with old Gid. He was a top hand, and he could take the snakes out of the meanest bronc. I thought the world of Gid Redding. Well, old Gid, he became the last horseback bank robber in the United States. He robbed the banks at Hatch and Santa Rosa, N.M. They say old Gid had seven lawyers at his trial but did all the talking himself."

In 1931, not long after his winter with Gid Redding, Mr. Patterson—who cowboyed "four full years, seven full summers and a lot of weekends"—took the $22 his boss owed him and hightailed it to Alpine, where he enrolled in Sul Ross State Teachers College. "What gave me the burning yearning for learning," he says, "was a big old gray horse that jobbed my head into the hard side of a hill. When I came to, I was wanting to do something else."

To finance his education, Mr. Patterson worked in a boardinghouse fourteen hours a day, cooking, slopping hogs, and cleaning rooms. "I was envious of old Gid," he says, "up there in New Mexico, robbing banks, doing what he wanted to do, and doing it on horseback."

For the rest of his working life, Mr. Patterson taught journalism, Spanish, history, and civics in the Trans-Pecos towns of Marfa, Sanderson, Crane, and Sierra Blanca, sometimes cowboying summers and weekends. "I was sort of a miscellaneous man," he says.

A Legend Runs Through It

In Crane, one of his students was Elmer Kelton, now one of the best living practitioners of the Western novel. In Sanderson, Mr. Patterson courted and married another young teacher, who had grown up in the East Texas Piney Woods. "When she moved to the Pecos country, she cried for two days and nights," Mr. Patterson says. "It was thirty miles between towns and farther than that between trees. But she learned to love it."

The origin of the word "Pecos," he says, is unknown. He thinks it may come from the Spanish *pecoso,* which means "freckled." "I figure the old Spaniards must have seen the sun glinting off the water and were reminded of freckles," he says.

He pauses, trying to remember something. "Sometimes my train of thought derails," he says, "and I never catch the next one out."

Then he says: "You know, in the old days, when the men were off working cattle, a lot of women would be left by themselves for long periods. Some of them would lose touch with reality and lose their minds. Some of them were too crazy to know daylight from dark."

Lloyd Goodrich, a bachelor, lives on the land his grandfather homesteaded in 1906, and in the same weathered frame house. Sometimes he raises alfalfa in a field across the road. His farm is near Mentone, around a bend in the road from Mary Belle and Punk Jones. Mentone is the only town in Loving County. About twenty people reside there. About a hundred live in the entire county. That averages out to seven square miles per person, which makes Loving the most sparsely populated county in the lower forty-eight states.

"There's not much in Mentone now except the courthouse," Mr. Goodrich says. "You never know whether the damned café is going to be open or not since Newt Keene died. I don't even know who has it now. I go to Mentone maybe

Part II—Texas, Our Texas: Some People and Places

twice a week to get the mail, and that's about it anymore. I don't circulate much. Hell, there's nobody to circulate *with!*"

Loving County lacks more than people. There's no school and no church. There's no cemetery. The last person laid to rest in the county was a cowboy who was dragged to death by his horse in 1929. He was buried on the lone prairie. Loving County's dead go to Kermit and Pecos for burial now. There are four hundred oil leases, which make Loving a wealthy county, but drinking water must be trucked in. Like people all along the Pecos, Loving County residents talk a lot about water and the lack of it.

"Hell, no, it's not as dry as it was in the fifties," Mr. Goodrich is saying. "Who told you that? It's nowhere close. In 1956 it rained on September 9, and it didn't rain again for eighteen months. Not a goddamn drop. Now that was *dry!*"

The scarcity of water in the Pecos country inspired a sixteen-year-long court battle in which Texas accused New Mexico of taking more than its share from the river. In 1988 the U.S. Supreme Court agreed. It ordered New Mexico to pay $14 million in damages.

"The Texas attorney general's office took $200,000 off the top for legal fees," Mr. Goodrich says. "The rest is in Treasury accounts, and the interest on it is divided among the seven water districts in the Red Bluff Water Control District. They spend most of it on legal fees. Damned lawyers. They're worse than the salt cedars."

Salt cedar is a scrubby bush introduced to the Pecos many years ago. It was supposed to reduce soil erosion. Now the riverbanks are choked with it. The line of dusty green salt cedar that runs across the desert like a scar is how you tell where the river is. An acre of it sucks up a million gallons of water a year.

Red Bluff, built in the 1930s, is the only reservoir on the Pecos in Texas. It's just south of the New Mexico line. Mr. Goodrich and other farmers irrigate out of canals from the reservoir.

A Legend Runs Through It

"Trouble is, Red Bluff has only been full one time," Mr. Goodrich says. "The problem with farming along this river is that we don't have a reliable water supply. You might have water for six or seven years, then you might not have any for two years running. The trick is, you've got to get big enough or be small enough. It's the guys in between that are hurting. I've been out here a long time. I've learned I don't have to be rich. All I have to do is survive."

Mr. Goodrich, who is fifty-eight, can recall a time of less mesquite on the land and fewer salt cedars along the river. "I remember what it used to be when there was a lot of farming going on. I remember the smell of green alfalfa fields. Some people older than me remember cottonwood trees along all the ditch banks, and the river running most of the summer."

Now he's all that remains. He's the only farmer left in Loving County.

The Girvin Social Club has a rusty sheet-iron roof and, inside, walls decorated with cow and sheep skulls, neon beer signs, and old license plates. There's a pool table in the back room and a wood burning stove in the front. The owner is Walter Bohanan. His customers are cowboys, oil-field hands, and a few welders who have been imported to install a new boiler at a nearby West Texas Utilities plant.

Near the bar, six or eight flyswatters hang from a nail. Mr. Bohanan explains the reason for so many: "It's a game we play. You get a flyswatter and sit down at a table with three or four other fellows. Whenever you see a fly, you swat it and rake it into your pile. When it's time for another round, the fellow with the fewest dead flies has to buy. Then you rake them off on the floor and start over. You have to watch some of these guys, though. When nobody's looking, they'll reach down and pick up some of the dead flies and put them back on the table."

Part II—Texas, Our Texas: Some People and Places

The Girvin Social Club has been open since 1956. Mr. Bohanan, who also operates an oil-field pump and supply business near McCamey, took it over in January 1998. More and more, he says, he conducts his other business from his table at the club. "This place," he says, "is an oasis in the middle of nowhere."

It's also all there is to Girvin, except the home of Burl and Frankie Pringle, out behind the club. The Pringles, Girvin's only residents, raise goats. Twenty or thirty of them move about their pens, constantly in search of food. There's also a llama, a rooster, a friendly German shepherd named Fancy, and another smaller dog.

Fourteen people lived in Girvin when the Pringles moved there in 1984. "Then the oil fields slowed down and some of them had to pursue jobs elsewhere," Mr. Pringle says.

"The rest died off," Mrs. Pringle says.

⊱ ★ ⊰

South of Girvin the land begins to change. The mesquite and greasewood are joined by juniper, yucca, and cenizo. The flat desert gradually yields to rocky hills and mesas, the range of goats and sheep.

On October 28, 1926, the fabled Yates Oil Field blew in, revealing that the barren rocks covered an ocean of oil. More than a billion barrels have been pumped out of the field since then, and it's still going strong.

Iraan, a little town kept prosperous by the Marathon Oil Co., which operates the Yates Field, was named for Ira and Ann Yates, owners of the land on which the discovery was made. The town has a small museum full of fossils and oil field and ranching memorabilia. Edna Brooks, who is ninety-three, runs it. She and her husband ranched for many years along the Pecos, she says. She tells visitors of cows stuck in quicksand, of horses swimming in the swift current, of floods rising thirty-six inches deep into her house, of her sister dying of a heart attack

A Legend Runs Through It

as a result. "It was just too much of a shock to her, seeing the river like that," she says. "But I wouldn't take any of it back. I wouldn't change it. I'd go back and live it again the same way."

A few miles outside the town, Dickie Dell Ferro has turned her grandfather's beautiful old house on the Parker Ranch into a bed and breakfast.

When he settled the land in 1907, Oliver Wendell Parker lived in a two-room cabin. When the Yates Field came in, he leased his land for drilling and built the big two-story house with the red tile roof. Ten years ago, his ranch was divided among his heirs, and Ms. Ferro got the part with the house on it. She runs a few cattle and has four rooms to let, and a rental house where a writer is living, working on a novel.

In the fall, hunters come for the white-tailed deer, which live on the flats, and the mule deer, which live in the hills. Orioles, cardinals, tanagers, wrens, warblers, flycatchers, hummingbirds, and wild turkeys sing a chaotic chorus in the yard shrubbery and the brush beyond. Near the old wooden windmill in the pasture, buzzards hunch over a dead javalina.

"Peace and quiet we've got, which in the world today is about the rarest thing there is," says the writer, Meredith Rolley.

"I've lived in Odessa, Mexico, Wichita Falls, Lubbock, and San Angelo, but this was always home to me," says Ms. Ferro. "I never liked anyplace except here. This is where I always wanted to be."

Toward its end, the Pecos widens and flows between majestic limestone cliffs several hundred feet high, looking again like a real river. It passes under the High Bridge on U.S. 90, which replaced a lower bridge wiped out by the flood of 1954, when the river rose to ninety-six feet.

It flows by Langtry (population about twenty), where Judge Roy Bean ruled as "the law west of the Pecos." Strangers

13

Part II—Texas, Our Texas: Some People and Places

from the East would step off trains there to drink beer at Judge Bean's Jersey Lilly Saloon and buy a round for his pet bear, Bruno. With a six-shooter and a seldom-consulted volume of the laws of Texas, Judge Bean brought an eccentric but somehow appropriate brand of justice to the wild and woolly Pecos of the 1880s and '90s.

The woman at the Texas Travel Information Center near the old saloon says 80,000 people a year drop in to watch a video about the old man and pick up a road map.

Then the river moves on past Comstock, a village not quite so small, and finally loses itself in the Rio Grande and Lake Amistad.

Amistad dam, built by the federal government in 1969, backed up the Pecos for eighteen miles and inundated hundreds of caves where the first human inhabitants of the region lived 3,000 to 4,000 years ago. On the walls of their shelters they painted beautiful and mysterious images of beasts and shamans, indecipherable records of their deeds or dreams.

Some two hundred fifty painted caves remain, but the humidity created by the lake eventually will erase them all.

At Seminole Canyon State Park, where a few of the shelters are open to visitors, Robert Slaton, an employee, is talking about water. "We're due another flood," he says. "We had a flood in '32. We had a flood in '54. We had one in '74. We haven't had one since. So we're due one. And we need it. We need something to break this drought. We're looking at five years of drought so far. Since '92."

After living in their shelters for thousands of years, the Pecos River cave dwellers left. Nobody knows where they went. Nobody knows why. Maybe they couldn't take it anymore.

Cattle Proud
The Longhorn

*E*ven if you've never seen him before, Amigo Yates looks familiar. Reddish hair. Big brown eyes. He's eleven years old, weighs maybe 1,300 pounds. His horns measure 103 inches from tip to tip and spiral outward in what old-time cowmen call a "Texas twist."

Amigo Yates is a longhorn steer, a champion of his kind, a classic. He could be the model for the longhorn that shows up everywhere in Texas on signs, billboards, TV commercials, menus, company stationery, business cards, and calendars.

In Dallas, at least thirty-five businesses named Longhorn sell cars, copiers, fences, loans, wheel alignments, drywall, foundation repairs, gaskets, motorcycles, liquor, barbecue, insurance, guitars, pet supplies, pipe, tires, tours. Fort Worth —Cowtown—has twenty-three. Across Texas, such longhorn enterprises number in the hundreds, maybe thousands. There's a football team in Austin called the Longhorns.

The longhorn is the totem of Texas, its sacred beast, its quintessential symbol. The reason: A few generations ago, the longhorn lifted the state from the ruin of war, then became the foundation of a vast economic empire. Because of the longhorn, the horseback laborer who tended him became America's most popular folk hero. Because of the longhorn, the world thinks of Texas the way it does.

Part II—Texas, Our Texas: Some People and Places

All of which means nothing to Amigo Yates, standing under the broiling sun in a pasture outside Tuscola, a tiny town south of Abilene. He sees his owner, Fayette Yates, roll down the dusty ranch road in a truck. He thinks maybe Mr. Yates is bringing him something to eat. A small summer afternoon treat. He trots toward the truck.

"Nothing for you," Mr. Yates tells him. "You're greedy."

Amigo Yates hangs around awhile anyway, huffing, still hoping, then moves slowly off toward the trees.

Mr. Yates takes off his gimme cap, wipes the sweat from his thinning white hair, and gazes admiringly after the steer. "Ain't he nice?" he says. "Real full-blood longhorns like him are getting pretty scarce. I doubt that there's 3,000 or 4,000 of them in the United States."

Well, it depends on whom you ask.

Tim Miller of Great Bend, Kansas, president of the Texas Longhorn Breeders Association of America, disagrees with Mr. Yates. The longhorn is doing just fine, he says. The great-horned beast, believed to be near extinction only fifty years ago, now numbers in the tens of thousands.

"When our association started in 1964, there were only 1,400 longhorn cattle left in the world," Mr. Miller says. "But since then we've registered 250,000 head. And those are only the best animals. There are thousands more that their owners don't consider fine enough to register. But they're real longhorns, too. Today's longhorn is the same animal that was going up the trails in the 1860s and '70s. They're just not slab-sided and rail-thin like they were then. They're taken care of now."

Mr. Yates, whose grandfather Ira drove thousands of longhorns up the Chisholm and other great cattle trails, scoffs at Mr. Miller's optimism: "One of them TLBAA dudes asked me, 'How long you been in the cattle business?' I said, 'Going on seventy-six years.' I was born to it. I've ate more cattle than them sumbitches have ever seen." He tucks his thumbs into the pockets of his jeans and leans back into a high-pitched laugh that almost brings tears. "So I know a real longhorn when I see one. Them cattle they're calling longhorns ain't longhorns. Their heads ain't right, their bodies ain't right, their necks ain't right, their tails ain't right. I went to their so-called world longhorn show in Fort Worth, and what I saw there made me sick."

"The Hereford, the Angus, and all other breeds were created by man, through selective breeding," Mr. Miller says. "The Texas longhorn is the result of natural selection and survival of the fittest. It's a product of evolution. It's the only cattle breed in this country that nature created."

Its evolution began in 1493, when Columbus brought a load of cattle from Spain to Santo Domingo on his second voyage to the New World. Two centuries later, Franciscan friars drove cattle across the Rio Grande into Texas to provide beef for their missions. Over the years, some of the animals strayed or were chased away by Indians. They became wild animals, breeding in the wilderness.

By the 1830s, when English-speaking settlers were spreading over the newly independent Republic of Texas, wild cattle roamed all the country from the Rio Grande north to the Red River and between the Sabine and the Brazos rivers. Some of the English breed cattle brought by the Anglos strayed or were driven into the brush as the Spanish cattle had been. Others escaped during cattle raids that the Texans and the Mexicans constantly inflicted upon one another's ranches. All contributed to the bloodlines of the wild kind. Only the smart and the strong could survive the rigors of the harsh Texas wilderness and weather. Over time they developed into a new type of cattle: the Texas longhorn, a breed as tough as the land that spawned it.

"They do so well on their own that people don't have to mess with them," says Walter Schreiner, whose family has

Part II—Texas, Our Texas: Some People and Places

raised longhorns for four generations on the YO Ranch near Mountain Home, Texas. The YO's herd of 1,500 is the largest in the world. "They live a long time. They produce a calf every year. They have very strong mothering instincts and will gang up to protect their calves from coyotes and panthers. They can walk a long way to water. They can survive on marginal land during a drought. They'll eat out of the trees like a deer. When it gets real, real dry, they'll even eat cactus."

The YO's cattle are docile, but the old wild ones were no more domestic than the buffalo and antelope that shared the prairie with them. Prince Carl von Solms-Braunfels, founder of New Braunfels, reported that his German colonists hunted longhorns like big game, but they were very hard to kill.

Before the Civil War, Texans drove herds to New Orleans and other Mississippi River ports for shipment to the East by boat, and up the Shawnee Trail, through Dallas and the Indian Territory, to towns in Missouri. But longhorns spread tick fever—to which they themselves were immune—to other cattle and jumped fences and bred with farmers' stock along the way. Gun-toting Missourians began turning away Texas drovers at their border.

A few years later Texan troops returned from four years of civil war to find the old Cotton Kingdom dead, nearly all their neighbors broke, and five million wild cattle roaming the land, free of charge to anyone who could catch them.

But no railroads were in Texas yet. There was still no profitable way to get the cattle to urban markets in the North and East.

A young Illinois entrepreneur named Joseph McCoy created the solution. At Abilene, Kansas, a village of a dozen huts, two tiny stores, and a saloon perched beside a railroad on the empty prairie, he built a complex of cattle-shipping yards and sent messengers to Texas to tell ranchers about them. In 1867, the year his yards opened, 35,000 longhorns moved up the soon-to-be-famous Chisholm Trail from South Texas.

18

At first, it appeared Mr. McCoy had made a disastrous mistake. "Texan cattle beef then was not considered eatable, and was as unsalable in the Eastern markets as would have been a shipment of prairie wolves," he wrote. But once reluctant Yankees tried Texas beef, they liked it. Soon tens of thousands of longhorns were moving, not only to Abilene, but to Dodge City, Newton, Ellsworth, and other Kansas railheads, where such men as Wild Bill Hickok and Wyatt Earp tried to keep order. During the next decade, a dozen dust clouds—each representing a herd of longhorns—could be seen at once from any point between Texas and Kansas.

Before long, Texas cowboys were driving longhorns not only to Kansas, but to new ranches in the Texas Panhandle, New Mexico, Arizona, Nebraska, the Dakotas, Wyoming, Montana, Colorado, Nevada, Utah, Idaho, and even into Canada, to grazing land left empty by the slaughter of the buffalo.

Between 1866 and 1890, ten million cattle moved over the trails out of Texas. They added 200 million golden nineteenth-century dollars to the state's economy and lifted it from the poverty the war had wrought.

But farmers were moving west and homesteading the land. They were building fences around their farms and across the cattle trails, setting up the plots of hundreds of Western stories and movies.

In 1876 a barbed-wire salesman named John W. "Bet a Million" Gates built a corral in Military Plaza in San Antonio and put a small herd of longhorns in it to demonstrate that his wire would hold them. It did. He claimed cattlemen gave him orders for one hundred carloads of wire that day.

The open range was doomed. So was the longhorn, it seemed.

Ranchers no longer needed a cow that could walk miles to water, fight off coyotes, and eat anything but rocks. They

Part II—Texas, Our Texas: Some People and Places

needed one that would stand quietly in a fenced pasture and get fat in a hurry. They imported the Hereford, the Angus, and other breeds that man had created to be beef. The nature-created longhorn, like the buffalo, was headed toward oblivion. "It was eaten almost to extinction," Mr. Miller says. "It was just slaughtered out. In 1927 a group of old ranchers petitioned Congress to put a few of the remaining longhorns on a preserve and try to save them."

Congress allocated $3,000 and three game rangers to gather a herd and move it to the Wichita Mountains Wildlife Refuge near Cache, Oklahoma. "The men who went down to South Texas and Mexico to find longhorns spent two or three months and came up with only twenty-seven head," says Joe Kimbell, the U.S. Forest Service biologist who now cares for the herd.

The Forest Service, which has kept careful breeding records on the herd since it was started, now maintains about three hundred pure longhorns and sells its excess calves to ranchers every fall. Most of today's longhorns are descendants of the Wichita Mountains herd. A few Texas ranch families, including the Yateses and the Schreiners, also kept a few longhorns for sentimental reasons. They maintained careful records on them, kept their bloodlines pure, and helped enlarge the gene pool of the Wichita Mountains herd.

In 1964 those cattlemen organized the Texas Longhorn Breeders Association of America. Charles Schreiner III, Walter's father, was its first president. Fayette Yates was the first member to sign up.

"They hired an inspector," Walter Schreiner says, "and if you wanted to join the association, he had to come to your ranch and inspect each of your cattle. If he considered them to be pure, he would let them in. If he didn't, he would kick them back."

During the Texas boom days of the 1970s and early '80s, longhorns became novelties for rich weekend ranchers, who would buy a few head and graze them near their country

Cattle Proud

homes, to look at during morning coffee. Others were sold to parks as museum pieces, and as rodeo stock. As Southwestern decor became popular, longhorn heads, skulls, and hides brought premium prices as decorative pieces.

Meanwhile, health-conscious Americans were seeking out foods with less fat and cholesterol than the beef they had been eating, unwittingly giving the longhorn a new importance in the cattle business. "Longhorn beef has 33 percent less cholesterol than flounder," Mr. Miller says. "It has 30 percent less fat than the English breeds you get at the supermarket. It has 20 grams more protein than regular beef. It's very healthy, and the taste is great."

But not enough longhorns are left to make them the beef supply they were a hundred years ago. "If you rounded up every Texas longhorn alive—registered and unregistered—they would last the beef industry only one day on the kill floor," Mr. Miller says.

The TLBAA now has about 5,000 members in almost every state and several foreign countries. But many of them now breed longhorn bulls and heifers with the European varieties, trying to breed the longhorn's newly desirable characteristics into the more common beef animals' offspring.

"A lot of those breeders don't care about preserving the pure longhorn," Walter Schreiner says. "If people keep trying to make the longhorn bigger to produce more beef and compete in cattle shows, then twenty years from now it may be hard again to find a pure longhorn."

⚜ ★ ⚜

Because of squabbles about exactly what a real longhorn is, two additional registries—the International Texas Longhorn Association and the Cattlemen's Texas Longhorn Registry—have splintered away from the TLBAA. Fayette Yates, the TLBAA's first member, now is an outspoken leader of the more conservative CTLR, which requires every animal it registers to

Part II—Texas, Our Texas: Some People and Places

be blood-typed to affirm that is hasn't been tainted with the blood of other breeds.

"The TLBAA would never agree to that," Mr. Yates says. "They say it's too expensive. It costs $30 a head. Hell, they spend more than that on one drunk. I've looked at thousands and thousands of their cattle and, by God, the longhorn's just not there. I told my daddy that as long as I lived, I would keep the old-time longhorns. But their future looks pretty bleak. It takes more than long horns to make a real Texas longhorn, you know."

Serving the Lone Star
The Texas Rangers

*T*ucked into the corners of Christine Nix's makeup mirror are postcard pictures of the Lone Ranger and Tonto and John Wayne, sent to her by a friend.

She's looking into the mirror, putting on lipstick. The Lone Ranger, Tonto, and John Wayne gaze back at her, tight-lipped and steely-eyed. "I've been working on that look, but I can't get the hang of it," she says.

Sergeant Nix laughs more easily than your typical Texas Ranger, the kind of laugh that makes other people laugh, hearing it. And she's shorter than your typical Ranger, standing 5-foot-1 without boots and hat. "When I walk through the door, people look over my head," she says. "They're expecting a much taller Ranger."

The Texas Ranger of song and story has been tall, Anglo, and male. He has been on horseback, with a Colt six-shooter on his hip and a Winchester in his saddle scabbard, a lonely champion of law and decency confronting evil on a savage frontier. On the silver screen, John Wayne, Clint Eastwood, and Nick Nolte have played him, on radio Joel McCrea, on TV Clayton Moore.

But times and Texas have changed.

Sergeant Nix, of Company F, stationed in Waco, is one of two women serving as Rangers now, and one of six African-

Part II—Texas, Our Texas: Some People and Places

Americans. Among the one hundred five Rangers scattered across the state are also fourteen Hispanics and an Asian-American.

And today's Ranger rides airplanes and helicopters more often than horses, carries semiautomatic weapons instead of the thumb-buster Colt and the saddle carbine. The roar of gunfire is less familiar to him than the tip-tap of his fingers on his laptop computer.

A Ranger now investigates white-collar crime frauds and corrupt public officials more often than he tracks cattle rustlers or quells riots. Most days, he's assisting a local sheriff or police department, but maybe working on a task force with the FBI, DEA, ATF, or Border Patrol. "A Ranger's life is 99 percent hard work and 1 percent excitement," says Lieutenant Clete Buckaloo of Company F. "And there's a lot of paperwork."

Even on TV, the Texas Ranger has changed. His modern fictional reincarnation is an urban figure, played by Chuck Norris. "*Walker, Texas Ranger,* is the *Lone Ranger* for the nineties," says Byron Johnson, director of the Texas Ranger Hall of Fame and Museum in Waco. "Instead of an Indian sidekick, Walker has an African-American. Instead of riding the horse Silver, Walker drives a Dodge Ram. Instead of silver bullets, Walker uses kung fu."

Nevertheless, in the rough country west of the Pecos, shadows of the Old West survive. A Ranger there still carries chaps and spurs in his car trunk, in case he must resort to horseback. And two members of Company E, Sergeant Gerry Villalobos of Fort Stockton and Sergeant Dave Duncan of Alpine, participated in six horseback manhunts in 1996 alone. One lasted three days and ended in a shootout.

The territory of Company E, headquartered at Midland, stretches 550 miles from El Paso to Eastland and includes forty-eight counties of mountains, deserts, and wide-open spaces. Some of them are larger than whole Eastern states.

Serving the Lone Star

And every Ranger, whether stationed in the city or the desert, still wears a white Western hat, boots, and a silver star fashioned from a Mexican coin.

Even a Ranger who's 5-foot-1, black, and female.

The Texas Rangers are the oldest state law enforcement organization in America. They cherish their history and tradition, but they've always been able to change—sometimes radically, sometimes reluctantly—when it was necessary.

So the Rangers arrived in 1998 at the 175th anniversary of their origin. In celebration, the Hall of Fame and Museum sponsored a symposium about their history and their place in American popular culture. Scholars lectured about several real-life Ranger heroes, and one talked about movie and TV Rangers, who, after all, are responsible for much of the Rangers' fame.

The first Ranger movie was made in 1910, a silent film called *Ranger's Romance*. Since then, dozens have appeared. Some are classy productions with big stars. Others are B-movie shoot-'em-ups such as *Rough Riding Ranger* and *Ride, Ranger, Ride*. The museum has thirty-five Ranger films in its archives.

Rangers were heroes of radio, too. "Return with us now to those thrilling days of yesteryear!" an announcer boomed in 1933. "From out of the past come the thundering hoofbeats of the great horse Silver! The Lone Ranger rides again!" Twenty years later, the masked man—sole survivor of a Ranger company ambushed by the cowardly Butch Cavendish gang—still roamed the audio waves with his loyal Indian sidekick, Tonto. Then he switched to video, where still he's spotted from time to time.

Joel McCrea played Ranger Jace Pearson on another fifties radio show called *Tales of the Texas Rangers*, based on real cases from Ranger files. M.T. "Lone Wolf" Gonzaullas, the famous

25

Part II—Texas, Our Texas: Some People and Places

captain of Company B in Dallas, was the show's technical adviser.

The Walker TV show, filmed in and around Dallas, has been shown on CBS since 1993 and is seen in nineteen countries.

Texas Rangers are the heroes of hundreds of Western novels and stories. Walter Prescott Webb's classic history *The Texas Rangers: A Century of Frontier Defense* has been in print for more than sixty years. Ranger biographies and autobiographies, some of them written almost one hundred years ago, still sell well.

"The popular appeal of the Rangers is staggering," says Mr. Johnson. "People from all over the world come into the museum, and they all know about the Rangers. The other day, a member of the Russian parliament was here. He pulled out a picture of his kid in Moscow, dressed like a Texas Ranger."

But many of the visitors think the Rangers were heroes of a mythic past, like the Knights of the Round Table. They're surprised to learn they're still with us.

So are some Texans. Sergeant Lee Young of Company B, stationed in McKinney, tells of a time he and a couple of colleagues were having lunch at a Dallas restaurant: "A guy at another table kept glancing at us. Finally he got up and came over. He said, 'Are you guys really Texas Rangers?' We said, 'Yeah, we sure are.' And he said, 'I thought you were all dead. I thought you went out with the Old West.'"

From time to time during the Rangers' turbulent history, groups of angry Texans have called for their abolition as relics of a barbaric frontier era. Their image sometimes has suffered through political ups and downs, charges of racial oppression, incidents of corruption and pure meanness, and accusations of excessive machismo and sexual discrimination.

But the Rangers are likely to be around for a long time. Texas law authorizes the Department of Public Safety to do away with the Highway Patrol, the Drivers License Division,

Serving the Lone Star

the Narcotics Division, or any other part of itself that it considers no longer necessary.

Except the Texas Rangers.

"It would be hard to imagine Texas without the Rangers," says Mr. Johnson.

John Tumlinson was killed on July 6, 1823, by a Karankawa Indian. He was the first Ranger to die in the line of duty. On January 22, 1987, Sergeant Stan Guffey was shot while helping another Ranger rescue a kidnapped child from a murderer. He was the most recent.

Rangers Tumlinson and Guffey lived in different centuries and different cultures and were doing different kinds of jobs. When Tumlinson served, Texas was still part of Mexico. He had responded to a call from Stephen F. Austin for "ten men to act as rangers for the common defense" of his infant colony, the first Anglo settlement in Texas. During Indian troubles, the volunteers—most of them teenagers—"ranged" the colony, protecting beleaguered settlers. When the Indian threat was over, they returned to their farms and families.

In 1835 the provisional government of revolutionary Texas created a more official "Corps of Rangers" to defend the frontier. Most of them later served as scouts for Sam Houston's army. During the years of the Republic, the Rangers were the frontier's only defense force.

When Texas joined the Union and war broke out between the United States and Mexico, the Rangers joined in. The commander of the American army, General Zachary Taylor, despised them for their bushy beards, barbaric dress, and lack of discipline. The Rangers kept marauding ahead of the regular troops, attacking villages and taking scalps in the manner of their home enemy, the Comanches. The Mexicans called the Rangers *los diablos Tejanos*—the Texan devils.

27

Part II—Texas, Our Texas: Some People and Places

During the Civil War, the Rangers served in the Confederate forces. After the war, federal troops took over the fight against the Indians, and the Reconstruction government created a highly political State Police. For almost a decade, Texas had no Rangers.

When Reconstruction ended and the State Police were disbanded, a plague of feuds and banditry raged across the state. The legislature created two Ranger forces to bring order out of the chaos. The Special Force was to tame the Nueces Strip, the land between the Nueces River and the Rio Grande, which some Mexicans still considered part of their country. The Frontier Battalion was to rid the state of outlaws.

The Special Force brought order to the Nueces Strip, but its methods created a racial bitterness between Hispanic citizens and the Rangers that still lingers in South Texas. It was the Frontier Battalion that made the Ranger the enduring white-hat hero and Texas symbol that the world would embrace. Its men roamed the state, putting down feuds, protecting black citizens from lynch mobs, tracking cattle thieves and fence-cutters, and pursuing robbers and murderers.

As the frontier faded away, so did the Frontier Battalion. But in 1901 the legislature turned the Rangers into a sort of state police force, authorizing four new companies to be chosen by their captains.

One of the captains, W.J. McDonald, was a colorful character with a silver tongue. In 1909 Albert Bigelow Paine, a famous writer of the time, wrote a biography of him. The often quoted "One riot, one Ranger" of Texas folklore apparently originated from tales Captain McDonald told Paine. The captain also spoke what since has become the Rangers' unofficial credo: "No man in the wrong can stand up against a fellow that's in the right and keeps on a-comin'."

Paine's book was hugely popular, which made Captain McDonald and the Rangers popular, too.

The new Ranger companies battled Mexican bandits and later, during the Prohibition era, liquor smugglers. Simultaneously, wildcatters discovered that Texas was floating on a sea of oil. Grifters, doxies, and thugs, frantic for the fast buck, rushed to the gushing oil fields. Oil town populations swelled by thousands overnight, and desperate local officials called for Rangers to establish order. They raided illegal saloons, shut down gambling dens and brothels, and rounded up thieves and holdup artists. When the jails were full, they handcuffed prisoners around telephone poles.

But the Rangers had become highly political. Governors were handing out Ranger commissions to cronies without regard for qualifications or character. Many Rangers were themselves bootleggers and gambling bosses or were on the take. Ranger corruption reached its zenith during the administration of Governor Miriam "Ma" Ferguson, who took office in 1933. She replaced her husband, James, who had been impeached for his crookedness. Forty Rangers and their commander, Adjutant General William Sterling, resigned immediately after her inauguration.

Mrs. Ferguson commissioned Rangers by the legion and appointed some 2,300 unofficial Special Rangers, who used their badges as a license to steal. Some of them were ex-convicts.

By 1934 Texas had had enough. The legislature passed a law that combined the Highway Patrol with the Rangers to form the Department of Public Safety.

In his book, published in 1936, Walter Prescott Webb predicted the new arrangement would spell the end of the Ranger service. "It is safe to say," he wrote, "that as time goes on, the functions of the un-uniformed Texas Rangers will gradually slip away."

But he was wrong. The same year his book was published, Texas staged its huge Centennial Exposition in Dallas, and the headquarters of Company B was set up in a log house at Fair Park. The hatted and booted, tight-lipped, steely-eyed Rangers attracted newsreel cameramen covering the exposition. They appeared on movie screens all over America and were

Part II—Texas, Our Texas: Some People and Places

cemented into the public's mind as the symbol of rugged, masculine Texas.

⚜ ★ ⚜

When Captain "Lone Wolf" Gonzaullas called Lewis Rigler into Company B's log house and swore him in, he assigned the new Ranger to Gainesville, where he would spend his entire thirty-year career. As Private Rigler was about to leave Dallas, the captain gave him his orders: "Don't be bothering me. You know what to do. If you have to shoot somebody, call me."

"In those days, Rangers were pretty much their own bosses," Mr. Rigler says. "There was no such thing as a certified police officer. Most sheriffs knew nothing about investigating crime. There was no school for sheriffs, no school for deputies. The Ranger had more knowledge, so he was called in for the investigative work."

Texas had matured and was more or less civilized. The Rangers were no longer fighting wars or shooting it out with horseback bandits. Ranger work became less bloody and more routine, similar to that of any modern investigative agency. But there was still plenty to do. Mr. Rigler remembers working eighty hours a week on some cases. "You worked on a case until you got it done," he says.

When the federal government forced the Rangers to conform with the wage-and-hour laws and limit the number of hours a Ranger could work each week without overtime pay, many old-time Rangers resented the change.

"The DPS didn't have the money to pay overtime," says another retired Ranger, Joaquin Jackson. "The federal government forced the Rangers to become liars. For years, the philosophy had been, if a man's qualified to be a Ranger, he don't need to be supervised. If a citizen or an officer called me and said, 'Ranger, I need help,' I was going to be there. I didn't count up how many hours I had worked that week."

Mr. Jackson served twenty-seven years, all of them on the border, first at Uvalde with Company D, then at Alpine with Company E. He adjusted to the Rangers' growing bureaucracy and the wage-and-hour laws and the proliferating paperwork. He even learned to use a computer. He intended to serve until the end of the century. But in 1993, when Governor Ann Richards mandated that women be hired into the Ranger service, he retired.

"I and a few other Rangers decided, 'Well, it's time for an old-timer to go,'" Mr. Jackson says. "It was politics, and I never liked politics. Queen Ann said Joaquin doesn't like women. That's wrong. I just don't think they belong in law enforcement. The Rangers have changed. The whole world has changed. And there ain't nothing we can do about it."

There was a big stir in the press in 1988 when Lee Young became the first black man ever to "pin on the cinco peso," as the Rangers say. "I was a bit overwhelmed by all the attention," he says. "I wasn't trying to make history. I was trying to get a job that I had wanted for many years. It didn't matter to me whether I was the first or not. But looking back on it, I have a good feeling." The men of Company B welcomed him. "I had no problems with race when I came into the Rangers," he says.

The inclusion of women, however, wasn't so smooth. Of the four women promoted into the Ranger service since 1993, only two remain. One resigned a year after her appointment, charging the Rangers with sexual harassment and discrimination. After an investigation, the Texas Commission on Human Rights ruled her claims were unfounded. Another turned down her appointment, accusing the senior captain then commanding the Rangers of a "calculated effort... to force me to work in a demeaning and diminished capacity" because she was a woman.

Sergeant Young became mentor to one of the remaining women, Sergeant Marie Garcia, now serving with Company D in San Antonio. "I showed her the ropes," he says. "She's

Part II—Texas, Our Texas: Some People and Places

doing well. She's as rough and tough as the guys are. That's what you've got to be if you're a Ranger."

The other, Sergeant Nix, calls herself "a happy camper" who wants to be a Ranger until she retires. "Early on, some people told me they were appalled to hear of women in the Rangers," she says. "They were civilians. And I'm not going to say there wasn't resistance inside the Rangers, too. But they certainly don't show it now. If something needs to be done, they're as likely to call on me as any other Ranger.

"Change takes time to get used to. But when you're there to help people, they don't really care how tall you are."

The Leather Throne
The Saddle Maker

When Rector Story started working there, Concho Avenue in San Angelo was a rough-and-tumble place. Ranchers and cowboys from all over West Texas went there to knock back a few beers, throw a few punches, visit Miss Hattie's whorehouse, and maybe buy a new saddle at R.E. Donaho's shop, where Mr. Story was building them.

The street is different now. Texas Rangers sealed Miss Hattie's door in 1946, her fiftieth year at the same location. The unpretentious brick buildings that housed the cowboys' saloons and cafes are antique shops and food boutiques selling pasta and healthful sandwiches.

At 8 East Concho, the writing on the plate-glass window still says "R.E. Donaho Concho Saddle Shop," but the saddlery that has occupied the building since 1890 is a small fraction of what it used to be. The front rooms, where saddles, blankets, bits, spurs, and other cowboy equipment were offered for sale, have been rented out as an antiques and gift shop. In the back, where seven or eight saddle makers and their helpers used to work, the present owner labors alone.

Mr. Story, who sold the shop in 1995, says, "When I went to work down there each man was expected to make four saddles a week. We were expected to start four saddles Monday and finish them Saturday."

Part II—Texas, Our Texas: Some People and Places

The kind of saddle that Mr. Story made has been called "the leather throne," because it made its owner feel like a king. Although he was only a hired agricultural laborer, a cowboy with a good horse and a good saddle under him felt superior to anyone who had to walk. In those days, when almost every cowboy was young, single, and poorly paid, his saddle and the clothes on his back often were his only possessions.

"His saddle was the last thing a cowboy would sell," Mr. Story says. "Unless he was an alcoholic. Then he would sell it for a drink."

Mr. Story was born in San Angelo in 1919, about four blocks from the R.E. Donaho Concho Saddle Shop. He apprenticed himself to Mr. Donaho in 1938 and learned from him how to build saddles. In 1939 he married the boss's daughter, Maxine, who kept the shop's books. In 1954, when Mr. Donaho died, Mr. Story bought a half interest in the business and became partners with his mother-in-law. When she died, he bought the remaining quarter interest from Maxine's brother and continued to run the shop until he retired.

During all those years, Mr. Story never considered changing the name of the place. "Mr. Donaho established the reputation of the place," he says. "I was never proud enough to put my own name out front."

He has no idea how many saddles he made during his fifty-eight years there, or how many apprentices learned the craft from him. The standard saddle maker's apprenticeship was five years, but most apprentices would stay only a couple of years, then go off and start a shop of their own. "Most of them didn't like working for other people," Mr. Story says. "They would go to some little town and set up a little old shop. A lot of them could build a good saddle. But a man working by himself can't build enough saddles to get much of a reputation. I don't know what happened to those boys. Hell, most of them are dead."

But the last apprentice Mr. Story took under his wing stayed with him for seventeen years and still is building saddles. David Smith, who is forty-six, is shop foreman for Coats Saddlery at Wall, a few miles from San Angelo. He also does fancy tooling on every saddle made there. He draws intricate designs of oak leaves, acorns, or flowers on the leather and shapes them with knives, hammers, and stamps. He works about sixty-five hours on each saddle.

"Rector put me into his room and taught me saddle making," says Mr. Smith. "I worked with him maybe two years before he turned me loose on my own. We would build saddles together. It was a real good education, working with Rector. I'd be in that old Donaho shop yet if old Rector was still running it."

Mr. Story and Mr. Smith have seen a lot of changes in their craft in recent years. Saddles have changed. The people who buy them have changed. Even horses have changed.

"When I went to work for Mr. Donaho, saddles weren't as intricate as they are now," Mr. Story says. "Today it's mostly show. They don't care much about how long saddles are going to last because they don't ride them much. In my early days, cowboys were horseback all the time. They would get up before daylight and ride maybe fifteen or twenty miles to where they were going to work. And they might stay out there a month. Those boys wanted a saddle to last just as long as it could because they couldn't afford one anyway."

The advent of the pickup truck and four-wheel drive changed the way a cowboy goes about his business. "Now he'll put his horse in a trailer and drive over there and unload his horse. When he finishes up the day's work, he loads his horse into his trailer and drives home to supper."

Also, most of the West Texas ranches no longer are as huge as they used to be. When an owner dies, his lands often are divided among heirs. When the next generation dies, their smaller spreads are divided again. "When they get too small to be real ranches, they're sold to doctors and lawyers who use them as places to have parties," Mr. Story says. "Those people like fancy saddles, with a lot of silver and stuff on them. They

Part II—Texas, Our Texas: Some People and Places

take a little ride for pleasure maybe once a week. Then there's the steer ropers, barrel racers, and cutting-horse men. They use the saddle for maybe an hour a day and put it up."

And the doctors and lawyers don't ride the same kinds of horses that Mr. Story's old cowboy customers did. "Back then," he says, "there were only two kinds of horses out here: the big American thoroughbred type and the little ponies from Mexico. They all had high withers."

The withers, the high point at the base of a horse's neck, kept the saddle from sliding forward. "Then they started breeding the withers out and getting the quarter-type of horse. The saddle would slide around. The horse widened out. So did the seat of the saddle," he says. "It's harder to fit a saddle to a horse today than when I started. The rider's weight must be spread equally over the horse's back. If a man's not comfortable, he's always moving around, trying to find a comfortable seat. And that tires out the horse, you see. A short-legged man has a hard time riding one of those wide quarter horses."

In his time, Mr. Story built a number of fancy saddles for celebrities and other rich folks. He built one for Western swing musician Bob Wills and one for B Western movie star Big Boy Williams. The last saddle he built before he retired was for country singer Tanya Tucker. But he's prouder that nearly all his saddles were ridden by working cowboys and ranchers. "That's what made our shop different from the others," he says. "We stayed with the rancher. We made a ranch saddle. We made it from a hide that was three-eighths of an inch thick, and it was expected to last a lifetime."

The catastrophic Texas drought of the 1950s spread the fame of the Donaho ranch saddle to the far reaches of the cattle kingdom. West Texas was dry for four years, then for seven years it didn't rain at all. Many ranchers couldn't survive such a drought. Those who had the money moved their stock out of Texas temporarily to some place where it was raining. They took their saddles with them.

Mr. Story still is amazed as he recalls those days:

"We started getting orders from North and South Dakota! Montana, Washington, Oregon, California! Arizona, New Mexico, Colorado! And we got orders from the East! Florida, Mississippi, Louisiana! Truckers hauling cattle from Texas to those other states would take four or five saddles with them and sell them at the other end. At one time the biggest markets we had were Florida and North and South Dakota. The people in those places had never seen a handmade saddle. They were using mass-produced saddles. The handmade saddle was a Texas thing."

When he started in the 1930s, a handmade, tooled saddle cost $85 to $100. When he retired in 1995, the price was $1,700 to $2,000. Coats Saddlery gets $3,000 and up for some of the intricately tooled saddles that David Smith creates. And there's no lack of demand. Mr. Smith and his small crew work fifty hours a week.

"Saddles aren't made the way they were when Rector taught me," says Mr. Smith. "We're highly mechanized. It's big business. The horse industry is really huge now. Not just in America. Even over in Europe. Cutting horses are popular in France and Germany. The competition in the saddle business is steep."

Because of the North American Free Trade Agreement (NAFTA), much of the competition is from south of the Mexican border. Some large American saddleries cut a saddle's pieces and send them to Mexico for assembly. And several Mexican companies now are building their own saddles for the American and European markets.

"But they don't have to worry about seeing the customer," Mr. Smith says. "Just throw it together and get it out. Cut and run. And under that NAFTA or whatever the hell that is, they don't even have to stamp 'Made in Mexico' on it anymore. But on this side of the river, you've got to face your customer. If your saddle is hurting a horse's back, you've got to take care of it or you're not going to be building saddles in Texas much longer."

Part II—Texas, Our Texas: Some People and Places

However, Rector Story says, many of the saddle maker's modern customers go for the flash and can't tell a bad saddle from a good one. "The people I sold to were used to a good saddle and could tell one just as quick as I could. Those people are easier pleased than the people that don't know saddles. People that don't know are awfully hard to please. Somebody has told them something, and they believe it. 'Old Joe Blow told me so-and-so,' they'll tell you.

"Well, maybe the fellow that told them doesn't know a damn thing about a saddle. Maybe old Joe Blow was just blowing. But the ranchers and the ranch hands—the people that rode them all day long—they could tell the difference between a bad saddle and a good one."

The Kingdom and the Fading Glory
The Ranch

Sallie Reynolds Matthews buried her oldest child, Annie, in 1881. She was three years old. Her grave was the beginning of the cemetery.

A few yards from Annie lies Mrs. Matthews' youngest child, Watt. He was ninety-eight when he died in 1997, one hundred sixteen years after his sister.

The cemetery is in a pasture on Lambshead Ranch, about thirteen miles north of Albany, Texas, on the Clear Fork of the Brazos River. It's a silent, serene spot, fenced off from the grazing cattle.

Between Annie and Watt, seven other Matthews children were born and died. Some lie in the cemetery. So do various grandchildren, cousins, in-laws, and Bill "Tige" Avery, who's there because, his gravestone says, he was a "Fine Black Cowboy."

Annie's stone is small and intricately decorated, featuring a lamb. The others are taller and plain, perhaps reflecting the family's austere Presbyterian faith. Watt's grave is marked only by a crude cross, formed of two sticks tied together, and a horseshoe.

On an autumn weekend in 1998, the monument company delivered Watt's gravestone to the ranch, but the Matthews family, who had planned a small ceremony for its installation,

Part II—Texas, Our Texas: Some People and Places

sent it back. Its shape didn't match the others, its lettering was wrong and the two cattle brands carved into it—the Spanish Gourd and the open-A-lazy-V—were the wrong size.

"It's unfortunate," says Watt's nephew, Bob Brittingham, "but it's got to be right. It's going to be there for the ages."

People along the Clear Fork say Watt Matthews himself was one for the ages. Lawrence Clayton, who wrote his biography, calls him "the last of the cattle barons." Whether last or not, he was one of an increasingly rare breed, says Watt's neighbor, Bob Green.

Mr. Green lives on the ranch where he was born in 1923. He and Watt used to chat on the phone every day before sunup, about the weather and the cattle market. Resting in his cook shack after a morning's work, Mr. Green ruminates about the cow business in Texas and how it used to be and how it's changing:

"When we had family ranches around here, where the people who owned the land worked it themselves and defended it, if necessary—well, we were a much stronger people then. When I was young, every one of these ranches around here had a family on it, raising kids."

He takes a pull at his mug of steaming coffee and runs his fingers through his thin white hair. "Now families don't live on those ranches anymore. The younger generation isn't interested in the loneliness and privation it takes to run a big ranch. When the old owner dies, it's sold and the heirs divide up the money. Or it's put in trust and a big-city bank sends a highly trained Aggie out to manage it."

Even with the death of Watt, as everybody along the Clear Fork still calls him, Lambshead hasn't come to that. But even it isn't as it used to be. "For the first time in more than one hundred years, no member of the Matthews and Reynolds families is living on that land," Mr. Green says.

The heirs of the cattle kingdom live elsewhere and do other things, says Dr. Clayton, a Hardin-Simmons University dean

The Kingdom and the Fading Glory

and a scholar of Texas ranch history. "I guess it's strange to assume that just because someone is born into a ranching family they would want to continue that kind of work," he says.

܀ ★ ܀

In 1861 Sallie Reynolds was born in what is now Stephens County, just east of where she would spend her life. Her family was living on the edge of the frontier, and the land belonged to no one. Her father and the few other herdsmen along the Brazos grazed their stock wherever there was grass and, when there was none, moved on.

On Christmas Day, 1876, when she was fifteen, Sallie married John Alexander Matthews, a young cattleman, in her parents' parlor. Hers was one of five marriages between the Reynolds and Matthews families. Four of Sallie's brothers married two pairs of Matthews sisters. These unions created a large Celtic clan whose members would fight Indians, drive trail herds, claim land and grow rich together, and rear many children.

Branches of the clan established ranches in several Western states and other parts of Texas. In the 1880s, when settlers were claiming West Texas land from the state and fencing the range with the new barbed wire, John and Sallie began piecing together their own big spread on the Brazos.

They named their ranch for Thomas Lambshead, an Englishman who was the first white settler on the part of the ranch where John and Sallie established their headquarters. He had come there in 1859, but the Comanches stole and killed so many of his livestock that he lost courage and moved away.

"It is a land of broad prairies, quiet valleys, and vast distances," Sallie wrote of the place, "a land of bright skies, glorious sunsets, and most brilliant sunlight; a land where the hills and plains are gay with lovely wildflowers in the springtime, and where we have the everlasting hills unto which we may lift up our eyes."

Part II—Texas, Our Texas: Some People and Places

The Reynolds-Matthews story contains all the ingredients of the Hollywood Western epic: shootouts with Indians and rustlers, frontier weddings and parties, circuit-riding preachers, vigilantes, soldiers and buffalo hunters, cattle drives to California and Colorado, a brother murdered by the Apache Kid in Arizona, even the lynching of a brother-in-law gone bad.

But the main character would have been Sallie. Growing up in a series of stone shacks on the windy prairie, she taught herself to read out of her mother's New Testament; watched Indians steal the family horses; became a fifteen-year-old bride in an almost womanless society; delivered her sister's baby when she was seventeen because there was nobody else to do it; contracted malaria while nursing a dying neighbor; educated herself in botany, astronomy, history, and literature; and borrowed money to send her daughters on a European tour.

Two of her nine children died in childhood. Her last—Watt, born in 1899—she sent to Princeton. "We've got enough cowboys in this family," she told him. "One of you ought to be educated." He graduated in the Class of '21, but then came home to the ranch.

When she was old, Sallie wrote a book about it all, called *Interwoven*. She published it privately in 1936, intending it only for the children and grandchildren of the interwoven Reynolds and Matthews families. But it has been published since in three public editions and is a Texas classic.

Two years after publishing her story, Sallie died. Three years later, John followed. Ownership of Lambshead fell to their surviving children—Watt, his older brother John, and their five sisters. The sisters were married and lived elsewhere. John had other ranching interests of his own. But Watt lived on Lambshead and managed it for the family until his death fifty-six years later.

"Watt personified and brought into our own time what he saw in his father and uncles, who had been long dead," says Dr. Clayton. "They were rugged individuals. To think of getting on

The Kingdom and the Fading Glory

a horse and driving a herd of cattle to California! The nights those guys spent in a bed were few. They lived on the ground, camped out. Watt was intent on not modernizing his own psyche in a way that would move him away from that."

Watt's father, who was called "the Judge" because he had been a justice of the peace, didn't share his wife's enthusiasm for bookish learning and believed Watt's sojourn in the Ivy League wasn't good for his character. During a rare visit to Princeton, the Judge was watching students hurrying across the campus to their classes. He turned to his son and in derision said: "Look at them, tripping along with their books under their arms! Sleeping between white sheets and drinking ice water!"

Watt always laughed when he told the story, Mr. Green says, but he spent his life following in his father's Spartan footsteps. "No one ever combined the sophistication of an Ivy League college with the earthiness of the branding pen and made that combination work. Watt was a wealthy man, but he lived in a simple little room in the bunkhouse, with a concrete floor and a narrow iron bedstead. His office was an old desk in the corner of the cook shack, and he drove a plain Ford automobile."

Bill Cauble, who has worked on Lambshead for fifteen years, adds that Watt's room lacked even air conditioning and heating, except for a fireplace. "After he got old, I used to go and throw some mesquite in the fireplace and make him a fire in the winter so he could get up. He'd be lying there with his head covered up. In the summers, he'd sleep on that little old screened-in porch he had, just sweating. To me, that's the real character of a man, when he can have anything he wants but he doesn't want anything."

Watt wanted nothing, but he gave freely to others. He was a patron of the arts and all manner of civic causes in Albany and throughout Texas. He restored the little stone house where his parents were wed and other old structures about the ranch where ancestors dwelt, and erected plaques and monuments at

Part II—Texas, Our Texas: Some People and Places

historic sites on his land. He gave to his alma mater and his church. He gave to his friends. Guests at his frequent and legendary parties often numbered in the hundreds and included people from every level of society and many walks of life. He invited strangers to dine and proudly conducted them on tours of his ranch.

His epitaph, when his gravestone finally was installed, read: "A Generous Man."

"Watt reminded me of an English lord who managed his estate in a benevolent way and kept open the house and welcomed whoever came," says Dr. Clayton.

When he died, the last of his generation, he was buried in jeans and a faded denim jacket with his old felt hat beside him, in a plain pine box built by a friend.

He had never married. Lambshead was inherited by more than sixty people.

⋐ ★ ⋑

"The federal estate tax is 54 percent of the assessed value," says Mr. Green. "Unless you get yourself a good estate planner, you're in trouble when you die."

Many a Texas ranch is in trouble when its owner dies. Often, the heirs have to sell the land to pay the tax. They split what's left of the proceeds and go their own ways. Putting a ranch in trust is a way to avoid that for a while, but it takes control of the ranch away from the family.

Watt chose a third way. In 1981, when he was eighty-two, he created the Matthews Land and Cattle Co. The corporation owns the land and buildings of Lambshead. Its present shareholders are the children and grandchildren of three of Watt's sisters, Susette Burns, Lucile Brittingham, and Sallie Judd. There are sixty of them, more or less. Watt's other sisters and his brother took their shares of John and Sallie's legacy and departed the family business years ago. "They had their own

The Kingdom and the Fading Glory

ranches and their own lives," says Bob Brittingham, son of Lucile and president of the corporation.

The three sisters and Watt did business as the J.A. Matthews Ranch Co., a partnership that still exists. Many of the sisters' heirs participate in it, others don't. The partners are in the cattle and hunting business. They lease Lambshead's present 40,000 acres from the Matthews Land and Cattle Co. The oil and gas wells on Lambshead are still another separate business entity.

It's all a lawyers' baroque game.

"The corporation is a shell," says Mr. Brittingham. "It's just a device to hold Lambshead together. It isn't meant to pay dividends. It's not really to make money. But there are some shareholders who are asking, 'Why aren't we getting any dividends? We need to get something from this.' It's an awkward situation, but not terribly awkward. We've enough people in the corporation who see Lambshead as a great gift, not as a cash cow."

Mr. Brittingham, a pleasant, bookish man in his sixties, lived thirty-six years in New York, managing the Doubleday bookstore on Fifth Avenue, publishing science-fiction stories, and dreaming of writing the great American novel. "When I was growing up, I would come to Lambshead to visit," he says. "I wasn't a very good cowboy. I can't call myself a cowman. I'm a reasonably good businessman, though, and Uncle Watt loved me. He was probably closer to me than anyone else. But I was the black sheep, living up in New York." He moved back to Texas in 1989, when Watt's health began to fail, but he divides his time among Fort Worth, Albany, and another family business in Wilmington, Delaware. He doesn't live on Lambshead.

The family convenes at the ranch for business meetings twice a year, in March and October. They come from other lives in Houston, San Antonio, Galveston, Austin, Fort Worth, and points as far away as Massachusetts. They talk things over, argue, make decisions. Mr. Brittingham serves as troubleshooter and mediator.

Part II—Texas, Our Texas: Some People and Places

"It's hard, unless you're Watt, who ran Lambshead like his personal fiefdom, to make it all pull together," Mr. Brittingham says. "Watt never groomed anyone to take his place. With him gone, the family tends to pull apart."

The heirs trust the cattle operation to their ranch foreman, Terry Moberley, who has worked on Lambshead ever since he graduated from Albany High School. "Terry knows the land, he knows the cattle far better than anyone in my family, including those who are ranchers," says Mr. Brittingham. "We're lucky to have him."

Lambshead is still making money. A lot of money, if it belonged to only a few people. But divided among so many, "it's nothing," says Mr. Brittingham, who, like Watt, has no children of his own.

"But everybody values the ranch for what it is and wants it to go on," he says. "I'm confident that it'll survive beyond my time. I see among my nephews and nieces and cousins great, great love for the place, and in that huge group of people there'll be someone who will come forward and carry it on."

⋘ ★ ⋙

Bob Green says it's no wonder that more and more West Texas ranches are becoming toys of wealthy city people who use them for party places and hunting reserves, as the state's real cattle people follow Watt and his kind into history.

"Big government likes big business because they think alike," he says. "Ranchers by nature aren't very good at politics and lobbying. Three or four packers control the cattle market now. We raise the cattle, and they throw us a pittance for taking all the risk in raising them. They and the big supermarket chains are raking off the profit that we used to get. At one time, we got about 52 cents of every dollar spent on beef. Now we get 24 or 25."

West Texas is going through a drought cycle, too, these past several years. The ranchers are having to reduce their herds to preserve their range. Even the oil revenue that has propped up many of them is declining. Oil is cheaper than it has been in decades. "You need a little oil money so you can keep your fences up and your pastures clean," Mr. Green says.

His son is a lawyer. He works for an oil company in Fort Worth. Mr. Green has two daughters, too, but, he says, they aren't interested in ranching, either. So what will happen to the Green ranch when he's laid to rest in his own family's cemetery as his friend Watt was?

Mr. Green spreads his hands and shrugs. "I don't know," he says.

The Tower of Dreams
The Oil Derrick

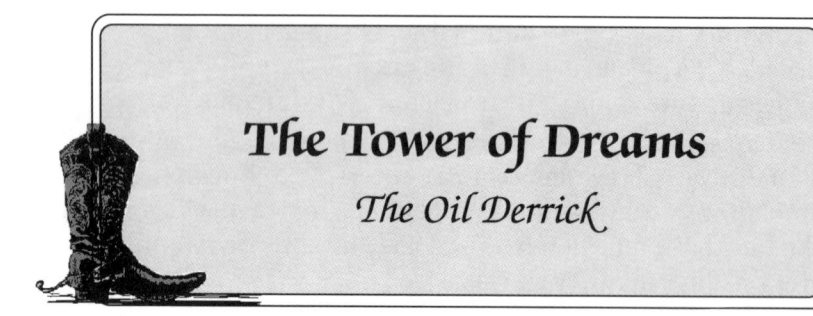

*I*n the collection of drawings and old black-and-white photographs of oil well derricks that adorns Dub Shivers' office wall is a large blueprint in a glassed frame. It's the plan for a derrick like those in the pictures, like those that Mr. Shivers used to build when he was young. But in a corner of the blueprint are the words "Warner Bros.," and it has been autographed by actor Robert Duvall.

"All the old derricks are gone now," says Mr. Shivers, who is in his seventies. "They've rotted away and the nails rusted out. The only place you see a derrick now is in the movies."

From the blueprint on the wall, Mr. Shivers and his family built four wooden derricks for *The Stars Fell on Henrietta,* a movie set in the Texas oil fields of 1935. In that 1995 movie, Mr. Duvall plays a dreamy, down-at-the-heels wildcatter bumming about the boom towns with his oil-finding cat, Matilda, looking for his big strike.

When the Hollywood people needed derricks, they went to the Spindletop/Gladys City Boomtown Museum in Beaumont and asked curator Christine Marino if she knew who built the derrick on display there. She sent them to Mr. Shivers, who lives in Hull. "As far as I know, I'm the only person left who knows how to build them," he says.

The Tower of Dreams

The oil field derrick—usually with oil gushing out the top—ranks with the longhorn steer and the cowboy on the bucking bronco among the enduring symbols of Texas. For almost a century it has appeared on road maps, restaurant menus, neon signs, in cartoons and book illustrations, anywhere an artist needs a simple image that says "Texas." For almost forty years it was the helmet logo of the professional football team that used to play in Houston.

But who among us remembers seeing a *real* oil field derrick? That is, one in a real oil field?

"They weren't building a lot of wooden derricks after World War II," says Mr. Shivers. "Steel derricks were becoming popular by that time. A few of those were being used until about 1960. Since then, they haven't used derricks at all. They use a cantilever or jackknife rig, which is portable. The last real wooden derrick I built was at Batson, Texas, in the 1940s."

When drillers with their portable rigs bring in a new well —an increasingly rare event in Texas these days—oil doesn't gush into the sky anymore. The industry many decades ago found ways to prevent that dangerous and wasteful spectacle.

But the first gushing oil well in America was in Texas. And its spectacular arrival made such an impression upon the world's psyche that the oil-spewing derrick and the state have been linked in the popular imagination ever since.

That gusher arrived at 10:30 A.M. on January 10, 1901, on a low hill called Spindletop near Beaumont, a sleepy Southeast Texas farming town.

It was a Sunday school teacher named Patillo Higgins who first suspected that oil in great quantities might be under the hill. On picnics there with his students, he would poke a stick into the ground and make a small hole. As natural gas hissed out of the hole, he would light a match and set it afire for their entertainment.

Mr. Higgins dreamed of making a big strike on Spindletop and becoming a tycoon. He raised the money to buy land on

49

Part II—Texas, Our Texas: Some People and Places

the hill and between 1893 and 1896 drilled three wells there. But he found no oil. One of the few who profited from the enterprise was Mr. Shivers' maternal grandfather, who rented Mr. Higgins the boiler that ran his steam engine on the 1896 dry hole.

Mr. Higgins' failures made him the butt of jokes in Beaumont, but even after he ran out of money, he persevered. He advertised in a business magazine for a partner to put up money for another effort. Only one prospect, a former Austrian navy officer named Anthony F. Lucas, replied. He came to Beaumont for a look, bought 90 percent of Mr. Higgins' interest in the business and raised the funds to drill.

Captain Lucas hired Curt and Al Hamill, brothers who had drilled several oil wells around Corsicana, Texas, to come to Beaumont with a new rotary bit they had developed. In October 1900 the Hamills and a friend, Peck Byrd, built a wooden derrick on Spindletop and started drilling.

For two months they struck nothing encouraging. Then, on the morning of January 10, their drill stuck in hard rock and wouldn't turn. Assuming that the bit had dulled, the drillers pulled it to the surface to replace it. As they were inserting the new bit into the pipe, a strange hissing sound issued from the hole.

Suddenly, a thick stream of mud erupted from the well, shooting sections of drilling pipe into the air like bullets. As mud, rocks, and four tons of steel plummeted toward the derrick floor, Al Hamill and Peck Byrd ran for their lives. Curt Hamill was working high on the derrick. "The first puff hit me and I was blinded by mud and oil," he told a folklorist many years later. "I had got to the ladder to climb down when the second puff or blow came.... I don't really know how I reached the derrick floor."

By 4 P.M., more than a thousand people had dashed to Spindletop Hill to see the Lucas Gusher, as it came to be called. The well spewed 100,000 barrels of oil 200 feet into the air for nine days—almost a million barrels in all—before the crew got it capped.

Already it was attracting merchants, developers, and laborers who hoped to establish businesses or get jobs in the new boom town, and the speculators, grifters, gamblers, prostitutes, and thieves who always fly to the sugar of sudden and easy wealth. Three months after the gusher blew in, Beaumont's population had grown from 9,000 to 50,000 and derricks of one hundred thirty-eight producing wells stood on Spindletop Hill.

The scene would be repeated in almost every section of Texas as wildcatters fanned out from Beaumont and made discovery after discovery. Thousands of oil field workers and the riffraff who preyed upon them moved with the play from town to town. Over the next few decades, Kilgore, Ranger, Cisco, Burkburnett, Borger, and dozens more farm and ranch communities suddenly exploded into boom town Gomorrahs. Their derrick forests were so dense that workers could walk from one end of a field to the other without stepping off their floors.

The modern oil industry had begun. Its pioneers—the go-for-broke wildcatter, the hard-working, hard-fighting roughneck, the sudden millionaire—entered Texas folklore and quickly attracted the attention of novelists and movie makers, culminating in the scheming wheeler-dealer oil executive J.R. Ewing of TV's *Dallas,* one of the few counties where oil was never found.

Dub Shivers' grandfather, William Gilbert Shivers, who had been working in the timber business, joined the boom as a laborer in 1909. By 1918 he was a rig-building contractor. "He built the wooden derricks for a dollar a foot," says Mr. Shivers. "A 64-foot-high derrick cost $64." It became the family business. Two more generations followed him into the fields, raising derricks all over Southeast Texas.

"But by 1957 it looked like the rig-building business was coming to an end," Dub Shivers says. "So I bought a service rig

Part II—Texas, Our Texas: Some People and Places

on credit and got into the well-servicing business." His son and grandson have since joined him in Shivers Well Service Inc. of Hull.

The only derricks Mr. Shivers builds now are replicas: the one at the Spindletop/Gladys City Boomtown, one in Ranger that blew down in a tornado, and those movie derricks in *The Stars Fell on Henrietta*.

"It doesn't take a lot of training or skill to build a derrick," he says. "You've just got to know how to do it."

Shooting Texas
The Movies

*I*n the 1928 silent movie *The Wind,* gentle Eastern lady Lillian Gish steps off a train into a West Texas sandstorm and asks: "Is this one of those... northers?"

Her cowboy interlocutor assures her it isn't. "If this was a norther," he says, "you and me 'ud be jest arms an' legs scattered over the prairie!"

In the old movies, gentle Eastern women always found it hard to deal with Texas. From Miss Gish's introduction to Sweetwater—which was filmed in the Mojave Desert—to Elizabeth Taylor in *Giant,* stepping off a train nearly thirty years later at windswept Reata, Hollywood almost always portrayed Texas as an endless expanse of blowing sand, tumbling tumbleweeds, heat, and violence.

And rugged, square-jawed men who loved it that way.

"To Hollywood, Texas was the ultimate West, the place of empire, where men who were bigger than life carved kingdoms out of the wilderness," says Don Graham, author of *Cowboys and Cadillacs: How Hollywood Looks at Texas.* "Texas was where the cowboys lived. That's why everybody outside of Texas thinks the whole landscape here is a sprawling, dusty plain where the main activity is raising cattle and maybe—as in *Giant*—drilling oil wells."

Part II—Texas, Our Texas: Some People and Places

But times and the movies have changed. From the huge, wild land where mighty heroes and villains fought epic battles against nature and each other, Texas in recent movies has shriveled to a tedious little town where small people live tiny lives.

"Four movies about Texas have come out in 1998—*Dancer, Texas Pop. 81, Still Breathing, Deep in the Heart of Texas*, and *Hope Floats*," says Dr. Graham. "Every one of them is about stereotypical, boring Hickville, Texas. And all of them are pathetic."

～ ★ ～

Near the beginning of *Red River* (1948), John Wayne says, after crossing that stream: "We're in Texas." And Walter Brennan replies: "It feels good to me."

The Howard Hawks film, based on a *Saturday Evening Post* short story, is considered by many fans and scholars the best Western ever made, and certainly one of the best Texas movies. Dr. Graham, who teaches Texas literature and culture at the University of Texas at Austin, calls *Red River* "the Texas foundation myth."

"The John Wayne character takes the land, kills Mexicans to hold it, then builds this great herd of cattle and drives it north to the railroad," he says. "That's the beginning of the Texas myth." *Red River*'s landscape, its characters, and the enterprise in which they're engaged are all gigantic. They lift the Texas Western far above the Saturday matinee shoot-'em-up.

Eight years later, in John Ford's *The Searchers* (1956), John Wayne plays another frontier Texan, this one a relentless Confederate veteran in pursuit of a band of Comanches who have stolen his niece. The five-year search takes Mr. Wayne through the usual Texas hazards—howling wind, withering heat, and vast, empty spaces—but Mr. Ford filmed it in the Monument Valley of Utah and Arizona, a distinctly un-Texan landscape.

Mr. Wayne came to the real Texas a few years later to shoot another of the state's foundation stories, *The Alamo* (1960), on a set near Brackettville that's still a tourist attraction because the Duke made his movie there. But the result was disappointing. Too many of *The Alamo's* 192 minutes are concerned with Mr. Wayne's Davy Crockett and Richard Widmark's Jim Bowie getting drunk and punching out whoever's handy while they await Santa Anna's arrival. "All the Alamo movies are wretched," says Dr. Graham.

It took Rock Hudson, Elizabeth Taylor, James Dean, and the big-sky country around Marfa to move the Texas story beyond its foundation myths.

"In *Giant* [1956], we are in the twentieth century, after everything has been consolidated," says Dr. Graham. "The Texans are still raising cattle, but they don't go on cattle drives anymore. They just ship their livestock at the local railroad."

But the incoming civilized Eastern lady—played by Ms. Taylor—still has to cope with wind-whipped sand, blistering heat, and barbaric natives. Her new Texan husband, Mr. Hudson, is as primitive as any but possesses certain merits that she finds appealing.

"Rock is virtuous because he's connected with the cattle industry, the older way of Texas life," says Dr. Graham. "James Dean, on the other hand, is associated with oil, the newer way, which is suspect. Oil is a form of gambling. It's a kind of unearned wealth. It's associated with negative things."

Edna Ferber, who wrote the novel on which the film was based, had little knowledge of Texas but despised it anyway. Her ridicule of the state and its cattle and oil establishment raised yelps of protest from the Rio Grande to the Red. But director George Stevens, by eliminating her attitude and adding the vast Cinemascope setting, turned her story into the National Movie of Texas.

Then along came native son Larry McMurtry and shot Hollywood's myth between the eyes. In *Hud* (1962), based on

Part II—Texas, Our Texas: Some People and Places

Larry McMurtry's first novel, *Horseman, Pass By*, Paul Newman speeds across the prairie and through the little ranch town in a pink Cadillac, raising clouds of dust and trouble wherever he goes. He's a hard-drinking, womanizing, conniving cad, not a hero. His aging father—who keeps a couple of longhorn bulls "for old times' sake, to remind me of how things was"—is the most unheroic of ranchers. His herd is threatened and finally doomed, not by Indians or rustlers, but by hoof-and-mouth disease.

"That's the finish of the ranching thing," says Dr. Graham. "At the end of *Hud*, you've got Paul Newman alone at the ranch house drinking a beer and there's nothing else living on the place. Everything is dead. In *Red River, Giant*, and *Hud*, you have the complete cycle of the glorious origin, the consolidation, and the decline of the Texas cattle culture."

And in *The Last Picture Show* (1971, based on another McMurtry novel), the last picture show shown at the Royal Theater before it shuts down is *Red River*. "In a way, *The Last Picture Show* is a goodbye to the movies as well as the cattle culture," says Dr. Graham. "The theater goes out of business. TV and the small screen have taken over."

When Mr. McMurtry published his own epic cattle-drive novel in 1985, no movie producer wanted it. *Lonesome Dove* wound up as a TV miniseries.

But in *The Last Picture Show* the wind, at least, endures. "I hate these northers," says the high school coach's wife, Cloris Leachman, to her teenage lover, Timothy Bottoms.

C⚹⚹

In the late 1960s, '70s, and '80s, as Texas evolved from a rural to an urban state and strangers were invading it from all directions, the plots and characters of Texas movies changed as well.

In *Bonnie and Clyde* (1967), Warren Beatty and Faye Dunaway turn the Depression-era Dallas criminals Bonnie

Parker and Clyde Barrow into romantic adventurers rebelling against the confines of bourgeois society. They even make a fool of a Texas Ranger—a sacrilege that wouldn't have been allowed in an earlier Hollywood.

In *The Getaway* (1972), another outlaw-couple-on-the-lam film, Steve McQueen and Ali MacGraw dash across Texas from the prison in Huntsville to the San Antonio River Walk to El Paso and finally to Mexico by train, bus, automobile, and garbage truck. The film's climax, one of director Sam Peckinpah's patented gunshot-and-gushing-blood ballets, takes place in a sleazy hotel in El Paso, where—honoring the great tradition—the sun is hot and the streets are dusty.

In *The Border* (1981), also set in El Paso, both the people and the land are meaner. The soft buzz of flies about Jack Nicholson's head adds a hint of stink to the heat and dust, and the desert landscape—magnificent in the earlier Texas epics—is merely bleak.

The Border is a tale of corrupt Border Patrolmen engaged in smuggling human beings into the United States. In it, law officers are crooked and murderous, their women are whining morons, the land is void of hope. Nothing is beautiful and no heroes are riding over the horizon. Evil rules.

"In Russia, they've got it mapped out so everyone pulls for everyone else. That's the theory anyway," says sleazy private eye M. Emmet Walsh at the beginning of *Blood Simple* (1983), the darkest of all Texas films. "But what I know about is Texas. And down here, you're on your own."

Joel and Ethan Coen, who later would win Oscars with *Fargo*, shot *Blood Simple* in Austin and Hutto. The banal suburbs and the seedy honky-tonk back room where its lust, murder, and double-cross take place make *noir* Texas a very scary place to be "on your own."

The themes of lust, corruption, and murder crop up again in *Lone Star* (1996), in which Kris Kristofferson plays a ruthless South Texas sheriff who runs his county as his personal

Part II—Texas, Our Texas: Some People and Places

fiefdom. Relations among Anglo, Hispanic, and black citizens in fictional Rio County are murky, complicated, dangerous, even incestuous. Shot in Eagle Pass, *Lone Star* is the first film to tackle the complexity of life in the Texas-Mexico border region—virtually a third nation between the United States and Mexico, with its own language, music, food, and rules.

At its end, Elizabeth Pena looks into Chris Cooper's eyes and speaks the line that puts John Wayne's second Texas foundation story in its grave:

"Forget the Alamo."

C✦⊃

But when Texas really starts to shrink on the big screen is when Debra Winger gives John Travolta the eye and asks: "Are you a cowboy?" He replies: "Well, it depends on what you think a cowboy is."

It turns out he *is* a cowboy, because in the Texas of *Urban Cowboy* (1980) a cowboy doesn't even work on a ranch. He lives in a trailer, works at a Houston refinery, drives his truck down to Gilley's every night for a longneck and a two-step around the dance floor, and demonstrates his male prowess by riding a mechanical bull.

Urban Cowboy inspired the "Texas chic" craze that had the whole country dressing in cowboy duds. For a time, Yankees in Boston were dancing the Cotton-Eyed Joe and New York ad execs were strolling Madison Avenue in Resistols and Tony Lamas.

Today, Texas movies are small. In *Hope Floats* (1998) Sandra Bullock returns to her little Texas hometown to recover from her bad marriage. *In Dancer, Texas Pop. 81* (1998) four high-school seniors must decide whether to move to Los Angeles together—as they vowed they would when they were eleven—or settle down among the terminally laconic men folk of tiny Dancer. "Some folks don't belong in a small town," one of the characters philosophizes. "Some folks don't belong anywhere else."

That's what Hollywood's vision of Texas has come to. If Walter Brennan were crossing the Red with John Wayne today, could he still say, "It feels good to me"?

"I don't know if we've lost our distinctness as a culture and a place," says Dr. Graham, "but I think we're in the process of losing it. Texas is no longer the strange and wild place it once was."

The wind doesn't even blow anymore.

A Whole Other Country
The Republic

*H*er father adored John Wayne, she says. He especially loved the Duke's movie about the Alamo. "I must have seen it twenty times," she says. "I knew all the dialogue by heart."

Twice every year, her father loaded up his twelve children and took them on a pilgrimage to the shrine. "We came for three days in March, and in the summertime we were here for a whole week," she says. "It's not true that all Hispanic Texans are embarrassed by the Alamo."

But back home in Laredo, where she was studying Texas history in elementary school, she and some of her friends sometimes felt uncomfortable. "The presentation of it was so one-sided," she says. "The Anglo heroes were so great, and the Mexicans were all butchers."

And for more than one hundred years after the events, many histories, poems, and novels portrayed the Texas Revolution as a triumph of a superior Anglo civilization over an inferior Hispanic culture.

Now Mary Alice Pena-Lopez is one of the lecturers who interpret the Alamo, its heroes, and their foes to the three million to five million visitors who mill through it every year, gazing at the names of its defenders on the bronze plaques, studying the old documents and guns and swords in the glass display cases.

A Whole Other Country

Working from memory of a script provided by the Daughters of the Republic of Texas—the custodians of the Alamo—Ms. Pena-Lopez passionately recounts the story of the thirteen-day siege, of the one hundred eighty-nine Texas revolutionists who defied the dictator Antonio Lopez de Santa Anna and his army of thousands, and died. She tells of the line that legend says Colonel William Barret Travis, the Texans' twenty-six-year-old commander, drew in the dirt when he finally acknowledged to his men that the Alamo was doomed. And of his exhortation: "Those of you who are prepared to give your lives for freedom's cause, cross over this line and come stand by me now."

Many historians say Colonel Travis probably never drew that line nor said those words, but myth doesn't die so easily. "Every single man crossed that line that day," Ms. Pena-Lopez tells the tourists, "except for one."

A few changes have been made at the Alamo, the most popular tourist attraction in Texas, since Ms. Pena-Lopez used to go there with her father. The picture of Davy Crockett that looked just like John Wayne is no longer on the wall. Neither are the old paintings of larger-than-life Anglos bashing Mexican soldiers with their rifle butts. Ms. Pena-Lopez's script is careful to identify the dictator Santa Anna, not the Mexican nation nor the Hispanic people, as the villain of the tale. For along with Travis, Bowie, Bonham, and Crockett also died Esparza, Abamillo, Fuentes, Badillo, Guerrero, and Losoya in the fort's defense.

Although toppling heroes from pedestals where myth and legend have placed them is common practice among historians these days, the story told by Ms. Pena-Lopez and the other Alamo interpreters has changed only slightly from generation to generation. The message and myth of the Alamo, she says, are bigger than mere history. "People need inspiration and motivation," she says. "There's so much sadness and grief and tragedy in the world today. People need to be reassured of the values that we stand for. Freedom. Justice. Democracy. And the

Part II—Texas, Our Texas: Some People and Places

Alamo is an excellent place for them to reflect on these things."

Sometimes visitors challenge her. "People have asked me, 'Why do you make such a big deal about these men? They were drunks and crooks.' And I say, 'Because they died for *us*. They weren't perfect in the way they lived, but they were perfect in the way they died.'"

❦ ★ ❧

When Stephen F. Austin led the first Anglo colonists into Texas in 1821, he had his first name legally changed to Estevan. He and his followers became citizens of Mexico, and so did the other colonists from the United States and Europe who followed other impresarios into the Texas wilderness.

According to Mary Austin Holley, a cousin of Austin who published a book in 1836 promoting his colony, the non-Indian population of Texas had grown to about 50,000 by then. Only 5,000 were native-born Mexicans. Many of the Anglo majority were rough, independent-minded frontiersmen who were always ready to fight anything or anyone. "Having lived mostly free from the restraints of law," Mrs. Holley wrote, "they are not apt to pay implicit obedience to its dictates, when contrary to their own views and feelings."

But when these frontiersmen took up arms against the Mexican government in 1835, they weren't alone. Theirs was only one of five similar rebellions in various parts of Mexico. Many Mexicans elsewhere were fighting Santa Anna, who had repudiated their country's liberal Constitution of 1824 and had abolished the rights of individuals and states that it guaranteed.

In the beginning, most of the Texan revolutionists saw themselves as loyal Mexican citizens fighting to rescue their country from the dictator. Branch Archer, who presided over the settlers' first meeting to discuss the situation, described their rebellion as "laying the cornerstone of liberty in the great

Mexican Republic." When Austin called the Texans to arms, the first organized troops were a company of *Tejano* volunteers led by Colonel Juan Seguin.

"Few people today know about those Mexican roots of the Texas Revolution," says Larry Spasic, director of operations at the San Jacinto Museum of History, which stands on the battleground near present-day Houston where the Texans finally defeated Santa Anna. "They don't know about the liberals of Mexico and their fight for a democratic government. They don't know the Texas Revolution was part of that larger struggle. It happened to be the one rebellion that succeeded."

Santa Anna put down the other revolts with cruel and devastating reprisals, especially in Zacatecas and Yucatan. As he turned his attention toward Texas, expecting an easy victory there, both Anglo and Hispanic settlers rallied to oppose him. And when Santa Anna's army laid siege to the Alamo on February 23, 1836, the flag its defenders raised was the red-white-and-green of Mexico, with "1824" in place of the eagle at its center.

But soon the aim of the rebellion shifted. Even as the Alamo battle raged, fifty-nine representatives who had convened in a raw new village called Washington-on-the-Brazos repudiated Santa Anna's rule and on March 2, 1836, declared Texas an independent nation. Among the signers of their declaration were Francisco Ruiz and Jose Antonio Navarro, the only Texas natives among the delegates. Lorenzo de Zavala, born in Yucatan, was named vice president of the new nation's provisional government.

As subsequent generations retold the saga of the revolution in books and movies, however, those names often were forgotten or ignored and the struggle for freedom became strictly an American-vs.-Mexican affair. Only in recent years have efforts been made to restore the Hispanic patriots to the Texas pantheon.

"I don't remember hearing anything about Juan Seguin or Lorenzo de Zavala when I was growing up," says Carolynne

Part II—Texas, Our Texas: Some People and Places

LeNeveu, who taught Texas history to fourth-graders at Spring Creek Elementary School in Richardson before she became a school counselor. "But we're more culturally aware today. Some people try to make an issue out of race in the Texas Revolution, but it was not about race at all. I did not teach my kids that the Alamo was about Americans fighting Mexicans. It was about people fighting for justice and their constitution. I taught my children to say, '*No rendirse, muchachos!*' It's a Spanish phrase meaning, 'Don't give up, boys!' The defenders yelled it at the Alamo."

Ms. LeNeveu, a Daughter of the Republic of Texas, says she learned her history first from her grandfather. And, of course, she learned it again in the fourth and seventh grades, when state law requires that Texas history be taught in the public schools.

Not long ago, *The Dallas Morning News* published an article about a recently auctioned document purported to be the diary of a Mexican officer who was at the Alamo on March 6, 1836, when it fell. The diary says Davy Crockett and a few other defenders didn't go down fighting in the bloody final assault, as every Texas schoolchild has been taught, but that they were captured at the battle's end, and that Santa Anna ordered them executed.

Ms. LeNeveu sent a letter to the newspaper, addressed "To my precious fourth-graders:"

"Do not be dismayed...," she wrote. "The fact cannot be disputed that Mr. Crockett, alongside a few others—both Anglo and Hispanic—made a commitment to face tyranny and dictatorship against all odds! Do not forget that their ideals of liberty, of patriotism, and of all that we hold dear to the American character are free to Texans today because of these brave men and women who chose to remain inside those walls."

A Whole Other Country

"Anglo and Hispanic neighbors went through a lot together during the Revolution," says Mr. Spasic at the San Jacinto Museum. "They helped each other and had respect for each other. They had a common bond. Some who came afterward didn't have that bond."

The museum is part of the San Jacinto Monument, a 570-foot stone shaft rising above the battlefield where on April 21, 1836, Sam Houston and his ragtag troops—including Colonel Seguin's *Tejanos*—surprised Santa Anna's army and, in only eighteen minutes, routed it. A half-hour multiprojector slide show in the museum tells the story of the battle that changed Texas, Mexico, and the United States forever, and its bitter aftermath for some of its Hispanic participants.

After independence was won, new settlers flooded into Texas from the United States and Europe. The Anglo majority grew larger. The Hispanic minority shrank. Some of the newcomers were adventurers and land-grabbers who used crooked bankers, politicians, and courts to rob Hispanic Texans of their lands. Many of the *Tejano* families who had helped finance and fight the revolution lost everything. Some were now laborers on land they had owned. Others—among them Juan Seguin—crossed the Rio Grande and settled in Mexico, feeling betrayed by the young nation they had helped create.

Anti-Hispanic prejudice and distrust increased with the U.S.-Mexican War, which broke out after the ten-year-old Republic of Texas was annexed into the United States. And, since history is written by the winners, much of Texas history, fiction, and poetry published during the following century was written with a distinct Anglo slant.

"There were population shifts after the Revolution," says Mr. Spasic. "And when a shift brings people with different histories and heritages and languages and religions together, there's going to be conflict. That will always happen. It is continuing to happen in the United States today. There will always be adjustments."

Part II—Texas, Our Texas: Some People and Places

Of the nearly seventeen million Texas residents recorded in the 1990 census, almost four million were of Mexican ancestry—a much larger percentage of the population than native Mexicans represented at the time of the Revolution or at any time since. This, says Mr. Spasic, is one of the reasons that the history of early Texas and its revolution is being reinterpreted at San Jacinto, at the Alamo, and in academic and popular histories. As the population of the state grows and becomes more diverse, it has become imperative that all sides be presented fairly.

"The goal in our life together is to get to the point where tolerance is the predominant view and the yardstick by which we act and react," he says. "And as new information becomes available, it should be included in our interpretations. I don't think any interpretation of history is finalized and completely truthful. There's probably a little bit of truth in everybody's view."

Part II

Texas, Our Texas: Some People and Places

The Pavarotti of the Plains

Don Walser was twelve when his mother died. When he would come home from school in the afternoons, he didn't want to go into the house where she no longer was, so he would climb into a tree in the yard, amongst the leaves in the spring of the year, and sing.

"If there was a lot of noise in the house and people around, I would stay up there until dark," he says. "I sang all them old songs that was on the radio."

Unbeknownst to the grieving boy, neighbors were bringing chairs into their yards and sitting in the darkness, listening to him, for his voice was beautiful.

For years, whenever he went back to Lamesa, Texas, old folks would come up to him and say, "I remember you. You're the boy who sang in the tree."

Mr. Walser is over sixty years old now, and he has kept on singing "all them old songs that was on the radio," performing anywhere he could get a gig: in high school auditoriums, Wal-Mart parking lots, VFW and American Legion halls, oil field fightin'-and-dancin' clubs, Moose and Elk lodges, and on local radio and TV shows in big towns and small all over West Texas.

"Some people have something they just have to do," he says. "Me, I have to sing. I can't keep from it."

Part II—Texas, Our Texas: Some People and Places

But suddenly there's a difference. Now that his children are grown and on their own, Mr. Walser has retired from his day job as a civilian employee of the Texas National Guard and launched a new career as a full-time performer. He's still singing the old songs, but now his performances are on nationwide tours, National Public Radio shows, and Caribbean cruise ships. He sings regularly at several of Austin's best music haunts. His CDs, released by Watermelon Records, a small but prestigious independent label in Austin, have received rave reviews around the country and are selling well.

Playboy magazine has hailed Mr. Walser as "the Pavarotti of the plains," a reference, perhaps, to both his pure tenor voice and his three hundred-something-pound bulk. The *Chicago Tribune* called him "the anti-Garth" in tribute to his simple, straightforward, traditional style, which is a world apart from the gimmickry and commercialism of mega-super-country-musician-marketer Garth Brooks.

And recently, Mr. Walser and Pat, his wife of more than forty years, bought a house in South Austin and moved out of the double-wide trailer they had occupied since 1984.

"I always knew I could play music for a living," he says. "But I knew, too, just from being around other musicians, that you've got to starve for a few years. I didn't want to do that. I had a family to raise."

※

Mr. Walser was born September 14, 1934, on a farm near Brownfield on the Texas South Plains. When he was about seven months old, his dad went to work at a cotton oil mill in Lamesa, a small town between Lubbock and Big Spring. There the boy grew up with his three sisters—two older and one younger than he—who all share the same birthday, April 21.

While his father was working the night shift at the cotton oil mill, young Don often was awake in his bed, listening to the powerful Mexican radio stations just south of the Rio Grande

The Pavarotti of the Plains

that were blasting the music of Jimmie Rodgers, Roy Acuff, Ernest Tubb, Eddie Arnold, the Carter Family, and other country greats of the 1940s and '50s to *gringo* audiences across North America, interspersing their songs with money pleas by weepy evangelists and commercials for quack medical remedies.

"I had a photographic memory for songs," Mr. Walser says. "I could hear one on the radio just one time and remember it. There was an old drugstore where we used to hang out in Lamesa. My cousins would make bets that they could play any song at all on the jukebox and immediately afterward, I would go outside and sing it perfectly. My cousins made quite a bit of money that way."

In 1948, two years after his mother died, Mr. Walser got his first guitar. A year later, he joined the Texas National Guard. Both events were the beginnings of long relationships.

"Me and another kid just wanted to be in something that had a uniform," he says. "We were fifteen, and I thought sixteen was the minimum age for joining the Guard, so that's how old we told the recruiter we were. But he told us you had to be seventeen to join up. He says to us, 'Next time I see you, you're going to have to be seventeen.' So we went out and walked around a little bit and come back, and the recruiter says, 'How old are you boys?' And we say, 'We're seventeen,' and he says, 'That's old enough.'"

Not long after joining the Guard, Mr. Walser and his two friends, Billy and Gene Richter, organized themselves into a band they called the Panhandle Playboys. "Billy and I played the guitar and Gene played the steel," Mr. Walser says. "We later added two fiddles and a bass and a piano, but we never could find a good drummer. We had this little old radio show there in Lamesa, and there was a DJ in Lubbock named High Pockets Duncan who used to put on music shows in high school auditoriums around the area—they called them shows 'jamborees'—and he'd ask us to be on. I didn't have a telephone, so when old High Pockets wanted me on one of his

Part II—Texas, Our Texas: Some People and Places

shows, he'd get on the radio and say, 'If any of you folks over there at Lamesa run into old Donny Walser, tell him I want him to be at such-and-such a place at such-and-such a time.' Somebody would tell me, and I'd show up."

Billed on some of the same shows as the Panhandle Playboys was a skinny kid with glasses from Lubbock. "He was Buddy Holly," Mr. Walser says, "but he wasn't famous yet. I met a lot of people on those shows. One night before Pat and I married, Hank Locklin sang 'Send Me the Pillow That You Dream On' and dedicated it to us."

Sometime in 1950, Mr. Walser's father went to Denison, Texas, to help build a new cotton oil mill there. When he returned to Lamesa in 1951, he brought a new bride with him. And a new teenage stepdaughter named Pat.

"I was away at a National Guard school at Fort Benning, Georgia," Mr. Walser says, "and when I got home that September, there was Pat. She had just moved into the house with my dad and her mama. Pretty soon we started dating, and in December we got married. I married my stepsister. I was seventeen at the time."

It was the beginning of an unconventional but loving family. The Walsers have reared two natural children—Donna and Allen—and two adopted children—Janie and Michael. And they've sheltered five foster children.

During the early years of his marriage, Mr. Walser worked around Lamesa at various jobs and performed with his Panhandle Playboys on the roof of the projection booth at the Skyview Drive-In Theater and other local nightspots. In 1957 the Texas National Guard hired him as a civilian mechanic to work on the Lamesa unit's trucks and other equipment.

Two years later the Guard transferred him to Midland, where he played in a band called the Texas Plainsmen and appeared on a number of local shows around the Permian Basin, including a TV program in Odessa where he shared the stage with a young rock-and-roller from Wink named Roy Orbison.

The Pavarotti of the Plains

During a two-year assignment to Port Neches, near Beaumont, Mr. Walser hung up his guitar and didn't perform. Then the Walsers were back in West Texas, in Abilene this time, and he was organizing another band.

A back injury in a car wreck ended his career as a mechanic, but the National Guard gave him a desk job in Snyder, then another in Sweetwater, then another back in Midland, then in El Paso, where he had a band called the El Paso Amigos.

Hopping about West Texas and performing with his various bands, Mr. Walser continued to ignore whatever was being played on the country Top 40 stations and kept singing and yodeling the old songs by Hank Williams, Bob Wills, Marty Robbins, Lefty Frizzell, Hank Thompson, Floyd Tillman, Tennessee Ernie Ford, Slim Whitman, Red Foley, and the other traditional country musicians who had provided his pleasure and comfort in the past.

"Country music was meant to come from the heart and to be played simple," he says. "The music that's on the radio today ain't really country music. In Nashville, they package singers just like they do meat or fruit, and they tell them what to do and what to wear and how to sing. They have writers that go into an office every day and get together in committees to crank the songs out. To me, that's all vanilla. How do you write something if it ain't coming from your heart?"

From time to time over the years, Mr. Walser has added to his classical repertoire a song that he has written himself, out of the quiet within him. "I've written about a hundred songs, but so many of them aren't any good," he says. "I'm really proud of maybe fifteen or twenty of them."

A few of those tunes are approaching classical status themselves, at least in the minds of his Texas fans. One of them, "The John Deere Tractor Song," brings tears to the eyes of many an old dirt farmer. Another, called "Cowboy Ramsey," relates the deeds of a West Texas heller whom almost anyone from the ranch country will swear he used to know personally:

Part II—Texas, Our Texas: Some People and Places

He was a lover and a fighter and a wild bull rider,
A pretty good windmill man;
Was a fair fence-mender when he wasn't on a bender,
Best working cowboy in the land.

"That Cowboy Ramsey was something else," Mr. Walser remembers. "They had a place in Lamesa called the Frontier Café, and he was there early every morning. He'd be setting in there and he'd have that big old ten-gallon hat pulled way down where he couldn't even see. And they'd serve him coffee, and he'd pour it out in the saucer and blow it. He worked for my dad down at the oil mill at night some. Him and his wife went over to Big Spring one time, and about four old boys kept eyeing him up, and when they come out of the joint, they jumped him, and he whipped them all. He was quite a character."

C⋆⋆⋆Ↄ

Finally, in 1984, the Texas National Guard named Mr. Walser an internal auditor and transferred him to Austin, where his destiny lay.

"I kept seeing his name pop up in the paper over and over again, and I began to ask, 'Who is this?'" says Heinz Geissler. "Then I heard the three cassettes that he was selling at his gigs around Austin. I said, 'This is really cool.' So we signed him."

Mr. Geissler is president of Watermelon Records. In July 1994 his company released *Rolling Stone from Texas,* a CD starring Don Walser and his Pure Texas Band performing such country standards as "Shotgun Boogie," "Don't Worry About Me," and "I'll Hold You in My Heart," along with several of Mr. Walser's own songs, including "Cowboy Ramsey," "The John Deere Tractor Song," and the CD's title song, which Mr. Walser wrote when he was seventeen.

Watermelon threw two parties to celebrate the release, one at the Broken Spoke, Austin's country-music equivalent to Carnegie Hall, and Emo's, the Sixth Street alternative rock club, headquarters of the young tattoo-and-ugly-haircut set. Huge crowds showed up at both. "We expected a lot of people at the Spoke," Mr. Geissler says, "but the crowd at Emo's was just as big or bigger. They say it was the second largest crowd in the history of the club."

In December 1994 Mr. Walser was on both *Fresh Air* and *All Things Considered* on National Public Radio within two weeks of each other. In one month after that, Watermelon shipped more than 10,000 copies of *Rolling Stone from Texas*.

"From California to the East Coast, nobody could keep it in stock," Mr. Geissler says. "Don totally bucks every trend in the country music business these days. That's one of the reasons I like him, because I really despise what's coming out of Nashville. What I find fascinating about Don is that people who don't care about country music love him, from the minute they sit down to listen to him. My nephew, who's seventeen, went to a birthday party the other day, and he took two CDs. One was a Snoop Doggie Dog. The other was *Rolling Stone from Texas*."

So anyone who happens to be at Babe's or Jovita's or Emo's or the Broken Spoke when Mr. Walser and the Pure Texas Band are there shouldn't be amazed at the cross-section of Austin that shows up, from the boots-and-jeans crowd to gray-haired grandmothers in sensible pant suits to the shaved-head-and-nose-ring bunch.

"In Nashville, they've taken away the fiddle, they've taken away the steel, they've taken away the banjo to try to make country music palatable to a commercial audience," says Mark Rubin, one of the tattooed persuasion, who plays string bass and tuba in a band called the Loose Livers. "But now the young kids are discovering real country music again, because of Don. And he doesn't do it for personal gain. He does it because he *has* to. A lot of younger musicians have keyed in on Don's ethic: Work your band, put out your own records, and what's popular be damned. Be true to yourself."

Part II—Texas, Our Texas: Some People and Places

As Mr. Rubin is speaking, Mr. Walser settles his large Western-clad body onto a barstool near the front of Babe's. Backed by the fiddle, steel guitar, drums, and bass of the Pure Texas Band, he breaks into "Invitation to the Blues." His crystal voice, the fiddle's plea, the wail of the steel fill every cranny of the place. His yodels swoop and soar like invisible eagles. Soon the small space between the band and the bar tables fills with humanity of many kinds, dancing, swaying, singing along on the old traditional tune, lost in the ecstasy of the moment.

"I tell a lot of people that Don is my spiritual leader," says Fred Noelke, who, with his companion Catherine Meador shows up wherever Mr. Walser plays in Austin. "Before I began following him, I hated dancing. Then one night I heard him, and his music just overtook me, and suddenly I wasn't self-conscious anymore. I was enjoying it. It was great. Don has transformed my life."

"His voice, when he yodels, is ethereal," says Ms. Meador. "I like to watch people who've never heard him before. Some of them look like they're in shock."

"I worry about him becoming famous," Mr. Noelke says. "I've waited forty years for Don Walser. I don't want to lose him now."

Mr. Walser comes to the end of his song. He grins at the applause. "Thanks very much, by gollies," he says.

Medicine Ball Man

*I*f you're in Fort Davis and find yourself in need of a leather medicine ball or a communist certified public accountant or a convenient place to dump an unwanted dog or just want to spend an afternoon enthralled by a huge collection of unusual art, you'll likely end up at Lineaus Lorette's house.

It's on a hill on the edge of town, next to the abandoned town dump. You'll know you're at the right place when you see the dogs. You can't help seeing them. There are twenty-two, Lineaus thinks, and they surround your car when you pull up. Big dogs, little dogs, old dogs, young dogs, white dogs, brown dogs, spotted dogs, quiet dogs, loud dogs, dogs of long and short hair, all of whom found their way to Lineaus' door either by themselves or in the company of someone who drove off quickly.

Despite their number and energy, they leave you alone when Lineaus tells them to. "That's Julius, and that's Ethel, and that's Rosa," he says, introducing a few of the closer ones.

He named them for the Rosenbergs?

"Yeah." Lineaus smiles. He's a tall, well-set-up man, dressed in red shorts, white T-shirt, and red-and-white knit cap on a sunny December day. He looks maybe fifteen years younger than his fifty-one years and is brim-full of a curiously contagious energy.

77

Part II—Texas, Our Texas: Some People and Places

He's strong, healthy-looking, and sunny, a product of his own product, the old-fashioned leather medicine ball, with which he and a buddy over at Sul Ross State University in Alpine exercise regularly. "Throwing a medicine ball is really aggressive exercise, so it's really great for stress management," he says. "The down side is that you can't do it alone. You've got to have someone to catch the ball."

Still, he says, the medicine ball is a much better way to strengthen the body than the torture-chamber-looking machines that are so popular nowadays, especially if you learn the routines taught by the book *Medicine Ball Exercise Cycles,* by Lineaus Hooper Lorette.

The red sign on a big sheet-metal building down the hill from Lineaus' house reads: LINEAUS ATHLETIC COMPANY. Inside, the air is redolent with the aroma of new leather. The late afternoon sunlight, filtered through a shaded window, casts a golden glow over benches and tables cluttered with tanned cowhides, the products Lineaus makes from them, and a sleeping cat, whose duty it is to guard the leather against mice.

There's a device Lineaus designed for Penn State University that allows a javelin thrower to practice indoors without skewering somebody. There's a six-pound football like the ones Lineaus made for Tom Landry's Dallas Cowboys and the University of Southern California, to strengthen the arms and the grip of receivers through off-season exercise. There's a $2,500 leather punching bag that he's making for somebody right now, and, of course, medicine balls of various weights and sizes.

"There was this wonderful man named Robert Jenkins Roberts Jr., who was director of a Boston YMCA," Lineaus says. "He was responsible for the Boston Marathon. He was the first person to go to the beach and bring home sand and make a sand pile for kids to play in. He invented the Indian club."

Medicine Ball Man

In about 1895 Robert Jenkins Roberts Jr. invented the medicine ball, which is simply a heavy, round leather bag filled with remnants of thread and laced with a leather thong.

"When I was a kid, there was a medicine ball in every high school gym," Lineaus says. "In basic training in the military during the Depression, they used medicine-ball exercises. But leather got expensive, the balls got expensive, and people stopped using them."

In the 1960s and '70s, the Russians and the East Germans began using the medicine ball in track-and-field training, and their success in international competitions later piqued renewed interest in the United States. "Almost all professional sports teams have medicine balls now, when in 1980 they didn't have any," Lineaus says. "They just didn't exist."

In 1982 Lineaus had an accounting practice in Austin and was running for the U.S. Senate on Barry Commoner's left-wing Citizens Party ticket. One day, while exercising with a friend at a YMCA, he found an old medicine ball.

"We developed an exercise routine with it, and I taught a conditioning class with it," Lineaus says. "One day in 1983 I went down to a sporting goods store to buy one, and there wasn't one. Rawlings had made the last leather medicine ball in 1964."

So Lineaus made one for himself. Soon other people were asking him to make medicine balls for them, too. He went into the business. He now makes about one hundred fifty medicine balls a year. His customers have included not only the Cowboys, USC, and Penn State, but also the New York Giants, Green Bay Packers, Chicago Bears, Houston Oilers, New Orleans Saints, Miami Dolphins, Cleveland Indians, Harvard University, and most of the big Midwestern universities.

The typical Lineaus medicine ball weighs about thirteen pounds, but he makes them larger or smaller if the customer wants. They typically cost about $250 for a men's ball, about $220 for the smaller women's version.

Part II—Texas, Our Texas: Some People and Places

"I'm the only person who makes a leather medicine ball," he says. "I have no competition. Every European country makes a rubber medicine ball. And in California—this is disgusting—they make a plastic silicone thing that just is awful. But everybody in sports knows I make this great leather ball that, God, it's expensive, but it lasts a long time. In fact, they last so long that I don't get a lot of repeat business. I sold a ball to Harvard, and ten years later they told me it was as good as the day they got it. Balls I made in 1983 are still being used. The leather I use is very open grained, and if you oil it, it will not wear out. It just gets better and better."

So it's fortunate that he didn't give up his accounting practice when he moved to Fort Davis, into the house where his parents had planned to spend their retirement. "My father was an oxymoron—an honest oil man," Lineaus says. "He was vice president for operations of an oil company, but never owned any production himself. He thought it would be a conflict of interest. My mother taught art in the Odessa public schools. I was raised in Odessa, which is a very egalitarian society. In Odessa, if you think you're better than anybody else, you get the shit beat out of you. Or you move to Midland."

For years, his parents collected art, and they designed their retirement house with a huge main room in which to display their collection. When they changed their minds and decided to stay in Odessa, they told Lineaus they would give him the house if he would move there. So in 1991, he did.

"I thought I would lose all my accounting business when I moved out here from Austin," he says. "But people like their accountants. They develop long relationships with us. I lost only one client. So I operate an Austin accounting business in Fort Davis. I've got a fax and a modem, and I'm OK."

His leftist political leanings notwithstanding, he has picked up clients in the conservative old cowtown of Fort Davis, too. "Yes!" he says. "I'm a communist CPA! Isn't it great? My maternal grandfather was a member of the first graduating class of Baylor Medical School. He practiced

80

medicine in Oklahoma Territory. And he was a communist! My family never talked about it because of the Red Scare. I wasn't told until 1982 when I was running for the U.S. Senate on that leftist ticket. A cousin of mine took me aside and said, 'Well, I guess it's time we told you...'"

Lineaus doesn't think the family secret had much bearing on his poor showing against Lloyd Bentsen.

"I'm not a member of the Communist Party," Lineaus says, "and I'm not a Marxist-Leninist. I'm just a communist genetically."

He has written a small book, called *Communitarianism: A Prospectus for Revolution,* which outlines his own plan for a future utopian world order, to be achieved through nonviolent, democratic means.

And to his parents' collection of decorated cattle horns, bronze sculptures, oil paintings, pottery, and etched portraits of every president from Washington through Cleveland, Lineaus has added a number of wood burning works by Addie Levine, an artist and fellow political leftist, formerly of Fort Davis, now living in Marathon on the edge of the Big Bend. They are whimsically humorous tributes to the likes of Sacco and Vanzetti, Emma Goldman, Anne Frank, Julius and Ethel Rosenberg, Pancho Villa and Emiliano Zapata, the organizers and martyrs of the Wobblies, the martyrs of the 1960s civil rights movement, Frieda Kahlo, the Beat poets of the fifties, Freud, Marx, Einstein, and the French Revolution.

And a framed copy of Richard Nixon's resignation letter.

"Isn't it great?" Lineaus says, spreading his arms as if to embrace it all. "I wouldn't live anywhere else."

Weeping Mary

Many years ago a black woman named Mary owned a parcel of land. A white man beat her out of it. The woman wept so constantly over her loss that her neighbors took to calling her Weeping Mary. They also named their new church after her, and the settlement that grew up around it took its name from the church.

Nobody remembers the grieving woman's last name or the year in which the wicked land deal was done, but the Church of Weeping Mary still stands among the trees beside a narrow road near Alto in Cherokee County. It still houses a thriving congregation of Baptists. And the houses and trailers that line the road are home to descendants of those who named the woman and the church.

"We used to *celebrate* Juneteenth," says Bessie Mae Parker, who is seventy-four. She sits on the front porch of her white-and-green frame house in Weeping Mary on a bright, sweltering afternoon, enjoying the shade with her daughters, Ella Ree Payton, Emmie Lee Martin, and Janice Martin. "Juneteenth was the only holiday I ever knowed until these later years. We always worked on the Fourth of July because they told us the Fourth of July was for *white* folks and the nineteenth of June was *our* day. And that's all I ever knowed. We always went to the woods. The men killed hogs, cows, goats and barbecued them. Papa barbecued all night long. And people from far and near came, and they'd set down, and they'd eat dinner and have a good time. Next day, they'd be right back in the fields, pulling watermelons, chopping cotton, hoeing peanuts, cutting fodder, stripping cane."

Such celebrations as Mrs. Parker describes are part of Weeping Mary's vanished past now. So are the fields and the work from which the celebrators were resting. Where the cotton, watermelons, and sugar cane then grew, grass and trees have long since reclaimed the land. The breadwinners of Weeping Mary drive to town jobs in Alto and Rusk and Jacksonville now, some as far as Nacogdoches and Lufkin and Crockett.

"Everybody does their own thing on Juneteenth now," says Janice Martin. "Some go to the lake. Some have family get-togethers. Some go swimming."

"They don't know what's good," her mother counters. "The people don't get *together* to celebrate no more. But you see what they *is* doing. People can't even come together for a game of ball without somebody starting a fight. People don't live like they used to."

Before June 19, 1865, when Major General Gordon Granger of the Union army came ashore at Galveston and ordered that "in accordance with a proclamation from the Executive of the United States, all slaves are free," the black people of Texas had little idea what the end of the Civil War meant for them.

And for many, the freedom proclaimed on Texas Emancipation Day—"Juneteenth," the former slaves would call it—had little immediate meaning in their lives. The slaves simply became sharecroppers, working the same fields for the same white landowners, with little more reward for their labor. Even those who hired out as field hands in more modern times made barely enough in wages to stay alive. "Ten cents an hour," says Mrs. Parker. "That's all they was paying us. Some was getting five cents an hour. They wasn't making fifty cents a day for ten

Part II—Texas, Our Texas: Some People and Places

hours of chopping cotton. Some farmers didn't want to pay that."

But some of the sharecroppers eventually were able to buy farms of their own, often the same acres they had worked for somebody else.

"They raised big families, and by all the family working, they could raise enough money to buy little plots from *Massa*," says Janice Martin, smiling wryly at the word. "But sometimes they would have a bad crop and they couldn't pay their taxes, and the white people would go up to the courthouse and pay the taxes and get the land back."

Against the odds, some succeeded. Two sisters named Nancy Ross Lockhart and Emily Ross Skinner, born in slavery, somehow bought not only their own plot but others as well, and later sold home sites to the families who live in Weeping Mary now.

"I remember them well," Mrs. Parker says. "I ate cooking what they cooked. They set up and talked with us when we were kids and told us about slave days, how they was treated. They was little girls in slavery. They said they'd cook and pour their food in an old tray, and all the children had spoons, and they all had to eat out of the same tray. They said some of them women, some of them master women over them, when the kids would go round the tray to eat, if the kids were talking or fussing, the master woman would take her hand and hit them so hard it would knock them plumb over that tray. My grandfather was their little brother. He was born the year slavery broke up."

The sisters are buried in St. Thomas Chapel Cemetery, about a mile from the land they owned. Their graves are unmarked. "It was hard times," Mrs. Parker says. "People couldn't hardly buy headstones."

Within sight of Mrs. Parker's house, Bill Hodge, who is ninety-two, is lounging on his own porch, listening to a cock crow into the drowsy air. His high cheekbones, Roman nose, and bronze, shiny skin lend him the aspect of an ancient

Weeping Mary

Egyptian pharaoh. "My sister, Eula Mae Ross, died last year at ninety-eight years old," he says. "Me and her was the oldest people down in here. That leaves me."

Mr. Hodge fathered seven children, two of them born dead. His wife died in 1971. All his children except one live in other places. He waves his arm at the dwellings across the road, which all house more distant kin, and says the names of those who live in them. "These people," he says, "they growed up, their parents all died, and they just stayed here."

He isn't a member of the Church of Weeping Mary, but he remembers when it also served as the one-room school for the black children. His attendance there was brief. "I quit school when I was in the second grade," he says. "The teacher wanted to whip me one morning because she didn't think I was walking fast enough. She was just like a big train from hell, marching us all up the road to the school. It was cold, and me and another boy fell behind. She had a switch. She said, 'I'm going to whip you if you don't step it up.' When we got to the schoolhouse, I went in and took off my coat. She come in, and she hit me two licks, and I said, 'I'm going home.' I got my dinner bucket and my coat and walked out the door. I never went to school again."

Mr. Hodge's nephew, Elijah Skinner, lives in the trailer across the road. He was a pupil at the school almost thirty years after his uncle quit, but the cold mornings were no different. "We didn't know what it was like to ride a school bus," he says. "We walked from back down yonder where we lived, and by the time we got to school, icicles would be frozen in our hair."

He recalls the women who followed one after another as his teachers: "Miss Beulah. Miss Ettie. Miss Bessie Howard. Miss Johnnie. They all was *hard*. These children now, they come home without no books at night. We had nine books in our hands whenever we left that schoolhouse. History. English. Geography. Arithmetic. Spelling. You had it under your arm when you went home."

Part II—Texas, Our Texas: Some People and Places

In the 1940s Booker T. Washington School was built in Alto. All the black children of Cherokee County were bused to it, and the Weeping Mary school was shut down.

By then the farms around the settlement were dying, too. "It kept slacking off, slacking off, slacking off until it was like it is now," Mr. Skinner says. "The farmers wasn't getting paid for what they was raising. All this land, from creek to creek, ain't nobody raising nothing on it now. Just cattle grazing."

So he, one of twenty-seven children in his family, left Weeping Mary to find a job. "I went to Nacogdoches, Dallas, Jacksonville," he says. "I stayed gone for forty years. I came back to Weeping Mary five or six years ago because my health failed me. I've had nine operations on my eyes and two for cancer."

From the doorway of his trailer, he can watch his nephew, Cherry Jenkins, working in his open-air shop. There's no sign that says so, but the shop is called the Oil Pit, Mr. Jenkins says. It's the only business in Weeping Mary, and his is the only job. "I work on any of it. Cars, trucks, mowers, TVs, VCRs," he says. Parts of these machines lie in piles everywhere, crowding the dark shed. To a post near his workbench Mr. Jenkins has nailed a hand-lettered sign:

> *To whom it may concern. No credit no checks. Too many hot. I work for cash not fun! So have the money when work is done. Not responsible for accidents fire or theft. Anything left over 30 days will be junked or sold. No credit so don't ask.*

Gospel music blares from an unseeable radio among the piles of metal. Mr. Jenkins pauses in his work and sips a beer. It's very hot. He was injured badly in a car wreck in 1988, and he, too, has had a number of operations to mend his bones and joints. It's hard for him to lift things. If something is really heavy, his son must come and help him. "But I build all my motors, do all my welding," he says. He shows off the engine he has installed in a pickup truck. "I built this," he says.

Later in the afternoon, Bessie Mae Parker walks down the road to visit her elder sisters, Minnie Ross Skinner and Cynthia Ross Thacker. Mrs. Skinner has been reading her Bible on the porch, but she puts it aside when Mrs. Parker arrives. Her favorite books in the Bible are Psalms and Revelation, she says. "I especially love to read Revelation. It explains what if we don't do, what's going to happen to who."

All the sisters have been members of the Church of Weeping Mary since they were children. "Whenever the door opened, we went," says Mrs. Skinner. "If we hadn't had something to hold to, we'd have been gone off the scene. But I'm thanking God that I had something to hold to. I held onto the Master. The one in heaven, I mean. And I'm still holding to him. He said, 'Man will *fail* you.' But the Master won't fail me."

After a while, the sisters' conversation moves into a kind of chant: "I've heard many a rooster crow," says Mrs. Skinner.

"I've wrung the neck of many a chicken," says Mrs. Thacker.

"Sure did," says Mrs. Parker.

"Pulled many a catfish out of the ditch."

"Oh, yes."

"Stripped many a stalk of cane."

"Yes, Lord."

"Killed many a rabbit."

"Oh, yes. Possum. Coon. What else?"

"Chopped lots of cotton."

"Oh, yes."

"Ten cents an hour in the hot sun all day."

"How many hours?"

"Ten hours."

"And we made it."

"We made it."

"We made it. Thank the Lord."

Part II—Texas, Our Texas: Some People and Places

Then Mrs. Skinner says, "I think of them as the good old days. I was happy then."

A handmade banner hangs over the pulpit in the Church of Weeping Mary:

The Lord Has Brought Us From a Mighty Long Way, it says.

A Postcard from the Past

I'm browsing the aisles of a book and paper show at Market Hall in Dallas. This show happens twice a year. Dealers in old and rare books, magazines, comic books, movie posters, picture postcards and the like set up shop in the huge hall for a couple of days, and bibliophiles, ephemera collectors, and other musty eccentrics go there and putter through the stuff, gnaw the fat with the dealers, and maybe buy an item or two.

So I'm at my friend Glenn Butler's table, looking through his thousands of old picture postcards, searching for photographs of the Mexican Revolution and West Texas small towns, two categories I collect in a casual way. And I run across this card from my hometown.

The description on the back reads: "Barbecue party on the patio at Indian Lodge, Davis Mountains State Park, Fort Davis, Texas."

In the center of the picture, a bunch of teenage boys and girls are gathered about a table, putting fixings on hamburgers. To the left, a smaller group—all girls—is seated on a low wall. The girls have already been to the table. They're holding paper plates on their laps, with fully constructed burgers. Another small group—all boys—is standing at the right edge of the picture near a huge agave cactus. The boys are holding empty paper plates, awaiting their turn at the grub.

89

Part II—Texas, Our Texas: Some People and Places

I can tell the picture was taken in the 1950s. There's a yellow wooden case of Coca-Cola in little green bottles on the wall near the seated girls. The kind of Coke that had a little kick to it. They don't make it anymore. Haven't for a long time.

Also, the kids are wearing typical 1950s West Texas teenager party clothes. All the girls are shod in the low-heeled shoes they called "ballerina slippers" back then. And one is wearing the most godawful fashion atrocity of that decade: a wide, flaring skirt with several stiff crinoline petticoats underneath.

The petticoats aren't visible in the picture, but anyone who was around in the fifties would know they're there. Lord, how I hated them. Trying to dance with a girl wearing half a dozen crinoline petticoats was like steering a tree about the floor. And when I stuffed her and her petticoats through the door of my mother's Plymouth, they took up three-quarters of the front seat, making it impossible for her to slide over and snuggle under my outstretched right arm while I drove with my left, which is what dating was about in those days of bench-style car seats and no safety belts.

West Texas boys' party style back then was pretty much what it is now: clean pants, clean shirts, and short, ugly haircuts.

It's a dull postcard. It doesn't show the viewer any of the beauty of the Davis Mountains or even of the Indian Lodge. The party is at night, and the patio is flooded with the harsh glare of the photographer's light, casting shadows on the white wall. He shot it from the top of a ladder, and the kids' facial features are washed out and indistinct. Nobody in the picture is doing anything interesting.

I can't imagine a tourist buying the thing and mailing it to the folks back home in Memphis or Tuscaloosa. Indeed, if this particular card ever got bought, it never got sent. There's neither message nor address nor stamp on it.

But as I look at the picture, the hairs on the back of my neck begin to rise.

"Hey, Glenn," I say. "Do you have a magnifying glass?"

Glenn gets a small pocket magnifier out of his briefcase. I scan the card with it.

Yes. The tall, skinny kid with the sandy crew cut. At the hamburger table. The one wearing the long-sleeved white shirt with the cuffs rolled back two turns, precisely between the wrists and the elbows. So cool. Only one guy wears his sleeves like that, only one guy that cool.

It is I. Bryan Woolley. Age seventeen.

I'm talking. Probably making a wisecrack, for I am a teenage smart-ass. The other kids, intent on their food or each other, don't seem to be listening.

In the group on the left, the girl in the bright green dress. My steady, Julie, from Marfa. She'll later become my first wife and ex. And near her, Barbara, another girl I date sometimes. And the girl in the black-and-white dress? My sister, Linda? I can't be sure.

I am sure about Albert, though, in the back of the picture, dead these twenty years, talking to his girl, Mary June. And Frank, in the plaid shirt and the big ears, at the center. And Horace, the husky, smiling fellow in the group by the cactus. My buddies. My companions in a thousand adventures.

But who are those other kids? Most of them seem younger than my crowd. I don't recognize them. Why is this bunch at a party together? Are we a school group? A church group? Is it somebody's birthday? Is it just a summer get-together? Many of our parties were at the Indian Lodge, and nearly all of them involved hamburgers.

There we all are, frozen in a moment more than forty years gone. It must have been an important moment for us then, but now it's as lost as an evening among the Etruscans or the Aztecs.

Part II—Texas, Our Texas: Some People and Places

Why has this humdrum postcard survived all these years? How has it come to be on Glenn Butler's table in Market Hall in Dallas on this particular December day? How does it happen that I, of all the hundreds browsing through the hall, pick it up and see my young, smart-ass self?

Is it fate? Mere chance? Does it mean anything at all?

I buy the card. Glenn charges me 75 cents for it.

The Pride of Cross Plains

Sixty years later, Jack Scott still remembers the four lines of verse he found in the typewriter after Bob Howard shot himself:

All fled, all done,
So lift me on the pyre;
The feast is over,
And the lamps expire.

On the sunny morning of June 11, 1936, Mr. Scott, still in his twenties, was editor, publisher, and the only reporter of the town's newspaper, the weekly *Cross Plains Review*.

As soon as word reached him, he rushed to the little white frame house where Robert E. Howard lived with his physician father and his sickly mother.

A few minutes earlier, a nurse had told Mr. Howard that his mother, who had lapsed into a coma, was about to die. He immediately went to his room and typed the verse, then walked to his car, climbed in, got a revolver from the glove compartment, put the muzzle to his head, and pulled the trigger.

A crowd already had gathered in the front yard when Mr. Scott arrived. The justice of the peace was standing on the porch.

93

Part II—Texas, Our Texas: Some People and Places

"He was kind of gazing off into the distance," Mr. Scott remembers. "Then he saw me and motioned for me to come into the house. He took me back to a little room where there was a typewriter on a table. There was a sheet of paper in the typewriter. He said, 'Read that.' I read it, and he said, 'What does it mean?' I said, 'Well, it seems to me it's the last thing Howard wrote. It seems to me he wrote that, went outside, got in his car, and put the gun to his head.' And the JP said, 'But what the hell is a pyre?'"

Today the house is a museum, and in the little room is a typewriter on a table, and in the typewriter are Mr. Howard's last words on a sheet of paper.

One summer weekend every year, dozens of pilgrims from all over the country and several foreign countries come to Cross Plains to pay homage to the young man who put the gun to his head. The Howard Festival, as the weekend is called, is the work of Project Pride, an organization that "tries to keep Cross Plains from dying and not let what few things we have that might be of interest to other people just go away," says Billie Ruth Loving, the local librarian. The Cross Plains Library bought the decaying Howard house a few years ago and transferred it to Project Pride, which has repaired and repainted it and furnished it in the style of the 1920s and '30s, when the doctor and his family lived there.

"For years, people traveling through here have stopped and asked if there was a museum or landmark or something related to Howard," Miss Loving says. "In 1986, on the fiftieth anniversary of his death, quite a lot of people gathered here, but we didn't have much for them. Now we do."

Mr. Howard, who was only thirty years old when he killed himself, was the most famous person who has ever lived in Cross Plains, and one of the most popular writers ever to work in Texas. Much of his work is still in print today, and his stories have been reprinted in several foreign languages. "He's big in Poland, big in Bulgaria, in England, Italy, France," says Glenn Lord, a Howard bibliographer and the former agent of his literary estate. "He's probably even bigger in Europe than he is in this country."

One of the hundreds of characters Mr. Howard created—Conan the Barbarian—has been the hero of an animated TV show, a series of comic books, and two movies starring Arnold Schwarzenegger. More than fifty novels about Conan have been written by other writers since Mr. Howard's death. All these properties are licensed by Conan Properties Inc., a company formed years ago by his literary heirs to perpetuate and promote the Conan character.

But during the nineteen years Mr. Howard lived with his parents in Cross Plains, most of the townspeople regarded him as odd, not special.

"I was sixteen at the time," says Miss Loving. "People were saying that Dr. Howard's crazy son had killed himself. That's the general impression that people had. He was withdrawn, and he was different. He was dominated by his mother. Nobody in Cross Plains understood him. But there's no telling how high his IQ was."

Robert Erwin Howard was born in 1906 in Peaster, Texas, the son of Dr. Isaac Mordecai Howard and his wife, Hester Jane Erwin. During the early years of his son's life, Dr. Howard moved his family from boom town to boom town across the West Texas oil patch. In 1919 he opened an office in the back of a drugstore in Cross Plains. He liked the town, so they stayed.

Desperately bored with life in the tedious little cotton-and-oil community, Bob Howard became a voracious reader. Local legend has it that when he ran out of stories to read during the summer, he broke into country schools and "borrowed" their books. "He always took them back," Miss Loving says. "He didn't do it to steal."

He wrote his first story at age nine and published his first work of fiction when he was eighteen. During the twelve years before his death, he wrote hundreds of stories, cranking out

Part II—Texas, Our Texas: Some People and Places

four or five a week for the "pulps," the cheap magazines with lurid covers, printed on rough wood-pulp paper, that provided tales of mystery, adventure, horror, and romance for the lowbrow masses of the 1920s, '30s, and '40s.

In July 1925 *Weird Tales*, one of the more prestigious pulps, which specialized in fantasy fiction, published a story by Mr. Howard called "Spear and Fang," for which the magazine paid him $16. It was the beginning of a long relationship. *Weird Tales* published many of Mr. Howard's best stories, including all the Conan yarns, paying him a penny a word.

Conan is a barbarian warrior from a prehistoric land called Cimmeria. Neither the places nor the time of his adventures ever existed. Sorcerers, monsters, gods, scantily clad women, and bloodthirsty warriors inhabit his world. Conan constantly is hacking at the minions of evil in dark, ruined temples and lost cities, rescuing women from sacrifice on the black altars of jewel-eyed idols, and escaping down hidden corridors and secret tunnels, pursued by man-eating gorillas, werewolves, and gargantuan snakes.

The stories are a stew of Norse myth, Arthurian legend, and Arabian fantasy, with dashes of Homeric and Virgilian epic stirred in. There isn't a tittle of existential angst, moral introspection, or any emotion except rage in Conan or any of his adversaries. The tales are pure, exuberant, uninterrupted action and mayhem from start to finish.

One of them describes the hero as "a tall man, mightily shouldered and deep of chest, with a massive corded neck and heavily muscled limbs.... His brow was low and broad, his eyes a volcanic blue that smouldered as if with some inner fire." To a friend, Mr. Howard wrote that he found the ingredients for the character among the people he knew in Cross Plains: "Some mechanism in my subconscious took the dominant characteristics of various prizefighters, gunmen, bootleggers, oil field bullies, gamblers, and honest workmen I had come in contact with, and combining them all, produced the amalgamation I call Conan the Cimmerian."

The result is comparable to Tarzan, says Mr. Lord, the Howard bibliographer. Or to Superman, says Donald M. Grant, a current publisher of the Conan stories. "I think the appeal of this kind of character is universal," says Mr. Grant. "People are looking for heroes, and Conan—with all his faults, even—is a hero."

Surely no comic book, movie, or TV hero ever swashbuckled with more verve than he: "Conan ripped a heavy ax from the rail and wheeled catlike to meet the rush of the sailors," relates *The Hour of the Dragon*. "They ran in, giving tongue like hounds, clumsy-footed and awkward in comparison to the pantherish Cimmerian. Before they could reach him with their knives, he sprang among them, striking right and left too quickly for the eye to follow, and blood and brains spattered as two corpses struck the deck."

Conan's creator was "a big, strong, robust guy," himself, remembers Mr. Scott. "He looked like a prizefighter, but I never knew of him having a fight. He didn't play ball. He didn't go to dances. He didn't like many people. He just didn't have much in common with them."

He stayed at home, taking care of his mother, who had tuberculosis. She controlled his life, says Miss Loving, and discouraged his budding romance with the only woman he ever dated, a local schoolteacher named Novalynn Price.

"His mother committed him when he was six years old to taking care of her," Miss Loving says. "He was a teeny little boy when she told him, 'Mother is taking care of you now, and when she's old you'll take care of her.' He often said he didn't want to outlive his mother."

The few outsiders allowed into the house told of hearing Mr. Howard in his tiny room shouting, "Die, demon from hell!" and other such lines, testing them in the hot West Texas air before committing them to the page.

"To the best of my knowledge," he wrote in an autobiographical essay, "I am the first writer to be produced by a

Part II—Texas, Our Texas: Some People and Places

section of the country comprising a territory equal to that of the state of Connecticut.... I was the first writer of the post oak country. My work's lack of merit cannot erase that fact."

"I have lived in the Southwest all my life," he wrote, "yet most of my dreams are laid in cold, giant lands of icy wastes and gloomy skies, and of wild, windswept fens and wilderness over which sweep great sea-winds, and which are inhabited by shock-headed savages with light fierce eyes.... Always I am the barbarian."

Mr. Howard's mother died the day after he shot himself. They had a double funeral.

The Star Party

Every evening when Sandra Schoonmaker came home from her shift at the Red Lobster, she would drop $5 of her tip money into a coffee can. When there was $100 in the can, she would mail it.

Every month, when he received her payment, the man who was selling her his telescope would send her a piece of it. By the end of nine months, Ms. Schoonmaker had assembled the complete instrument.

"So this is my baby," she says, wiping dust off it with a soft cloth.

It's near sundown. Ms. Schoonmaker is setting up her "baby" in a pasture. Across the ranch road, on the other side of a strong fence, a few buffaloes and longhorns chew their cuds and gaze incuriously in her direction.

For sixteen years, Ms. Schoonmaker has waited tables at the Wichita Falls Red Lobster restaurant. But when the sun goes down and she takes off her apron, she's an astronomer. The message on her T-shirt says it: A Woman's Place Is in the Observatory. For her, the stars are a passion.

Every May during the dark of the moon, she and hundreds of other obsessed amateur astronomers head for the Texas Star Party in the Davis Mountains of West Texas, where, as the old song says, "the stars at night are big and bright." They erect

99

Part II—Texas, Our Texas: Some People and Places

their telescopes and their tents, endure the torrid sun and the dust devils that dance across the land like miniature tornadoes, and—defying the wishes of the surrounding drought-stricken ranchers—hope it doesn't rain. Here they eat, sleep, and breathe astronomy without pause for a solid week.

"I don't even mind the dust and the wind," Ms. Schoonmaker says. "I would be the most miserable person to work with if I had to be at the Red Lobster while this was going on. Nobody could get along with me. I couldn't even be nice to my customers."

She didn't acquire her telescope until 1990, but astronomy has been her passion since 1957, when the Soviet Union launched *Sputnik I*. "Every single night, I was outside trying to spot it as it went over," she says. "And I kept seeing these stars—three stars in a row—and I didn't know what they were. I kept asking people, but nobody knew. I went to the library and found out they're Orion's belt. Then I started reading about stars. I found out that different stars have different colors. I learned they have names. I thought, 'Wow! This is neat!'"

In 1985 Ms. Schoonmaker came to the Star Party. "There weren't many women out here that year," she says. "I was one of the first."

The first Star Party was in 1979 when about fifty astronomers gathered in Davis Mountains State Park, only a few miles from the world-renowned McDonald Observatory on Mount Locke. They studied the heavens at night, slept late in the mornings, and visited in the afternoons.

Three years later the party was outgrowing the park's capacity, so it moved a couple of miles to the Prude Guest Ranch. In the years since, it has become recognized as one of the three major annual events for amateur astronomers in the United States. The other two, in Vermont and California, are primarily for telescope makers. "They're for getting together and looking at gizmos," says Keith Shank of Allen, one of the honchos of this year's Fort Davis get-together. "The Texas Star

Party is the only major astronomical gathering in the United States that's made for observing. What we have here is 5,000 feet of altitude and the darkest skies in North America. With that, you can do some serious astronomy."

More than seven hundred astronomers showed up this year, many with spouses and kids along. Some drove nonstop from Minnesota, Washington, Florida, or Connecticut, hauling their gear in vans and trailers. Several flew from Great Britain, Brazil, Canada, France, Italy.

"It's awesome," says Romano Genocchio, from near Venice, taking a gaze at an invisible-to-the-naked-eye galaxy through somebody else's 36-inch telescope. "To see the stars this clearly in Italy, you would have to go far into the mountains, and it would be about zero degrees."

Mr. Shank says his Dallas friends don't believe his claim that Venus casts shadows in the Davis Mountains. "But it does," he says. "One year we had some folks down from New Jersey. When the Milky Way came up over the horizon, they thought it was thunderclouds. It's so big and bright it's kind of scary."

The astronomers have the ranch to themselves for the week. Windows of its buildings are covered with foil. All necessary outdoor lights are fitted with the dimmest of red bulbs. The ranch gates are shut to traffic at nine each evening, just as the sun is going down, and no one inside the gate may drive about the ranch after dark.

During the mornings, a howitzer fired down the ranch road wouldn't hit a living being. Although the temperature inside their tents hits 100 degrees by 9 A.M. some days, the astronomers snore on unawares.

By noon they're beginning to emerge, scratching and yawning. They head for chow at the ranch dining hall, then to the area where vendors have set up shop, offering everything the amateur astronomer needs, from gadgets to red-lensed

Part II—Texas, Our Texas: Some People and Places

flashlights, books and star charts, and astro jewelry made of meteorite metal.

Later in the afternoons, some gather for lectures by invited amateur and professional astronomers on such topics as "Photographic Determination of the Eccentricity of the Earth's Orbit" and "Ektachrome 1600: The Ultimate Deep-Sky Slide Film?" and "How to Configure Your Home Video Camera and PC as a Fireball Motion Detector" and "The Challenge of Comet Hale-Bopp."

Near sundown they drift into the fields where their telescopes stand like cannon, wrapped in plastic or foil to protect them from sun and dust. They remove the covers, examine their mirrors and lenses for dust and dirt, lay out books and charts on tables equipped with red light, and aim their telescopes at the parts of the sky where they plan to spend the night.

"Some are looking at star clusters and nebulae," Mr. Shank says, "some at galaxies. Some are looking at things that have never been visually seen. Many things in the sky are photographed that have never been seen with the eye. Ninety percent of professional astronomers never look through a telescope. They look at data. Some of the larger telescopes here are connected to computers. You can spend tens of thousands of dollars on this hobby. A lot of people do. It just depends on how much the disease affects you. If you're not careful, your life will center on it. Some folks, on the other hand, come out, throw down a lawn chair, take out a pair of binoculars, and look at the sky. I think maybe they have the most fun."

Many speak of their first encounter with the stars in tones that others might employ in describing a religious experience. Mr. Shank recalls lying in his backyard in Irving when he was a child, looking up at the stars, and reading a certain book that taught him the constellations. "It was like turning a switch," he says. "I've been 'Go' ever since."

Dave Clark of Austin, one of the founders of the Prude Ranch party, tells of borrowing a little telescope from a neighbor when he was a child. "One night I pointed it at a bright thing and looked into the eyepiece, and there was Saturn and its rings. That's all I needed. I still have almost mystical experiences sometimes, looking at celestial objects. Especially Saturn."

Larry Mitchell of Houston, whose 36-inch, 14-foot-tall telescope is one of the largest on the ranch, has spent many thousands on his hobby. "I went to a Halley's Comet party in 1986 and saw people with these humongous telescopes. I've been into it ever since. I keep buying bigger scopes. I like snooping around in other galaxies. But I've reached my limit," he says, stepping onto a 14-foot ladder to climb to his eyepiece.

As the sun sinks beyond sight, the sky dims and the spectacle for which so many people have traveled so far begins to unfold: first, Venus, bright as a headlight above the western horizon; then the brighter constellations—Leo in the west; Castor and Pollux, the twins, to the right of him; the two Dippers directly above; Scorpius in the east.

As the darkness deepens, more stars, smaller seeming, unimaginably far away, brighten into sharp needles of light until the vast black dome seems full of them, thousands beyond thousands, prodigally flung.

By full dark, an upward-gazing earthling can imagine himself flying by night into a great metropolis, its thousands of lights brilliant, the plane upside down. Quiet falls over the fields where the telescopes stand. Work bulbs glow like far-off exit lights. Gazers bend over their eyepieces, beginning their night's work and pleasure.

Mr. Mitchell says he and his Houston friends must drive eighty miles out of the city to find a sky free enough from light pollution to allow them to see anything. Mr. Shank and his Dallas buddies have to drive clear to Oklahoma.

"Most of the children in our cities have never seen the stars," Mr. Clark says. "Some of them never will. That's sad."

In a League of His Own

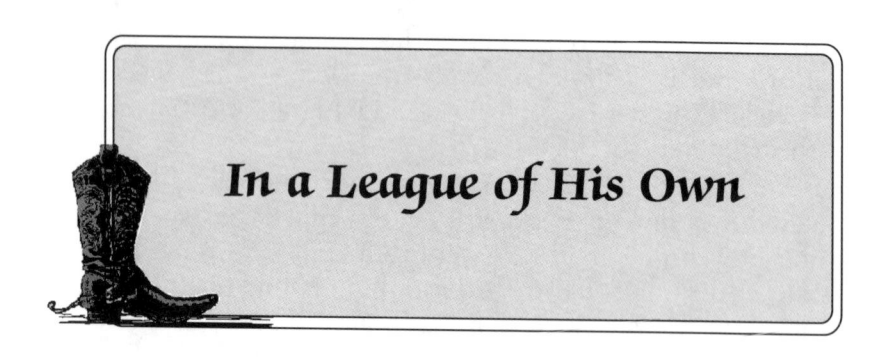

One day pitcher Jerry Craft of the Wichita Falls Stars was warming up for a big game when a commotion broke out in his team's dugout.

Amidst a lot of screaming and cussing, Mr. Craft's teammates were removing the uniform from a new player who had joined the Stars just that day. When he was wearing nothing but his jockey strap, they tossed him onto the field before the hooting crowd. He fled the ballpark and never returned.

"What in the world was that all about?" Mr. Craft asked a teammate.

"He said some bad things about you," the teammate replied. "We were just taking care of you."

During the summers of 1959 and 1960, when the civil rights movement was beginning to heighten racial tensions throughout the South, Mr. Craft was a star pitcher in the semiprofessional West Texas Colored League.

He also was the league's only white player.

"They were two of the best summers of my life," he remembers. "Except for that one time, race never entered into it. The crowds never booed me. Nobody was ever rude to me. They threw beer bottles sometimes when I would strike out the home team, but they did that to the black pitchers, too."

In a League of His Own

Today Mr. Craft is mayor of Jacksboro, board chairman of the Jacksboro National Bank, and a successful rancher. In 1959 he was twenty-one years old and would graduate from Texas Tech in a year. He had played baseball at Tech when he was a freshman but had quit after he joined a fraternity. "Being on the baseball team required discipline," he says. "I was having too much fun playing softball and chasing girls."

But when he returned to Jacksboro each summer, he would play for one of the many semipro baseball teams in the area. "Almost every town had one," he says. "Baseball was a community thing back then."

Just home from school in 1959, he got a phone call from a Mr. Carl Sedberry, a businessman who lived in Graham. He asked Mr. Craft if he was planning to play ball that summer. Mr. Craft said he was but didn't know yet for which team. Mr. Sedberry said, "Well, we'd like you to play for us."

"And who are you?"

"The Wichita Falls Stars."

"I never heard of you."

"We have a really good ball club, except we don't have any pitching. And we're in a really tough league."

"I never heard of you guys."

"We're playing the Abilene Blues Sunday at 2 o'clock. Come on by and pitch for us one game and see how we do."

Mr. Craft had never heard of the Abilene Blues, either, but he showed up at Spudder Park in Wichita Falls, where many semipro games were played. "The stands were full of black people," he says. "I thought I had gone to the wrong address."

He drove to a couple of other ball fields, but nobody was playing there, and nobody could tell him about the Wichita Falls Stars. So he returned to Spudder Park.

A black man in a suit, necktie, and snap-brim hat approached him. "Are you Mr. Craft?" he asked.

"Yes, I am."

Part II—Texas, Our Texas: Some People and Places

"I'm Mr. Sedberry."

Mr. Craft's mouth dropped open.

"Obviously, you didn't know I was black," Mr. Sedberry said.

"No, sir," Mr. Craft said.

"Have you ever played for a black ball club?"

"No, sir," Mr. Craft said. "I've never even played against a black ball club."

"Do you have any prejudices?"

"I don't guess so. As long as I get to play ball. Will the black people resent my playing for you?"

"I don't know. It'll be a good experiment. We'll pay you $75 a game."

"That's OK with me."

"Well, go warm up."

The Stars had never beaten the Abilene Blues, but Mr. Sedberry had developed a strategy for Mr. Craft's first game. He would start his worst pitcher, allow the Blues to score a few runs and get very confident, as usual. Then he would put in his secret weapon, Mr. Craft.

"By the second inning," Mr. Craft says, "the Stars were behind 7-0 and Abilene had the bases loaded and one out. Mr. Sedberry turned to me and said, 'I think it's time to put you in.' I said, 'I think it's way the hell too late, Mr. Sedberry.' He said, 'Trust me, Mr. Craft.'"

The first batter hit a hard line drive past Mr. Craft's ear, but the second baseman caught it and stepped on the bag for a double play, ending the inning. "When I got up to pitch the third inning," Mr. Craft says, "the first batter stood on home plate. I mean right on it."

Mr. Craft appealed to the umpire but lost the argument. "Go on and pitch, white boy," the umpire said.

The batter walked on four pitches. So the next batter stood on the plate, too. Mr. Sedberry came to the mound and said,

"Well, Mr. Craft, you're going to lose this game unless you hit one of them in the head."

"I didn't want to do that," Mr. Craft says. "I decided to hit him on the shoulder. But he turned into the pitch instead of away from it, and I hit him right in the heart. He fell over and his legs kicked and his eyes rolled back in his head. I thought I had killed him. The rest of the batters stood so far from the plate that they couldn't touch it with the bat. I pitched a no-hitter the rest of the game. The final score was 17-9. It was a great victory. They carried me off the field on their shoulders. Mr. Sedberry said, 'Well, what do you think?' I said, 'I've never had so much fun in a baseball game.'"

So Mr. Craft pitched for the Stars the whole season, and the next season, too.

When his team played in Wichita Falls, they were the Wichita Falls Stars. When they played in Graham, where Mr. Sedberry lived, they were the Graham Stars.

"I always called him Mr. Sedberry, and he always called me Mr. Craft. We really did like each other," Mr. Craft says. "The other players always called me White Boy, but it was kind of affectionate. We also had a shortstop called Fat and an outfielder called Rabbit."

Caravanning about Texas and Oklahoma in cars and pickup trucks, the Stars defeated all the other teams in the West Texas Colored League—the Abilene Blues, the Hamlin Pied Pipers, the Waco Tigers, and the Grandfield, Oklahoma, Zebras.

"That first year, we all furnished our own uniforms," Mr. Craft says, "and they were all different. I wore an old canvas uniform with the name of the Midway Falcons on it, a team I had played on earlier. But we had a large entourage because we never lost a game, and a lot of money was bet on us. The second year I played for the Stars, we had real uniforms, all alike."

Sometimes they played non-league games against white teams, too. "The black folks would sit on one side of the

Part II—Texas, Our Texas: Some People and Places

stands," Mr. Craft says, "and there would be a 10- or 20-foot empty strip, and the white folks would sit on the other side. I guess I was naive. I had never thought about it. The schools in Jacksboro were segregated, but some of the earliest pioneers in the town were black because of Fort Richardson on the edge of town and the black soldiers who had served there. Consequently, we never had any area of town where the black people were concentrated. They lived all over Jacksboro. We played football and baseball together in my parents' yard. We swam together. But I never once wondered why the schools were segregated."

Then one night in 1960, the Stars were returning from a tough game in Waco, where they had lost to the Tigers, 2-1. They stopped for dinner at a black restaurant in West.

"The owner came up to me and said, 'Sir, you're going to have to leave. We don't serve white people here.'

"Mr. Sedberry said, 'Well, if he can't eat here, none of us can eat here.' So he canceled all the orders and we left.

"My teammates slapped me on the shoulder and said, 'Welcome to our world, White Boy.'"

Mr. Craft pitched eleven games for the Stars in 1959 and won them all. He was 8-2 in 1960. But in the course of that season, the team began falling apart. "Players started showing up late for games, or not showing up at all," he says. "It got to the point where we were recruiting people out of the stands to fill out the team. During a particularly bad game in August of 1960, I put on my warm-up jacket, shook hands with Mr. Sedberry, and said, 'It's been a real pleasure, but this is it.'"

He went home and never played baseball again. His youth was over.

The Sacred Harp

The hellos have been said. The hands have been shaken. The hugs and greeting kisses have been exchanged. Now the chairman, B.E. Matthews, steps to the center of the square and announces the opening song.

Someone among the tenors sings the pitch, for there are no instruments here. Then the people sing the whole song in the syllables of the musical scale, *"Fa, la, sol, fa, mi, la, sol"* to ensure that everyone knows the tune. Then, without a pause, they repeat, this time launching robustly into the words:

Come, we that love the Lord,
And let our joys be known;
Join in a song with sweet accord,
And thus surround the throne.

Mr. Matthews has chosen the hymn at the bottom of page 31 in *The Sacred Harp*, the long blue songbook that he and all the people hold. As he sings, he pumps his right arm up and down in long, even strokes, setting a stately pace for the music. Others of the singers pump their arms, too, to keep themselves in time, or just for the pleasure of it. Some are almost rising from their seats in their enthusiasm.

About one hundred people, some young, some old, some rural, some urban, some religious, some not, have gathered at the Bethel Primitive Baptist Church in the tiny community of

Part II—Texas, Our Texas: Some People and Places

McMahan on this sunny Saturday for the annual Southwest Texas Sacred Harp Singing Convention, a tradition their ancestors began long ago. They'll sing at the top of their voices —there's no pianissimo in Sacred Harp music—for four hours a day for two days, making a joyful noise unto the Lord, with only two five-minute recesses and an hour-long break for dinner on the grounds each day.

"Some people run marathons," says Gaylon Powell, one of their number. "They work themselves up to running 26 miles. Likewise with our voices. We work until we can sing for four hours today and four hours tomorrow. We could go longer than that. In Alabama, singings sometimes last three or four days."

The singers have arranged themselves in a hollow square as they always do, the tenors in front of Mr. Matthews, the altos behind him, the basses to his right, the trebles to his left, all facing him.

"We're not a choir," Mr. Powell says. "It's not listeners' music. It's singers' music. We're singing to each other, not to an audience. And we can hear each other better in the square."

One after another, other leaders follow Mr. Matthews, moving to the center of the square, announcing the page numbers of the songs they want to sing. Leaders of all ages, from bashful children to revered seniors, take their turns. All are treated equally with attention and respect.

How tedious and tasteless the hours,
When Jesus no longer I see!
Sweet prospects, sweet birds and sweet flow'rs
Have lost all their sweetness to me.

Individually, few voices here are better than ordinary. But by what the musical folklorist Alan Lomax has called a "combination of musical skill and individualism," the singers invest their music with a rare passion and vigor. They sing their words with a conviction and joy that raise their sound to an almost angelic purity. Every verse is a hallelujah. In the rear

The Sacred Harp

of the sanctuary, where the nonsinging listeners sit, tears are welling in many eyes.

This is a kind of singing taught many years ago by itinerant masters who rode from village to village, teaching classes at churches and schools and courthouses.

The music is simple, with a scale of seven notes, but using only the four syllables fa, sol, la, and mi and missing the do, re, and ti of more usual music. And the notes that the singing masters taught have different shapes—a triangle for fa, a circle for sol, a square for la, a diamond for mi—a scheme devised in early America to teach singing to people who couldn't read music.

Unlike the choral music most listeners are used to, the melody in Sacred Harp isn't carried by the highest voices. It's sung by the tenors. The treble, or soprano, section—which includes both female and male voices—sings a harmony higher than the melody. Joined by the lower altos and basses, the singers create an ethereal but wild-sounding harmony seldom heard in modern times.

"Shaped-note music began in New England just after the Revolutionary War," says Charles Whitmer, a band director in the Conroe public schools and a devoted Sacred Harp singer. "The songs were indigenous American music, and they wound up in various songbooks that the traveling singing masters used. Their composers didn't follow the rules of the composers in Europe. But later, the Northeastern cities started importing the European style of hymnody and saw the American style as inferior and odd-sounding."

Eventually, shaped-note music was pushed out of even the rural areas of the increasingly "sophisticated" Northeast, but it traveled southward and westward with the frontier and landed in Texas in the 1850s with settlers from Alabama.

In 1844 Major Benjamin Franklin White of that state had published a shaped-note songbook called *The Sacred Harp*, containing more than five hundred songs that frontier people who

Part II—Texas, Our Texas: Some People and Places

had no musical instruments could sing in their worship services or for their own pleasure.

The words of the songs in Major White's book—which has been revised only a few times since its first edition—are religious. Some of them are in the regular church hymnals, many not. Some are set to ancient drinking and dancing tunes from the British Isles. Others were written in New England not long after the Revolution. Some crossed Cumberland Gap with Daniel Boone. Some were written on the Southern frontier or in old Texas.

The *Sacred Harp* became a favorite of the Southern singing masters, who taught from it and sold copies to their pupils. After a teacher moved on to another village, his former pupils would get together from time to time to sing the music they had learned, and they formed "conventions" to meet at regularly scheduled times at different churches and schools about the countryside. Before they sang the words of each song, they would run through the shaped notes as their masters had taught them, singing the fa, sol, la, mi syllables of each measure to make sure everyone knew the tune. That practice has been continued in the Sacred Harp conventions ever since.

Why should we start or fear to die,
When tim'rous worms we mortals are,
Death is the gate to endless joy,
But yet we dread to enter there.

Many of the singers at the Southwest Texas Convention are offspring of longtime Sacred Harp families. "My family taught in the singing schools of Alabama, where I was raised up," says Mr. Matthews, who lives at Thorndale. "We sang this music at home. We sang it in our churches. I learned it from my father and mother, from my grandfather and grandmother. I've been singing it for seventy years."

Mr. Powell, though little more than half Mr. Matthews' age, also was born into the Sacred Harp and has a lifelong association with the annual singings at Bethel Church.

The Sacred Harp

Organized by Alabama settlers in 1852, the church was chosen as the site of a singing in 1900. Every spring since, on the last Sunday of the first month with five Sundays, singers have gathered here. More times than not, members of Mr. Powell's family have attended.

"My great-great-grandfather on my mother's side came from Alabama in 1880," Mr. Powell says. "He became a Sacred Harp singing school teacher in Lampasas County. On my dad's side, a gentleman from this church, named Walter Reed, taught Sacred Harp schools among the Primitive Baptists of Texas. He taught in Llano County, where my ancestors on my dad's side were residing in 1907, and they would come over here to attend the singings at Bethel. My grandmother and grandfather married on May 1, 1936. On the fifth weekend in May of that year, there was a singing here. That was their honeymoon. I led my first song at this very church two weeks before my fourth birthday. They stood me up on a bench, and I led 'Amazing Grace.'"

Mr. Powell, who's a member of Littlevine Primitive Baptist Church in Austin, says *The Sacred Harp* songbook and Sacred Harp singings also occupy an important place in his denomination's history. "In the old days, the Primitive Baptists had circuit-riding preachers, and a congregation would have preaching only one Sunday a month. The other three Sundays, the church was vacant, so they would have singings there. Most hymns the Primitive Baptists sing now came out of *The Sacred Harp*, and we still don't have instruments in our services."

But Sacred Harp conventions have never been denominational affairs, and the twenty singings now held in Texas each year attract singers of many religious persuasions. "You'll find Baptists and Methodists and Presbyterians," says Mr. Whitmer. "And Catholics and Unitarians and Quakers."

"And agnostics and Jews," adds Mr. Powell.

Folk music enthusiasts from outside the Sacred Harp's traditional Southern and Texan territory also have been learning

113

the old songs, and singers gather for conventions now in such unlikely places as Chicago, San Francisco, and Denver.

    Early, my God, without delay,
    I haste to seek thy face;
    My thirsty spirit faints away,
    Without thy cheering grace.

For many of the singers at the Bethel convention, an annual singing isn't enough. They also participate in most of the other Texas conventions, and some travel to singings in other states as well. Barbara Moore, an elementary teacher from Thrall, says she attends a convention or at least one practice session almost every week. "There's a peace that comes over me when I sing Sacred Harp," she says. "The words of the songs are truths, are things that I believe in. The music is a bond that forms between the people. You meet someone, you go somewhere else, you see them again. You have no strangers. Once you travel a bit with this, you have friends wherever you are."

By the end of the first day, sixty-five singers have risen to lead their favorites. By the end of the second day, more than one hundred twenty songs have been sung, and the singers have elected Al Rogers of Austin to succeed Mr. Matthews as their new chairman.

Before they leave for home, they bow their heads in memoriam to those whose voices in times past rose with their own, but are silent now. "Let us remember those who have died with songs that they have sung and we have sung," Mr. Rogers says.

And he names their names.

    Dear friends, farewell I do you tell,
    Since you and I must part;
    I go away, and here you stay,
    But still we're joined in heart.

The Last of the Big Four

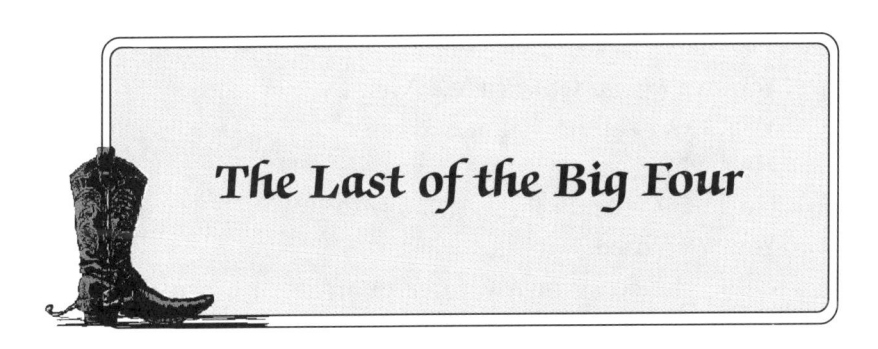

One summer day in 1923, when James Farmer was three years old, he went shopping with his mother in Holly Springs, Mississippi. "It was a great joy to me to walk downtown with her," he remembers. "I was holding onto one of her fingers, trudging through the red dust along the unpaved streets."

They reached the town square and went into a store. Mrs. Farmer bought a few things. When they returned to the blinding heat of the square, James told his mother he was thirsty. "Let's stop and get a Coke," he said.

"Son, you can't get a Coke down here," Mrs. Farmer replied. "We have lots of Coke in the icebox. Wait till we get home."

"I want one now," James said. "I have a nickel. Daddy gave it to me."

"It's not the money, son," Mrs. Farmer said. "Keep still. Wait till we get home."

Just then, James saw a boy go into the drugstore across the street. "Mother, see him?" James said. "I bet he's going to get a Coke."

He remembers pulling his mother across the street and looking through the drugstore's screen door. He remembers the boy was sitting on a stool and sipping a drink through a straw.

Part II—Texas, Our Texas: Some People and Places

"See there, Mother," James said. "Now let's go in and get my Coke."

"You can't get a Coke here," Mrs. Farmer said.

"Well, why can he?" James asked.

"He's white," she said.

"He's white. And me?"

"You're colored."

Telling the story nearly three-quarters of a century later, Mr. Farmer stops speaking for a moment, then sighs and continues:

"We walked home in silence. I held onto her finger all the way. When we got home, she threw herself across the bed and wept. I went out on the front porch and sat on the steps, alone with my three-year-old thoughts.

"This is my earliest memory of life."

☆

Mr. Farmer's father, Dr. James Leonard Farmer, was the first black Ph.D. in Texas. On January 12, 1920, when James Leonard Farmer Jr. was born, Dr. Farmer was pastor of a Methodist church in Marshall, Texas. But Methodists move their clergy around a lot. Six months after his son's birth, Dr. Farmer, a biblical scholar, was transferred out of Texas to Rust College, a black school in Holly Springs, Mississippi, as a professor and administrator.

In the son's autobiography, *Lay Bare the Heart*, he remembers the father: "A highly complex man, he projected three images, three distinct faces: to the black community, a savant and solon; to the whites, a 'good' Negro, compromising if not subservient, who knew his place; and to his son, a strong father who, perhaps unknowingly, fostered the spirit of rebellion."

Mr. Farmer's mother, Pearl, was educated to be a schoolteacher. She quit her job when she married the clergyman. The family occupied a position of prestige in the black community.

Her walk to town with her little boy and the Coke he couldn't buy would mark his life forever.

"Up through the years, I had a recurring dream about that day," he says. "I dreamed about it so much that I wasn't sure it had really happened. As I was approaching adulthood, I asked my mother about it. She remembered it as clearly as I. So it did happen. It was not just a recurring dream. It was a reality which had buried itself in the subconscious and had become a dream."

When he became a man, Mr. Farmer would devote his life to destroying the laws and customs that wouldn't allow a little "colored" boy to take a seat beside a little white boy at a soda fountain.

In April 1942 he and a few other activists—some black, some white—organized the Congress of Racial Equality (CORE). Its purpose was to use the nonviolent protest techniques of Mahatma Gandhi to end racial segregation in the United States. About a month later, at the Jack Spratt restaurant in Chicago, CORE began what Mr. Farmer believes was the first organized civil-rights sit-in in American history. It succeeded. The owner desegregated his restaurant.

On February 1, 1960, four black students began a similar sit-in at the Woolworth lunch counter in Greensboro, North Carolina. CORE volunteers joined the students and helped them keep the sit-in alive. It was the first major event of what would become the civil rights movement of the 1960s.

In 1961, after becoming national director of the organization he had helped establish, Mr. Farmer organized the Freedom Ride that took black and white protesters on Greyhound and Trailways buses from Washington, D.C. to Jackson, Mississippi. White CORE volunteers took the seats in the back of the buses, and the black volunteers sat in the front, where the region's Jim Crow laws forbade them.

In Alabama, the Ku Klux Klan beat several of the riders almost to death and burned one of the buses. In Mississippi,

Part II—Texas, Our Texas: Some People and Places

the state police arrested the riders and locked them in several jails and a state penitentiary.

About a year later, Mr. Farmer led another protest called Freedom Highways, in which black and white motorists traveling together staged massive sit-ins to desegregate restaurants along U.S. Highway 40. "One day we walked into a restaurant and the manager was standing in the door," Mr. Farmer says. "He said, 'You can't come in here! You can't come in here! We don't serve niggers here!' and I said, 'It's all right! We don't eat them, either!'"

In August 1963 Mr. Farmer couldn't attend the March on Washington with Dr. Martin Luther King Jr. and the other nationally prominent civil rights leaders because he was in jail in Plaquemine, Louisiana, where he had led a march protesting police brutality. A few days later, he almost was lynched by state troopers there. He escaped the town in the back of a hearse.

In June 1964, during the Freedom Summer in Mississippi, the Ku Klux Klan murdered Michael Schwerner, Andrew Goodman, and James Cheney, three CORE workers who had been trying to register black voters. Their bodies were uncovered weeks later in a shallow grave under a fake dam.

During the worst days of the civil rights protests, when violence met the nonviolent demonstrators at every turn, CORE was called "the Marines of the movement." Of those times, Mr. Farmer later would write in his autobiography: "If any man says that he had no fear in the action of the sixties, he is a liar. Or without imagination."

⚜ ★ ⚜

Mr. Farmer is sitting in a wheelchair in his red frame house, which sits on a hill in the countryside near Fredericksburg, Virginia. It's February 1997. The trees are bare, the sky gray and heavy. The thick snowfall of the previous day is beginning to melt.

The room used to be a living room or den, but now a hospital bed is there. Several medicine vials are grouped on the table beside it. Caroline Cotton, the nurse who tends Mr. Farmer every day, passes in and out, bringing him things, answering the phone.

He's a month past his seventy-seventh birthday. He lost his right leg to diabetes a little over a year ago. He's blind. He lost his right eye to retinal vascular occlusion in 1979 and the sight in his left several years later. "I wear the eye patch for cosmetic purposes," he says. "The right eye has deflated like a balloon." The patch looks dashing on him, and the dark left eye, though blind, still sparkles with intelligence and humor. His short hair is gray. His café au lait skin is unwrinkled, his voice rich, deep, and melodious. "I'm not really in peak condition," he says. "I've been fighting not only blood sugar but blood pressure." But he looks twenty years younger than he is. If it weren't for the wheelchair, he wouldn't seem infirm at all.

His schedule also belies his condition. He's midway through his twelfth year on the faculty of Martha Washington College, a state school of about 3,800 students in Fredericksburg, where he teaches a course titled "The History of the Civil Rights Movement." "I had to cut down on the number of students enrolled," he says. "I used to have 275 per semester, 550 for the year. But I've cut that down to 100 students per semester, 50 in each class, because of the load of term papers."

He likes young people, he says. He waves toward a green-and-white street sign that's displayed on the fireplace mantel beside his chair. "James Farmer St." it says. In July 1995 the City Council of Marshall, Texas, Mr. Farmer's birthplace, renamed Barney Street for him and his father. "The thing that I liked about it was that the city high school kids came up with the idea," Mr. Farmer says. "That's an integrated high school, you know. The kids put the pressure on, so the City Council discussed it and agreed to it."

It was in Marshall many years ago that Mr. Farmer met one of the most influential people in his life, a man who would give

Part II—Texas, Our Texas: Some People and Places

him a hard push toward his destiny in the struggle for racial equality and justice.

After his father's hitch at Rust College had ended, he had been transferred to Sam Houston College (now Huston-Tillotson) in Austin, then to Gammon Theological Seminary in Atlanta, then back to Texas as a professor of religion and philosophy at Wiley College in Marshall.

At age fourteen, James Jr. registered as a freshman at Wiley and fell under the spell of Melvin B. Tolson, a professor of English who also coached the debating team and directed the campus dramas. "He taught everything in his classes," Mr. Farmer says. "He made students study. He drove me to the library to look up things and to read books that had nothing to do with the class he was teaching. He would discuss those books with me. But I guess the most important part of my relationship with Tolson was that he pointed me toward the answer to segregation."

Mr. Farmer remembers a particular Thursday night and a bull session in the men's dormitory: "We were discussing segregation. I took the floor and orated about what a terrible institution segregation was. With my words I destroyed segregation! I ripped it apart! I cremated it and dug a grave for its ashes and wrote its epitaph in stone! I told the other men that segregation had to be destroyed and all of us had to do it!" Mr. Farmer's rolling voice stops. He chuckles softly. "I was so pleased with myself because the other men in that room were listening to me wide-eyed and with their mouths open. Afterwards, I felt so proud. I had done my duty! I had killed segregation!"

A few days later, Mr. Farmer told Professor Tolson of his oratorical triumph. The teacher greeted the news with a quizzical smile and turned the conversation to a movie that was playing at the Paramount Theater in downtown Marshall. He asked Mr. Farmer whether he had seen the movie and had he enjoyed it. Mr. Farmer replied that he had.

"Where did you sit?" Mr. Tolson asked him.

The Last of the Big Four

"I sat where we always sit. Up in the balcony."

Mr. Tolson said: "Now let me understand what you're telling me, Farmer. On Thursday night in the men's dormitory you destroyed segregation. You reduced it to ashes and buried it. And then Saturday you walked downtown in Marshall, Texas, to the Paramount Theater, you went around to the side entrance, climbed the back stairs, and sat in the buzzards' roost and watched a movie. You allowed yourself to be segregated. You paid your parents' hard-earned money for the privilege. Furthermore, you enjoyed it."

As he walked home that night, Mr. Farmer says, he remembered the incident in Holly Springs when he was three years old: "It hit me like a sledgehammer. When I was three, that incident had burned me up inside. But now that I was a teenager in college, something had happened to me. I had been segregated so often in the past years that it didn't bother me anymore. Each time I was segregated, it hurt less than it did the previous time. Now it didn't hurt at all. Going to that theater, I had passed more than a dozen stores that wouldn't have served me a Coca-Cola or anything else. And it didn't bother me. The old wound from Holly Springs had scabbed over or developed calluses. I felt no pain there anymore. It seemed to me that somehow I had to rub the wound raw again and make it hurt more each time I was segregated, rather than less. Finally we would come to a point where we would say to ourselves: 'No more! This is it! Never again!' Then segregation would be doomed."

C∈⋲ ★ ⋺⊃

Mr. Farmer majored in chemistry, intending to become a doctor. But during his senior year he discovered he couldn't stand the sight of blood. "Since then, I've seen more blood than I could imagine," he says. He graduated in 1938 at age eighteen and decided to follow in his father's footsteps. He enrolled in the Howard University School of Religion in Washington, D.C. There he met Dr. Howard Thurman, a theologian who introduced him to the writings of Mahatma Gandhi on the philosophy of nonviolent protest. Mr. Farmer received his bachelor of divinity degree in 1941, but when he learned what was happening in his denomination, he refused to be ordained.

"Three branches of the Methodist Church—the Methodist Episcopal Church, the Methodist Episcopal Church South, and the Methodist Protestant Church—were reuniting after splitting apart during the Civil War," he says. "The reunification plan was a segregated plan. In it there were five jurisdictions that were geographic, for the white-member churches, and a sixth jurisdiction, called the Central Jurisdiction, for all the black churches in the country. I did not see how I could preach the gospel in a segregated church. It was as simple as that."

Instead, he went to work in Chicago for the Fellowship of Reconciliation, a Quaker-sponsored anti-war, anti-violence group, making speeches against racism and segregation. He was twenty-one. A year later, he organized CORE.

During the 1950s, while serving CORE as a volunteer, he made his living as a labor organizer for the Upholsterer's International Union, and later for the State, County and Municipal Employees Union. In 1959 Roy Wilkins invited him to join the staff of the NAACP. He eventually became program director, but resigned in 1961 to return to CORE as national director.

During his early days as CORE's leader, he had a meeting with Vice President Lyndon Johnson and recommended an idea he called "preferential treatment" for black people trying to find places for themselves in predominantly white schools and workplaces.

"Prior to that time, the federal laws had been requiring color blindness of an employer," Mr. Farmer says. "My argument was that it was impossible for an employer to be oblivious to color because we had all grown up in a racist society. He would be most likely to hire someone who looked like himself. So we needed preferential treatment for blacks and other minorities to keep that from happening. Mr. Johnson thought the idea was great but the name was terrible. He said, 'Let's call it something positive, something affirmative. Yeah! That's it! Affirmative action!'"

When he became president, Mr. Johnson made affirmative action one of the foundation stones of his Great Society. It has been a powerful influence in American society ever since, but in recent years it has come under attack from some quarters as an outmoded, counterproductive policy that unfairly discriminates against white males.

Mr. Farmer believes affirmative action is still necessary. "If we didn't have it, I think the nation would drift rapidly back to the old system of blacks and other minorities being the last hired and the first fired," he says. "There *are* incidents where white males are done an injustice by the existence and use of affirmative action. I wish that were not so. I wish there could be some program that could eliminate social and economic injustice without injuring anyone. But I don't think that's possible. Affirmative action should be viewed as a temporary solution to the problem. When should it stop? When we have effectively eliminated gaps in education, housing, and all the other fronts in which racism affects the quality of life and living."

Mr. Farmer resigned as CORE's national director in 1966 and taught at Lincoln University in Pennsylvania, and later at New York University. In 1968 he ran on the Liberal Party ticket for a Brooklyn seat in Congress but was defeated by Shirley Chisholm. In 1969 President Nixon appointed him an assistant secretary of Health, Education and Welfare, a position in which he never felt comfortable. He resigned a year later.

In 1976 his wife, Lula, a white woman who had been an active fighter by his side throughout the segregation wars, died of Hodgkins' disease, leaving him to complete the rearing of their two daughters. He never remarried. The daughters, Tammy and Abby, are married now and live within easy driving

Part II—Texas, Our Texas: Some People and Places

distance of Mr. Farmer. They don't like to talk about the old civil rights days, he says, because they still have frightening memories of state troopers and Klansmen trying to lynch their father.

"They had it pretty difficult," he says. "It was pretty tough on them."

⊂∈ ★ ∋⊃

Dr. Martin Luther King Jr. of the Southern Christian Leadership Conference is dead. Roy Wilkins of the NAACP is dead. Whitney Young of the National Urban League is dead. Of the "Big Four" leaders of the 1960s civil rights movement, only James Farmer of CORE still lives.

Thirty years later, what does he think of race relations in the country? Did he expect them to be better by now?

"Oh, yes," he says. "We expected them to be substantially better by now. We had too simple a perception of the race problem. In those days, many thought if we could get the civil rights laws passed, it would change everything. We thought if we could get our kids into the same classrooms with white kids, then segregation would be over and the race problem would be solved. We got the front seat on the bus. We got to sit down at the counter and eat a hot dog. By and large, we killed Jim Crow. But we had not even battled against racism—the idea that physical characteristics such as skin color, hair texture, and feature shapes determine the intelligence, character, and morality of a person. That concept still exists. People still believe it. And it's passed down, by parents in most cases, from generation to generation."

At the end of his autobiography, Mr. Farmer wrote: "The tired among us must recharge our batteries. The uninitiated must learn to gird their loins. We have not finished the job of making our country whole."

Note: James Leonard Farmer died on July 9, 1999, in a Fredericksburg, Virginia hospital at the age of seventy-nine.

The Dog Woman

The day that Pat Arnold's life began to change was a rainy one, she remembers. She had stopped at a country store to buy gas and was standing in the downpour, filling her tank.

"This little dog crawled up to me on her belly," she says. "She was wet and shivering. I picked her up and put her in the car. I took her to the Humane Society. I was going to leave her. She looked sick."

Tears rise in Mrs. Arnold's eyes.

"I don't know why I'm breaking down like this," she says. "I guess because there are so many strays. It's so sad."

She was halfway home from the animal shelter when she thought, "They're going to put her to sleep." She turned around and got the puppy back and took her to a veterinary clinic, where the dog was treated for mange. "I thought, 'Surely we have room for one more dog,'" Mrs. Arnold says. "And that's what started it all."

Happy, as she named the stray, became the third dog in the Arnold household.

At the time—in 1993, she believes it was—Mrs. Arnold and her husband, Bill, were living in a "normal" house at Payne Point on Cedar Creek Lake. "But after that, it seemed that everywhere I would go, I would run into another stray dog." A year after that first stray, eight dogs were living in

125

kennels that the Arnolds had built on their one-acre lot. "The neighbors started to make it clear that we had a few too many dogs," Mrs. Arnold says.

So they looked for another place and found the ideal spot on a hill a few miles outside of Eustace. It was a 21-acre spread with a storage barn that had been converted into a cabin—and no nearby neighbors. The Arnolds bought it and built four 30-by-30-foot chain-link-fenced kennels around the cabin, and shelters for their eight dogs. Within a few years, there were eleven kennels and twenty-four dogs.

"I found Misty on a country road in the middle of nowhere. She was a puppy," Mrs. Arnold says. "I found Teddy Bear in a grocery store parking lot. Fluffy and Buffy were two little puppies about six months old we found on Highway 175. They looked too sick to move. Cars were just whizzing by those little fellows."

Every time Mrs. Arnold finds a stray, she takes it to the Lakeside Animal Clinic in Gun Barrel City, where Dr. Damon Stevens or Dr. Jim Collingsworth checks it out and treats it for whatever ails it.

"Fluffy had parvo virus, which is very deadly. She had to stay at the clinic five or six days. When we got home with her and her little brother Buffy, we had to keep them separate from the other guys for about six months. That was really something. We had to bleach everything and wear special clothes when we went out with the puppies. Little Lassie's owner just moved away and left her fenced in the yard. And then there's little Sandy that I found at the Humane Society, sitting in a cage all by himself in a dark room. He was holding up his little leg and had cuts all over him. I asked the woman what was going to happen to him, and she said he was going to be euthanized. It was so heartbreaking. So I said, 'Could I please take that dog?'" Spunky, the most recent arrival, had been shot. The veterinarian x-rayed him and put four pins in his shattered leg.

If a stray is healthy, it gets its shots and is spayed or neutered before it joins the crowd. The last thing the Arnolds want is a litter of puppies. "Humans domesticated dogs 10,000 years ago," Mr. Arnold says. "When we did that, we made a pact with them that if they would become tame, we would take care of them. Now we're breaking that pact. We're letting them run wild and multiply and die in misery. Conception control has to be achieved. It's stupid that we haven't solved this problem of stray dogs and cats before now. They could be controlled without using euthanasia, which is the way we control them now. It's just absurd. And it's unacceptable for Pat and me. So we've given up everything and are living in a little cabin now just to be able to take care of twenty-four dogs."

Although Dr. Stevens and Dr. Collingsworth give the Arnolds big discounts, their veterinary bills still average about $500 a month. The eleven kennels, which house twenty-two of the dogs (Toby and Blackie live in the house) cost $1,100 each to build, and the Arnolds spend about $400 a month for dog food.

Mrs. Arnold retired from her job at a Dallas printing company several years ago, so it's up to her husband to try to make ends meet. He stays in Dallas and works his customer service job during the week, then drives home every Friday with a carload of dog food. He works extra hours, too. "I volunteer for all the overtime I can," he says. "Luckily, I'm earning enough to keep our heads almost above water. We're surely not saving any money now. But what is the alternative?"

Meanwhile, Mrs. Arnold works twelve hours a day, 365 days a year, taking care of the dogs. At 7 o'clock every morning, she begins preparing their meals. "Two of the older fellows have hip dysplasia," she says, "so they get a home-cooked meal of grains and vegetables. It seems to help them. It takes about two hours to feed everybody."

After feeding time, Mrs. Arnold cleans all the kennels and fluffs up or replaces the straw beds in the shelters. While she cleans a kennel, the two dogs who live in it get to romp in the

Part II—Texas, Our Texas: Some People and Places

central play yard with a lot of doggie toys. When the kennels are clean, Mrs. Arnold walks all the dogs, two at a time, on leashes. It takes about three hours. After her own lunch, from 2 P.M. until dark, it's dog rounds again. The dogs get their dinner, then Mrs. Arnold brushes them all and gives each pair another romp in the play yard. "They're all healthy and happy," she says, "but I still feel that they're not getting enough attention."

The Arnolds haven't had a vacation in years, or even a day off. "We spend only two hours away from here even on Thanksgiving and Christmas," she says. "Our kids ask me, 'Mom, when are you going to start living a normal life?' Well, as long as these dogs don't have homes, I don't see how we could *ever* live a normal life."

The Arnolds used to advertise in the local newspapers, offering the dogs for adoption. The results were so disappointing that the effort wasn't worth the expense. "We adopted one out," Mrs. Arnold says, "but he came back. It was this wonderful young couple. They fell in love with the one we call Dallas, because we found him there, and they took him away. I called them about three times to see how things were going, and the woman said, 'Everything's fine. Everything's fine.' Two weeks later, she called and asked if they could bring Dallas back because they didn't think he was happy. Then little Lassie was going to just a wonderful woman. She was so sweet. But somebody gave her a dog and she could no longer adopt Lassie. So we've never given one away."

Still, they hope to find homes for their orphans. "If truly wonderful people wanted to take a dog or a pair of dogs, yes, they're up for adoption," Mrs. Arnold says. "But I would have to feel really comfortable with them. I know there are loving people out there. I just know. And our dogs could go to those people."

In All the Wrong Places

*T*he New York film producer says she's going to a wedding in Mexico City and is thinking of stopping off to take a look at Texas on the way. She could arrive at 11 A.M. and catch another plane out at 8 P.M. Is that OK?

She has optioned one of my novels for a movie, so I'm happy to oblige. I tell her I'll pick her up at DFW and drive her down to the country where the novel is set.

"It's near Houston, isn't it?" she says.

"No, it's southwest of Fort Worth."

"That isn't near Houston?"

"No."

"Where are you?"

"Dallas."

"How far is that from where we're going?"

"About one hundred miles."

"Oh, my God! Wouldn't it be closer if I flew to Houston?"

"Houston is a four-hour drive the other way."

"Oh, my God!"

We've never met. She says she'll be wearing a pink straw hat. "How will I recognize you?" she asks.

"I'm 6-foot-3. Shoulder-length sandy hair. Beard."

Part II—Texas, Our Texas: Some People and Places

"Isn't that what everybody in Texas looks like?" she says.

⋐ ★ ⋑

I stash her luggage and head the car past downtown Dallas into the prairie. My novel takes place on a Central Texas cotton farm and in a small nearby town during World War II. Carlton, the town I had in mind when I wrote the story, is almost a ghost town now. Only a few houses and not a single business survive. But Hico, only ten miles from Carlton, should suit her purpose. I explain that the country through which we're driving was cotton country during the 1940s but is mostly ranch land now.

"Running boards," she says. "We'll need cars with running boards." She takes a small notebook from her purse and starts writing. "A few things from your book will have to be changed," she says. "Your title will probably have to go. *Some Sweet Day* doesn't tell viewers what kind of movie it is."

While I'm digesting this, she tells me she's thinking of changing my novel's climactic scene, too, the scene that makes my novel, the critics and professors say, a powerful story. "It's too much of a shock," she says, looking out the window. "It makes people cry. Who milks all these cows?"

"They're beef cattle. Nobody milks beef cattle," I explain. She makes a note.

The last time I saw Hico, I had recognized it as the Hico of my childhood fifty years ago. In my mind's eye, I could still see the farm wagons and beat-up old flivvers lined up along its main street on Saturday. The humble stores and office buildings of limestone and red brick, dating from the beginning of the century or before, could have stood in any little town of the old cotton South.

But now I see the street has been gentrified. A slender plaza thing built of sissy pink brick divides the spacious thoroughfare into narrow halves. Flowers—pansies? petunias? —bloom in wooden barrel halves there, alternating with pseudo-antique street lamps of the sort on Currier and Ives Christmas cards. Through a speaker attached to one of the lampposts, Patsy Cline is singing "I Fall to Pieces." Antique shops and restaurants with cute names occupy the old storefronts.

On the back streets, though, we find a fine old brick building with a canopied driveway that was a gas station in the forties and several dignified, ungentrified business buildings, most of them vacant. They easily could be turned into movie sets.

The producer snaps pictures, but she looks dissatisfied. "Where's the Spanish influence?" she asks. "Didn't the Spanish settle Texas?"

"They stopped at San Antonio."

"Isn't that near here?"

"Two hundred fifty miles southeast."

"Oh, my God!"

"Texas is bigger than France," I say with chauvinistic satisfaction. "The parts are all different. The East is kind of like the South, the West is kind of like New Mexico and Arizona, the Panhandle is kind of like the Midwest. If you want to see a different kind of place..."

"France!" she says. "Have you read *A Year in Provence?*"

I drive on toward Fairy, a tiny community where my great-grandparents are buried in an old cemetery that nestles among hills covered with buffalo grass and juniper. There's a funeral in my novel, and I'm thinking Fairy might be the spot to film it. Along the way, we pass a mangled, bloody mess lying beside the road.

"What is *that*?" the producer asks.

"Dead armadillo."

Part II—Texas, Our Texas: Some People and Places

"They're *real*?" She writes in her notebook. "Promise me there won't be snakes," she says.

"Snakes are always a possibility, but not likely."

She doesn't like the cemetery. Too many people are buried in it. Their gravestones look too new. I point to one erected in the 1890s. My great-grandfather has been dead since 1911.

In desperation, I head for Carlton, eight miles away. We stop for her to look through the car window at a windmill. "I'd like a picture of it," she says, "but I'd have to walk through that grass. I don't know what's in there."

I get out and snap the picture. She thanks me. "There's a windmill in your book," she says. "What are they for?"

"Pumping water. From wells. In the ground."

She makes a note.

She barely glances at the ghostly buildings of Carlton, so I drive to the cemetery on the edge of town. It won't do, either. Too many people. Headstones too new. I show her the graves of my grandfathers: the one who put a shotgun in his mouth in 1935 after he lost a leg to diabetes; the other, the deputy sheriff, shot by robbers in 1932.

"Sheriff. Shot," she mumbles, writing. "Perhaps we can use that."

It's a quiet trip back. The producer seems lost in thought. But as I'm about to drive through the DFW tollgate, she says, "My perception of Texas was all wrong."

"What were you expecting?"

"I don't know." She looks at me with anguish in her eyes. "Where are the saloons? Where is Gary Cooper walking down the street in *High Noon*?"

At last I know what she's looking for. Hollywood.

The Limpia Creek Hat Company

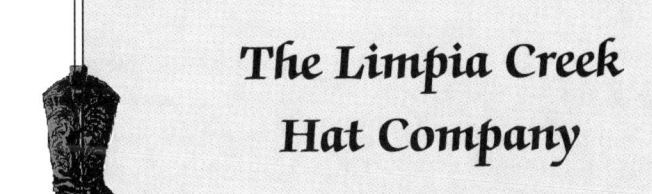

K.D. West and L.J. Jones walk into Buster Mills' place and belly up to the counter. "How about a little service," rumbles Mr. West, a burly Wilford Brimley look-alike.

"What can I do for you?" Buster asks.

"A new hat," answers Mr. Jones, a string bean of a fellow. "K.D.'s sick, embarrassed, and disgusted by this one."

The thing on Mr. Jones' head was a hat once, apparently gray felt, but barely qualifies as one now. It appears as if a pack of javelinas played hopscotch on it or a burro chewed it.

"He's ashamed to go anywhere with me," Mr. Jones says. "We went to El Paso yesterday and went in to eat, and he walked way ahead of me."

Mr. West mumbles unintelligibly into his heavy gray mustache. He used to be the police chief in Marfa, twenty-one miles down the road. Now that he's retired, he's a full-time saddle maker. Mr. Jones moved to Marfa from Tennessee only a little while ago. Mr. West has instructed him that Buster Mills is the man to make him a big improvement in the way of a hat.

"You want one just like that, but new?" Buster asks.

"I want one the same brim width," Mr. Jones says. "I want a five-inch crown with a John Wayne crease."

Buster goes into the back room and comes back with a picture of John Wayne. "Like this?"

"Naw, not that one. Like the one he had in *Rooster Cogburn.*"

This is the way business is normally conducted at the Limpia Creek Hat Company, which Buster operates in the old Carlton Grocery building on the main street of Fort Davis: The customer comes in and tells Buster what he wants, and Buster makes it for him.

"We built our reputation making good hats for working cowboys," Buster says. "And we have no desire to change that."

When a cowboy comes in to pick up his new hat, it has become customary for him to toss his old one onto the high shelf behind Buster's counter. A couple of dozen dusty, sweat-stained felt hats, high of crown and wide of brim, repose there.

"See that brown one there?" Buster asks, pointing. "I made that for Mike Williams in 1984. In 1994 he came over here and got another one. He said, 'I'm through with this one,' and just pitched it up there. Then everybody started doing it."

This is the way it usually is, the way Buster wanted it to be when he moved to Fort Davis from Pecos and started his company. "The working cowboy is what we're all about," he says.

From time to time, however, things can turn unusual.

One day in the summer of 1996, Buster was next door at the boot shop and somebody came in and told him, "Martha Stewart is over at your hat store."

"Who's Martha Stewart?" he asked.

The high priestess of the artsy-craftsy set hasn't had much impact yet out in the mountains and plateaus of the Trans-Pecos. But here she was, somehow, in Fort Davis, a tiny town a long way from nearly everything.

"She was down here doing an article on West Texas cooking and stuff," Buster says. "She bought sixteen hats and gave them to her camera crew and everybody. She was a neat lady."

Ms. Stewart posed in her own Limpia Creek hat for a full-page picture in the September 1996 issue of her magazine, *Martha Stewart Living,* and told her readers where she got it.

"We ended up with twenty-five calls or so from all over the United States because of that, from California to Boston," Buster says, "a lot out of Ohio for some reason."

There's also the movies: "We did the hats for all the main characters in that Larry McMurtry miniseries *Dead Man's Walk.* And I made a hat for Tommy Lee Jones when he was out here filming *The Good Old Boys.* The movie thing is just getting started around here. They just finished *The Rough Riders* a couple of days ago, and they're supposed to be starting another one in a couple of months. And we do the hats for the country band Ricochet, which had a No. 1 song, "Daddy's Money," not long ago. Two of the old boys in that band are from Pecos, and they talk us up wherever they go."

And there are the buses full of tourists who come to look at the mountains and the frontier army post and McDonald Observatory up the road. "We've probably got two hundred hats in Japan and China right now," Buster says. "The Japanese come in here by the busload. And the finance manager of Kerr-McGee Oil Company was taking a bunch of Chinese through here on a tour not long ago. His credit card was *real* good."

All in all, Buster figures that he and his able apprentice, Skeeter Roubison, a former bartender, build four hundred to six hundred hats a year, 90 percent of them custom-made.

"We haven't had time to build a lot of inventory hats to put on the racks and sell to the walk-in public," Buster says. "We were building us up some inventory stock for Christmas, but in October we had three tour groups come through in a week, and they wiped us out. That's OK. We're not complaining."

Buster has lived his whole life in the Trans-Pecos. He was born in Van Horn, lived on a ranch near Kent, moved to Pecos

Part II—Texas, Our Texas: Some People and Places

with his parents when he was small. Like many kids in the area, he went into the oil fields when he was old enough.

"I was roughnecking for ten years," he says. "Then in 1981 I started a Western wear store in Pecos. A couple of years later, the oil field decided I wasn't going to participate too much in the economy of Pecos anymore, so I had to supplement my income by doing boot repair and hat cleaning. I pretty much taught myself how to make hats. I just have a knack for it. Before long, that was a better way to go. I phased out the clothing."

Some branches of Buster's family have lived in Fort Davis since the 1880s, and he had always wanted to live there, too. So when the bottom dropped out of the Pecos economy, he pulled up stakes and moved south.

"They don't make movies in Pecos," he says. "There are no tourists in Pecos. In Fort Davis, I've been able to send hats all over the United States, where in Pecos it was just the local area."

His growing celebrity trade hasn't swelled the head under Buster's own hat, and he says it never will. He still prices his hats strictly according to the amount of beaver hair in the felt and its quality. He can make you a beautiful, soft 100X hat—100 percent beaver—for $750, or a 5X hat—all rabbit—for $99. "It would typically retail in stores for $140 to $150," he says. "Our 10X hat—50 percent rabbit and 50 percent beaver—would typically retail in stores for $225 to $240. We sell it for $165. That's the most popular one with the cowboys. It's a good quality hat that they can afford.

"Like I said, we built our business around the working cowboy. Those guys, they don't make much more now than they did ten years ago. Should they have to go down in quality because they can't afford today's prices? Not in my store. That wouldn't be fair."

Clyde's Sister

*A*round sundown, they would drive to some secluded spot outside Dallas and wait. Soon another car would come speeding down the road, dust billowing behind. It would pull up beside theirs, and everybody would get out. There would be hugging and kissing, talk and laughter.

"My mother always made red beans and corn bread and fried chicken," the woman recalls. "It was like a picnic. My brother loved red beans, and Mama could fry a chicken better than anybody I ever saw."

She never was afraid, she says. "We didn't think of danger. I guess we were all too danged ignorant to know. Clyde didn't think nothing about it, and we didn't either."

On the evening of November 22, 1933, they were waiting on a hill where the Irving Mall is now. The other car—a stolen Ford V-8—came speeding up the road, as usual. But this time it didn't stop.

"Clyde slowed down, then drove on by. Later he said he had a hunch there was somebody out in that field," she says. "He played his hunches a lot. He'd think something, and usually that's what it was. He had no more than passed us when they opened fire. I was stupid. I was young. I thought it was a

Part II—Texas, Our Texas: Some People and Places

bunch of firecrackers going off. It was a streak of fire across the sky. Then I thought, 'Well, I guess they're shooting at Clyde.'"

Marie Barrow was fifteen years old. She and her family had come to the hill to visit with her older brother Clyde and his girlfriend Bonnie Parker. When the Dallas County sheriff and three deputies opened fire with their machine guns, Marie was the only occupant of the waiting car who didn't duck to the floorboards. "I told Mama, 'They didn't get him. I saw him go over the hill.' But they had wounded him. A bullet went through his leg and into Bonnie's."

Her brother was the notorious Clyde Barrow of West Dallas, leader of the Barrow Gang, which also included his brother Buck and Buck's wife, Blanche, and Clyde's girlfriend Bonnie, a former waitress, along with several other gangsters from the area.

For more than two years, Bonnie and Clyde crisscrossed the South, the Southwest, and the Midwest in stolen cars, robbing banks and businesses, breaking out of jails, and trading gunfire with "the laws," as they called the police. During the chase, they killed between a dozen and eighteen officers and other citizens, depending on whose account you believe. Then a friend betrayed them, and on May 23, 1934, "the laws" gunned down Bonnie and Clyde in a roadside ambush near the tiny town of Gibsland, Louisiana. Clyde was twenty-five years old, Bonnie twenty-three. Despite their wishes to be buried side by side, their graves are in separate Dallas cemeteries.

"I think Mrs. Parker should have buried them together like Bonnie asked her to," Marie Barrow says. "She promised she would. I guess she was a little hot after Bonnie got killed. You know, somebody drags your daughter off and gets her in trouble. But maybe Bonnie was as bad as Clyde was."

During their brief and violent careers, they upstaged such notorious Depression-era outlaws as John Dillinger, Pretty Boy Floyd, and Machine Gun Kelly. Even before their deaths, they became legend, endowed by the press and the popular imagination with almost superhuman dash and cunning. Since their

138

deaths, dozens of books and numberless newspaper and magazine articles have been written about them. At least six movies for theater and TV—all of them wildly and willfully inaccurate—have portrayed them either as murderous monsters or as romantic fighters against an unjust and oppressive society.

"I don't guess people will ever let them die," Ms. Barrow says. "I really don't know why. Maybe it's because they were a boy and a girl and they were young and in love. But they didn't have as much fun as people think they did, I tell you."

She owns several items that belonged to her brother. They were saved in her mother's cedar chest, she says. Among them are the bullet-riddled shirt Clyde was wearing when he was killed, his tan fedora, his gold pocket watch, several crafts items he made in prison, and a sequined tam that belonged to Bonnie.

The youngest and last living member of her generation of the Barrow family, Marie has led a quiet married life in the Dallas area and has shied away from publicity. She still refuses to be photographed for publication. But she's willing to show the family relics now, she says, because she wants to sell them. A collector from Colorado already has bought the tan fedora. Ms. Barrow has turned down an offer of $30,000 for the riddled blue dress shirt. "I want to sell these things," she says, "but I also want to get what they're worth."

To the rest of the world, Clyde Barrow was a notorious—and, to many, a romantic—criminal. But to Ms. Barrow he was simply her brother, whom she adored. "It has always been difficult to be kin to Clyde," she says. "When I was just a kid going to school, the teacher would ask me every day if the police had caught my brother yet, if he had been killed yet. It was embarrassing, you know. I used to swear I was going to whip that teacher when I got big enough. Now I can't even remember her name."

To Ms. Barrow, West Dallas—a cauldron of poverty and crime—was simply "the neighborhood where we lived." Clyde's criminal buddies were "people we knew." And Clyde

Part II—Texas, Our Texas: Some People and Places

and his older brother Buck, who was killed by police only a few months before Clyde, weren't much different from anybody else's brothers.

"I don't remember them doing so much that was bad when they was young," she says. "Well, Buck did fight them chickens, you know. Cock fighting. I remember him putting them spurs on them. And he had an old pit bulldog he used to fight. Mama made him get rid of it. It tore out the whole seat of my dress when I was playing ball."

Her brothers' first entanglement with the law, in 1929 or '30, was for something they didn't do, she says. "It was about some chickens or turkeys. They had bought them from another boy, but the police arrested Buck and Clyde because they thought they stole them. But it was the other boy who had stole them."

There were seven Barrow kids, but Buck and three sisters already were grown and married when Marie was growing up. Only she, Clyde, and their brother L.C. still lived at home. L.C. was three years older than Clyde. Clyde was eight years older than Marie. "All the time, Clyde and L.C. were playing marbles," she says. "They carried their marbles around in tobacco sacks. They never would let me play with them."

The family lived in a tiny house attached to the gas station that Marie's father, Henry, ran in West Dallas. After the trouble about the poultry, the police developed a habit of checking on the Barrows whenever a car theft or a burglary was committed. "I remember Mama having fits with the police coming around all the time, coming to arrest one of her boys," Ms. Barrow says. "She always believed they hadn't done nothing. I never paid much attention to it. It was just the way life was."

Eventually, both Buck and Clyde became car thieves, burglars, and armed robbers and were sent to prison. Whenever they were paroled, their sister says, their records made them targets for police harassment, and it became impossible for them to hold honest jobs. "Every time Buck or Clyde would get work, the police would come around, pulling them in for questioning," she says. "Their bosses couldn't have that happening all the time, so they would get fired. My brothers' trouble with the law about run my mother insane. She was crazy about her kids, but there was nothing she could do about it. If the police hadn't hounded them so much, they wouldn't have been such bad boys, I don't think."

Henry Barrow, who worked at his gas station from dawn until dark, left the rearing of his family to his wife, Cumie. "He depended on Mama to spank us," Ms. Barrow says. "He'd say, 'Cumie, make that kid do this. Cumie, make that kid do that.' I don't remember my daddy ever hitting me in my life. He was easygoing. Just a real good old man. He said, 'If you can't say something nice about somebody, don't say nothing at all. Just keep your mouth shut.'"

He never went on any of the trips to the country to meet Clyde.

All the time they were on the run, both Clyde and Bonnie kept in contact with their mothers, writing them letters and postcards, sending them snapshots, phoning occasionally, meeting them for quick, furtive visits. "When Clyde wanted to see us," Ms. Barrow says, "he would drive by the station and throw out a Coca-Cola bottle with a note in it. Or he would leave a note in our mailbox. Or he would just stop and tell us. He come around there all the time. Mama used to mark on the wall how many times. He couldn't stay away, poor thing."

Sometimes Clyde would give Marie money, and she would go downtown to shop for Bonnie, who was about her size, "real tiny," and "kind of pretty." "She wasn't a beautiful girl. She was just a cute little old girl and had a nice personality. She had a way to make you like her."

Around his little sister, Clyde always was cheerful and happy-go-lucky. To her, the meetings on country hilltops at twilight were gatherings of a close and loyal clan, full of laughter and love, like any family's reunion.

Part II—Texas, Our Texas: Some People and Places

"He never seemed worried around me," she says. "He talked a lot to Mama, though. He told her more than anybody in the world. He and Bonnie knew they was going to get killed sooner or later. They told Mama that.

"I thought we was just having a big picnic. I didn't pay much attention. I was just a kid."

Clyde's Sister: A Sequel

On April 14, 1997, the shirt off Dallas outlaw Clyde Barrow's bullet-riddled back sold at auction in San Francisco for $75,000. His sister, seventy-eight-year-old Marie Barrow, said, "That may be more than he made all the time him and Bonnie was out," robbing banks and businesses in their two-and-a-half-year crime spree across a wide swath of Depression-era America.

Clyde was wearing the blue shirt with pearl buttons (neck size 14) on May 23, 1934, the day he and his lover, former Dallas waitress Bonnie Parker, were gunned down from ambush as they rode down a lonely Louisiana country road in a stolen Ford.

Whiskey Pete's, a casino in Primm, Nevada, bought the bloodstained rag, paying $30,000 more than the price estimated in the auction catalog. Ray Paglia, who represented the casino at the auction, said it will be displayed alongside a shot-up Ford, reputed to be Bonnie and Clyde's death car, that has been a tourist attraction at Whiskey Pete's for years.

"Was it a good deal? Absolutely," Mr. Paglia said.

The casino was the big buyer at San Francisco's Butterfield & Butterfield auction house, in a sale that has attracted international media attention. In addition to the shirt, Mr. Paglia bought a belt and a beaded necklace that Clyde made for his

Part II—Texas, Our Texas: Some People and Places

little sister, Ms. Barrow, while in prison for $3,750; a vanity mirror he made for a girlfriend for $1,900; and seventeen snapshots from the Barrow family album for $11,000.

Brent H. Hockman, a Charleston, S.C., dealer in rare documents, autographs, and relics, paid $28,000 for two letters that Clyde and his brother Buck wrote to their mother from prison; a group of photographs of the bodies of Bonnie and Clyde laid out on slabs at a Gibsland, Louisiana, funeral home; and a .45-caliber Army Colt semiautomatic pistol said to have been taken from the death car after the ambush.

An anonymous buyer paid $24,000 for a rifle Clyde owned as a boy—$20,000 above the estimated price. "It was probably the first gun Clyde ever shot," Ms. Barrow said. "He used it to play like he was Jesse James. Jesse was Clyde's hero."

Clyde's gold-filled Elgin pocket watch, which he was carrying when he died, went to an anonymous East Coast buyer for $18,000, six times the estimated price. A second lot of Bonnie and Clyde postmortem photographs sold to another anonymous buyer for $3,250.

Before the auction, Ms. Barrow told of her father bringing home Clyde's bloody shirt from the Louisiana funeral home where the bodies were taken after the ambush. Her mother had it washed and wrapped it up and put it in her cedar chest with her son's few other belongings. "It has been there all these years," she said. "My sister Nell got the cedar chest and all those things when my mother died, and when my sister died, I brought them home with me." Ms. Barrow said she felt "really sad" to be selling her brother's belongings now, "but I'm getting old, so I might as well let somebody have them that appreciates them."

Charles Heard, a Dallas collector who bought the shirt and Clyde's pencil-written prison letter from Ms. Barrow in 1996, said he paid her a "fair price" for it, but he acknowledged after the auction that he had made "a healthy profit."

"As a collector, it has been terribly exciting to own something so rare and unique as the Barrow shirt for a while," he

Clyde's Sister: A Sequel

said. "It has been fun. And I'm very happy for my brother, Steve, who was my co-investor. Now he has got a down payment for a house in Florida."

Ms. Barrow said she, too, was pleased with the sale. "I think I got a good deal," she said. "I really do. Of course, I should have kept the shirt until now."

Her total was $65,150; Mr. Heard's $79,500. Butterfield & Butterfield gets 10 percent of that, plus healthy buyers' premiums that are added onto the purchase prices—15 percent for sales up to $50,000 and 10 percent for everything over that price.

Gregg Martin, director of the company's Arms and Armor Department, spent the morning holding up the shirt for ABC, CNN, CBS, Fox News, and a German TV network. "Bonnie and Clyde were two of the most glamorous figures of the Depression era," he told them. "They were icons of their time. This shirt is a great biographical artifact. It tells a story just looking at it."

Mr. Martin said he was amazed at the number of calls from news media and potential bidders the auction house had received since it announced the sale. "When you have a star like General Custer or Elvis Presley, you're going to get media attention," he said. "But this has somehow attracted worldwide attention. It's right up there with Elvis Presley. We may have eclipsed General Custer."

Intrinsically, the Barrow artifacts were among the least valuable in the room. The pocket watch must have cost only a few dollars when it was new. The rifle, the women's belt, and the beaded necklace, vanity mirror, two letters, and yellowing snapshots of the outlaws all seemed poor and humble alongside the huge collection of beautifully crafted antique guns and cutlery.

Ms. Barrow was flown to San Francisco for the auction at Butterfield & Butterfield's expense. The youngest of seven Barrow children, she turned sixteen four days after her brother

145

Part II—Texas, Our Texas: Some People and Places

was killed. Now a silver-haired grandmother, she stood among the meager ruins of her brother's short life and tried to explain him.

"What was it like, growing up with Bonnie and Clyde?" a reporter asked.

"It was like growing up with a brother," she replied. "He was a good boy. He was good to his mother, and he was good to all of us. He bought me my first bicycle, and he bought me my first bedroom suite. And he give us money to keep us from starving."

"Are you saying he was a nice person?" she was asked.

"No, but I'm saying he didn't do all the things that they said he done."

"He killed over a dozen police officers."

"Well, maybe he did. I wasn't there."

The Chicken Dance

As she talks, Sylvia Ratcliffe's eyes get dreamier and dreamier. "You just let loose," she says. "You don't have any inhibitions. Sometimes it gets so crazy and wild you can't believe it."

Her boyfriend, J.R. Krauss, is wearing what appears to be a white Leghorn rooster on his head. Among the hundreds of people in the dance hall where he and Ms. Ratcliffe are drinking beer, dozens are sporting similar headgear. Chickens. Some of them flannel, some of a white, feathery material. They're sitting on people's heads. Some of the beer-drinkers also are wearing chicken beaks attached to their noses.

"This is where Sylvia and I met, twelve years ago," Mr. Krauss says. They've driven over from Houston to observe that anniversary, he says, and are getting sentimental.

"Did we do the chicken dance back then?" Ms. Ratcliffe asks, hugging his arm.

"Yeah. Heck, yeah," Mr. Krauss replies.

Every autumn, the old German-American Hill Country town of New Braunfels throws its Wurstfest, a ten-day beer-and-dancing party billed as a "salute to sausage." There's a lot of that around. And beer. And plenty of polka bands. More than sixty, each in turn oom-pahing its gig in the huge Wursthalle, where the dancing is done, or in one of the two

147

Part II—Texas, Our Texas: Some People and Places

outlying tents where people sit, drink beer, and sing along. Nearly all the bands play "The Chicken Dance" at least once during each performance. The crowds demand it. In the Wursthalle, it's played even more frequently, though not as often as some would like. "We ask the bands to hold 'The Chicken Dance' to not more than once an hour," a Wurstfest official says. "Some people want it all the time, just over and over again."

Rob Hearn of Arlington, who travels about the country selling $10 flannel chicken hats on weekends, says New Braunfels and Cincinnati are America's largest hotbeds of "The Chicken Dance," a spasm of terpsichorean madness imported from Europe by an unsuspecting New York music company in 1972.

"It's because of the large German populations in those towns," says Mr. Hearn. He's hawking his hats out of the back of a van in the Knights of Columbus parking lot. "'The Chicken Dance' drives Germans nuts."

Whenever a band leader announces "The Chicken Dance," loud cries of "Wooo!" and "Yee-haa!" rise from the assembled populace. Probably otherwise normal citizens, many with chickens on their heads, rush to the dance floor and begin behaving like chickens. They shape their hands into beaks and make squawking or clucking motions; they tuck their thumbs into their armpits and flap their arms like wings; they wiggle their posteriors as chickens do when scratching in dirt; they clap their hands.

They repeat all this four times, then grab each other's hands, spin in a circle, and repeat the whole sequence over and over as the band plays faster and faster. The circle expands throughout the dance as more and more dancers join in. It's as large as the dance floor by the time the band stops. White-haired grandfathers and grandmothers are there, young husbands and wives, even six- and seven-year-old children, all flapping and gyrating.

The Chicken Dance

"I'm a chicken-dancing fool!" cries Jim Bruce of Dallas, making his way back to his table with his wife, Lisa, after they've chicken danced for their first time. They learned it in about 15 seconds. "It has expanded my horizons incredibly," Mr. Bruce says.

The Bruces' companions, Sarah and Walter Wilcox, also of Dallas, have been chicken dancing for years, but, they say, experience doesn't necessarily make a chicken dancer better or worse. "The whole point is to act like a fool," says Mr. Wilcox. "It's the group participation thing that makes it fun—everybody acting like a fool at the same time."

"And you know it would embarrass your teenagers if they knew you were out doing it," says Ms. Wilcox. "That makes it even better."

Celebrants of every ethnic stripe are "acting like fools" at Wurstfest, but the chicken dance mania is particularly virulent among German-Americans and Czech-Americans because it's played mostly by polka bands. "We play it at weddings, at parties, sometimes at clubs if the dance floor is big enough," says Joe Kripps of the popular Denton polka band Brave Combo. "We do go to some places where people just look at us like we're crazy when we announce 'The Chicken Dance.' Like in Arkansas. But around Texas, it seems to be pretty widely known by everyone."

Many chicken dancers believe their dance is old and probably harks back to some Black Forest fertility rite, or originated among drunken sausage-makers or brewers of the Czech Republic or Germany. "I guess people have been doing it one hundred years or more," says Mr. Krauss, adjusting the Leghorn on his head.

"Wrong," says Stanley Mills, whose September Music Corporation owns the American publishing rights to "The Chicken Dance" music. "It was written by a couple of guys named Terry Randall and Werner Thomas. One is a Belgian and one is a Swiss, but I don't know which is which."

Part II—Texas, Our Texas: Some People and Places

Mr. Mills says he first heard the tune in 1972 at a convention that music publishers and record company people attend in Cannes, France, every January. He liked it and bought the American rights to it.

"When I picked up the song it was called 'Tchip, Tchip,'" he says. "I don't have a clue what that means. At the time, it was a medium-size hit in Europe. Then in the early eighties it became known as "The Birdie Song" and became a huge hit in England first, and then all over the Continent—Spain, Italy, France, you name it. They put bird whistles and chirpings in the recordings, and it was no longer just a song. It was this monstrous dance. In Italy it's called the "Dance of the Cock." In France it's the "Dance of the Ducks." In Spain it's the "Dance of the Little Birds." People went nuts over it."

Jeff Barnes of Brave Combo has heard that when the tune would come over the radio in Europe, drivers would pull over to the side of the road, get out of their cars, and do the dance.

"I called my version of it 'Dance, Little Bird.' I don't remember why," Mr. Mills says. "But I couldn't get it going in America. It just didn't mean much here because the music is like a polka, you know, and that kind of music never meant much here except in certain ethnic areas like Austin, Scranton, Cleveland, Milwaukee. In New York, it meant nothing. In L.A., it meant nothing. But it always stuck around. Then people started dancing to it at weddings and bar mitzvahs, and the local dance bands began to play it. A few local polka groups recorded it and sold it out of the back of the truck."

In 1994 a guy called Mr. Mills and said he was making a record of dance party favorites such as "The Alley Cat," "The Electric Slide," "La Bamba," and "Locomotion" and wanted to include "The Chicken Dance." "I said, 'I don't own anything called "The Chicken Dance,"' Mr. Mills says. "He said, 'Yes, you do. I'll play it over the phone.' When he did that, I realized it was my song. It got that name by itself. Don't ask me how. This record—called *Turn Up the Music*—became a huge success. It sold hundreds of thousands of albums."

The Chicken Dance

Since then, "The Chicken Dance" has been recorded on several similar albums, including Brave Combo's *Group Dance Epidemic*, and on a Walt Disney album for children. It has been performed on TV's *Drew Carey Show* and several times on *America's Funniest Home Videos* and in the movie *Grumpier Old Men*. It has been published as a piece for high school and college marching bands and concert bands to play, and as sheet music with lyrics written for September Music by Paul Parnes. It has been used in several local television commercials, including one for the Detroit Tigers, and in some cities fans are doing the chicken dance during breaks in ball games.

"It's amazing," says Mr. Mills. "Suddenly it's going in every direction. I'm now negotiating to have an orchestra version come out soon, and maybe a choral version. It appeals to everybody, from old people to little kids. I'm not able to retire on it, but it's doing very well."

Back in New Braunfels, Patty Schell—a competitor of Mr. Hearn in the chicken hat business—is trying to ride the humble chicken's tail feathers to riches, too. Her hats sell for $10 each. "I introduced my chicken hat to Wurstfest for the first time in 1996," she says. "We sold out by 9 o'clock on the first night. I ran home and called the maker, and he had workers working night and day to make hats for me. This year, I ordered plenty ahead of time."

"On Saturday night," says Joan Hannan, who is helping in Ms. Schell's booth, "as fast as we could take their money and give them back their change, we were selling chicken hats. For six or eight hours."

Inside the Wursthalle, Beth and Robert McMillan of Dallas are sitting, listening to the Cloverleaf Orchestra oompah up on the stage. They've never done the chicken dance. They've never even heard it played. But Ms. McMillan is wearing one of Ms. Schell's white Leghorn roosters, and she's ready.

"It's time we did it," she says. "We have four children. We work all the time. We have a full schedule. We never get away. This is our time. Yes. It's time we did the chicken dance."

Laos on the Prairie

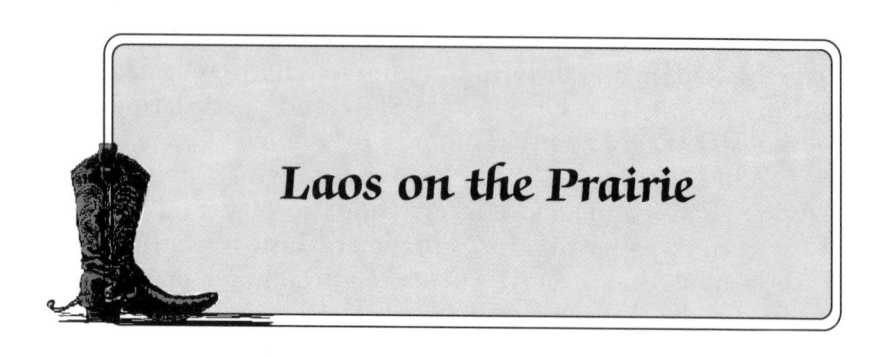

Outside, the white sun blazes down from the cloudless sky of a Texas August. Inside, two bald monks in saffron robes sit on the floor before a golden statue of the Buddha and chant in Pali, a language of ancient India. While they chant, one hundred people or more file singly to a long table and place food and money into a row of bowls. Behind the tables, men and boys remove the food and sort it into several plastic baskets—bananas into one, oranges into another, cookies and candy into another, Grape-Nuts and Rice Chex into another.

"Back in Laos, this time of year is the rainy season," says Leck Keovilay, one of the participants. "During the rainy season—from the middle of July until the middle of October—the monks don't go out of the temple, for religious reasons. So the people come to the temple and bring them food. That's what we're doing now. It's a holy season."

The season is called "Phaasa," he says, which means "rain."

It seems odd to celebrate Asian downpours in a Texas prairie village this Sunday morning while, not far to the west, Protestant ranchers are praying for relief from a way-too-long dry spell, the worst drought in forty years. But as recently as twenty years ago, few Texans would have believed that hundreds of Laotians would come and settle this countryside west of the small grain-elevator-and-railroad town of Saginaw. Or

Laos on the Prairie

build a Buddhist temple only a few miles north of Cowtown and Billy Bob's Texas.

"When the first of us came here, we had our temple in a mobile home," says Inpeng Soukhoumrath, president of the congregation. "Then we built our multipurpose center. Now we're building a real temple."

The old mobile home still stands at the back of the lot, but the ceremonies are now performed in the handsome multipurpose center, which also houses the two monks. (Buddhist monks live in their temples, says Mr. Keovilay.) The huge golden Buddha, recently arrived from Thailand, sits on an altar decorated with flowers and smaller statues. The monks' chants create a mesmerizing buzz, punctuated now and then by the clang of a gong. The worshipers, who have left their shoes at the door, sit in family groups on rugs spread about the floor.

Next door to the center, workers have just poured the concrete foundation of the new temple. Now volunteers will come every Sunday afternoon to help build on it. "Soon we will have our dancing ceremonies here," says Mr. Soukhoumrath, showing off the project. "Just as we did in Laos."

The first Laotian immigrants arrived in Tarrant County, where land and jobs were available, not long after Laos fell to the communists in 1974. Nearly all of them spent months or years in refugee camps in Thailand before they were relocated to Texas. They got jobs, saved money, and bought land. By settling in an unincorporated area, they didn't have to conform to city building codes or hire contractors and licensed electricians and plumbers. Friends and neighbors pitched in and helped one another build their homes, as earlier Texan settlers did a century and more ago, keeping construction costs low.

When other Laotians—many of them friends or relatives of the first immigrants—followed, they bought more land and built more houses, many of them large because several generations occupy them. Now about three hundred families live in what amounts to a Laotian village on the North Texas prairie.

Part II—Texas, Our Texas: Some People and Places

Although they're happy to be in Texas and are proud to be American citizens, they say, the Laotians don't want to forget the religious and cultural heritage of the ancestral home they left behind, and they want their children to avoid some of the dangers they've discovered in their new country.

In Texas, they say, too many Laotian children are yielding to strange new temptations. Like many other American children, they're succumbing to unhealthy pressures from their peers. They're rebelling against their parents. They're threatening the unity and discipline of their families.

The Saginaw Laotians, together with people from temples in Irving and Fort Worth, have formed an area-wide Buddhist youth group, which has about fifty members, most of them younger children. "We try to be a positive influence on the kids," says Nong Phommalay, the young man who leads the group, "so when they're older, they won't get into gangs and drugs and guns. We try to keep our kids together so they will always be friends. We try to get them to help out around the temple and to learn their own culture."

It's important, he says, that a Buddhist temple be built on the prairie. "The temple holds us together," he says. "It's the center of our life."

Sam and Lucy Vongxone (many Laotians adopt English first names when they become American citizens) and their two children had a good life in Laos. "We had a nice place to live," Mr. Vongxone says. "We had a normal family, a buffalo, a cow. But I had served in the army, and when the communists took over, it was a danger to my life. We had to decide whether we would go or stay."

In 1983 Mr. Vongxone, his pregnant wife, and their two small children crossed the border into Thailand and made their way to a refugee camp. Five months later, Mrs. Vongxone had her baby there. A month after that, the Vongxones were told they were to be relocated to Texas. "A refugee worker told me that in Texas there were lots of cowboys riding horses and shooting guns," Mrs. Vongxone says. "I was scared."

She also was told there were many jobs in Texas, even for people who couldn't speak English.

Soon the Vongxones were living in an apartment in a tough neighborhood in East Dallas, where they met Leck Keovilay, who had come from Laos several years earlier and was helping a number of his countrymen adjust to their new, strange lives. "When they first came to this country, they asked me, 'When are we going to have a house and TV?'" Mr. Keovilay remembers. "And I told them, 'Well, that's the American dream. You're going to get it sometime.'"

But not for a while.

Mr. Vongxone went to work for Dick Smith, owner of Art Forms at Olla Podrida, and learned to make jewelry and belt buckles. Now he designs and makes decorative copper water fountains for Mr. Smith, which are sold wholesale to the decorating trade at the Market Center in Dallas. Mrs. Vongxone works on an assembly line at Decibel Products, soldering antennas. They moved from East Dallas to a West Dallas housing project, and from there to an apartment in Garland.

Then one day a few years ago, Mr. Vongxone drove to Saginaw with a friend who was moving there from San Antonio. The friend had bought a lot and was building a house. Mr. Vongxone helped him. "It was a nice house," Mr. Vongxone says. "I wanted a house like him. So I bought some land and began building my own." Mrs. Vongxone's brother built his house next door.

Like most Laotians in the neighborhood, Mr. Vongxone built a large, comfortable brick house. Mrs. Vongxone's mother lives there with her daughter and son-in-law and her grandchildren. There's room in the back for a vegetable garden and a pen for chickens. There are two cars in the driveway and a large TV set in the living room. A china plate with pictures of

155

Part II—Texas, Our Texas: Some People and Places

all the American presidents sits on top of the TV. A pair of cattle horns decorates a wall. At dusk on this October day, an ice cream truck is moving down the street, its music box blaring a tinny rendition of "Home on the Range."

"Have you achieved the American dream?" the Vongxones are asked.

"Yes," Mrs. Vongxone replies.

Then they talk of Sekmouk.

Sekmouk was nineteen, the Vongxones' eldest child. "He was a good boy," Mr. Vongxone says. "He was doing well in school."

But one day in 1992, a friend of Sekmouk's arrived from Arkansas. Sekmouk's parents had never met this friend. "He was Vietnamese," Mr. Vongxone says. "He looked like a gang member."

That night, the Vongxone family went to a party at the Buddhist temple. They expected to see Sekmouk there, but he wasn't. They learned that he and two other boys from the neighborhood had gone to Houston with the friend from Arkansas. They had gone in Sekmouk's car.

"The Arkansas boy knew some gang members in Houston," Mr. Vongxone says. "The boys from Saginaw didn't know what was going on between the guy from Arkansas and the guys in Houston. The Arkansas guy tried to get some money from the Houston guys. Shooting broke out. Sekmouk and another boy from Saginaw were killed."

Mr. Vongxone shows photographs of Sekmouk, who was a handsome boy. Sekmouk's younger brother, David, who was born in the refugee camp, glances at the pictures, then looks away.

David, who is also called Douantyadeth, goes to Wayside Middle School in the Eagle Mountain-Saginaw Independent School District, where he plays forward and shooting guard on the basketball team. He makes A's and B's in school, he says, "and sometimes C's."

Laos on the Prairie

His sister, Phoukhont, graduated from Boswell High School in 1995, the first member of the Vongxone family to earn a diploma. Now she's studying at Tarrant County Junior College, making good grades. A night job helps pay her way.

Mr. and Mrs. Vongxone have been planning a trip to Laos to visit Mr. Vongxone's mother. He hasn't seen her since he was sixteen. It'll be their first trip back to their homeland since they fled. They can't afford to take David and Phoukhont with them, Mrs. Vongxone says. Besides, they would miss school.

David doesn't care. "My grandmother has shown me videos of Laos and told me stories about it," he says, "but it's a foreign country to me. I have no desire to go there."

C⋲ ★ ⋺Ↄ

When a Laotian family in Saginaw celebrates a birthday or commemorates a death (which is a Laotian custom), many people come to the party, not only from the surrounding neighborhood, but also from smaller Laotian communities in Fort Worth, Keller, Irving, and Venus. And almost three thousand people came to the Buddhist temple in April 14, 1995, to celebrate the Laotian New Year.

Their celebrations are generous and open to whoever comes. Sometimes their hospitality brings them harm. "The kids come to our parties, they case out the houses and come back later and rob them," says Jerry Rogers, who moved to Saginaw from California, where he had met and married his Laotian wife. He now has Laotian children, grandchildren, and in-laws living in Saginaw.

In 1992, around the time Sekmouk Vongxone and his friend were killed, Mr. Rogers' mother-in-law was babysitting with some of her grandchildren. "About five teenagers armed with guns came into the house, gagged them with duct tape, and robbed the house," Mr. Rogers says.

Part II—Texas, Our Texas: Some People and Places

About that same time, a gang member shot a teenager in the head during a celebration at the temple. "He lived," Mr. Rogers says, "but it took a year and a half for people to start coming back to their functions."

Because of their experiences with the communist government in their old country, many Laotians are reluctant to call the Tarrant County sheriff when crimes are committed against them. Instead, many families have built six-foot-high chain-link fences around their yards and put locks on their gates.

Some say these bad things are happening in their midst because their children don't respect and obey their parents as children did back in Laos. And they feel that the Eagle Mountain-Saginaw Independent School District isn't giving Laotian parents the support they need in trying to control their children. "According to our culture," says Edward Immanieong, "when the kids are at home, their parents are their parents; when they are in school, the teachers are their parents. But here it's different. The kids don't listen to the parents at home. They don't listen to the teachers at school. So they don't know what's good and what's bad."

Despite their problems with the communist government in Laos, there has developed among some residents of the Saginaw community a nostalgia for the ancient culture and family-centered life they left behind. And they've petitioned the Eagle Mountain-Saginaw school board to supply what they feel is lacking from their lives here. They want the schools to teach classes in Laotian culture and customs, offer bilingual education to young Lao-speaking students, teach Lao as a foreign language in high school, and teach the children to respect and obey their parents.

The approximately three hundred Laotian children represent nearly six percent of Eagle Mountain-Saginaw's student population. After Hispanics, they're the second-largest minority group in the school system.

"They also want us to hire teachers and counselors of Laotian descent to work in the school district so that they can assist in teaching their culture and customs," says Eagle Mountain-Saginaw Superintendent Truett Absher. "We've told them we will not be able to do those things." But, he says, the schools are trying to improve their communication with non-English-speaking parents. "We have eleven different languages represented in our system. We now have a telephone system that allows parents to call in and tell the school in their own language that a child isn't in school, and they can leave a message that they wish to be contacted by someone from the school. We're also sending communications to non-English-speaking homes in their native languages."

The school board has voted to hire a Lao-speaking teacher's aide/interpreter for Elkins Elementary School, which most of the young Laotian children attend. The aide also will serve as a liaison between the school and Laotian parents.

"We've had contact with other Laotian families who say they disagree with those who are making all these demands," Mr. Absher says. "They feel that teaching the culture, customs, and language and controlling their teenagers should rest with the family. We're trying to respond in a positive manner, even though we can't grant everything that some of them would like us to."

The problems worrying the Laotian parents are far more widespread than they realize, Mr. Absher says, and aren't unique to any of the nationalities and cultures struggling to coexist in America. "Many of their children don't know any English when they come into our school," he says. "But they learn it quickly, and as they grow older they become more and more Americanized. Often, they have to be interpreters for parents who don't speak English. This gives them power over their parents, and sometimes they take advantage of that. By the time they've become teenagers, the kids are very American, and their parents are not. Sometimes the kids become rebellious and disrespectful. They don't want to do what their

Part II—Texas, Our Texas: Some People and Places

parents tell them to do. They don't want to communicate with their parents. Does any of this sound familiar to you?"

Meanwhile, construction continues at the Buddhist temple. By early November the walls were up.

Tumbleweed Smith

About thirty years ago Bob Lewis got fired from his radio station job in Big Spring. So, with typical West Texas optimism, he turned his misfortune into opportunity. "I had always wanted to do something on my own, and getting fired prepared me for it," he says. "I decided, well, hell, I don't want to work for anybody anymore. It's too hard on the system."

So he recorded five brief radio shows and mailed the tapes to sixty-five West Texas radio stations. "I called the program *Tumbleweed* because the tumbleweed is such a strong symbol of West Texas," he says. "I ended each show with: 'This is Bob Lewis reporting for *Tumbleweed*.' And I made a sale! The Littlefield station, KZZN, bought my show. Then a station in Big Spring—not the one that fired me—bought it. So I had a network, man!"

Three months after he syndicated himself, Mr. Lewis was airing on five stations and a few months after that, ten. On April 1, 1970, he went statewide. Now he has about forty stations, all of them small. "Every now and then I get a big station," he says. "I was on KLIF in Dallas for a while, and WBAP in Fort Worth, and KPRC in Houston. But I know it's going to be a short run. They'll eventually say, 'What do we need in Dallas from Big Spring?'"

Part II—Texas, Our Texas: Some People and Places

In 1970 Mr. Lewis changed *Tumbleweed* to *Tumbleweed Smith* because people were forgetting his name and calling him by the name of his show. So he decided what the heck. But he didn't like the sound of "Tumbleweed Lewis." "Smith is my middle name," he says, "and I thought 'Tumbleweed Smith' had a better rhythm than 'Tumbleweed Lewis.' So that's how I became who I am."

The show is simplicity itself. It's two and a half minutes of some Texan just telling a story about something that happened once or some guy he used to know or explaining some unusual hobby he has, such as popping bullwhips. Tumbleweed introduces the storyteller and keeps the story moving along with a question or comment now and then. But mostly he just listens and laughs.

There's Pecos Pate Boone, for instance, a thirsty cowboy who used his boot as a bucket to get water out of a well and drew up a rattlesnake. When he shot the snake, his bullet severed the rope that he had tied the boot onto, and the boot fell into the well, with spur attached. And then some other interesting stuff happened.

Or there's O.C. Proffit, who claims he once caught a catfish that was "66 feet and 13 inches long." He invited all the residents of two counties to the fish fry.

Or James Wheat, who busted his Rolls Royce herding a heifer with it. Or Hence Barrow, who remembers a norther so cold it froze all the thermometers and the cattle died standing up.

Or Lela, proprietor of a café, who has had so many last names, she says, that "it doesn't make any difference what you call me." She has been a bride "half a dozen times, more or less," but all her husbands are dead. "I killed them all," she says. "I just loved them to death." She made nice tombstones for them out of cement and beer cans.

Tumbleweed's favorite story is about a boy who stuck his head into a churn and couldn't get it out. It was told years ago by Corbet Akins, then sheriff of Panola County. Sheriff Akins' account of the family's efforts to remove the churn, and his own odd laughter while he's telling it, bring tears of hilarity to every eye in every audience.

Starting out, Tumbleweed compiled a thousand ideas into a folder. Then he hit the road. "I was looking for people with a gleam in their eyes who liked to talk," he says. "As I traveled around Texas trying to sell my program, people at the stations would tell me about unusual characters and people who did unusual things. Pretty soon I had about seven folders. I divided the state into about thirteen districts and explored one area at a time."

Tumbleweed figures he has driven about a million and a half miles. "That's the equivalent of two or three trips to the moon," he says. "I've used enough audiotape to wrap twice around the borders of Texas." He averages about five interviews a day, but has done as many as fourteen.

Tumbleweed seems an easygoing sort, soft-voiced for a radio man, almost shy, but ready to smile or laugh out loud. Despite his white hair, he looks younger than his sixty-something years. "The time we spend laughing is added to our lives," he says.

He has recorded some seventy-five hundred people and kept the tapes. He believes they constitute the nation's largest privately owned oral history archive.

He recycles his material, too. He converts some of the interviews into weekly newspaper columns, which run in about twenty-five small-town papers. The show and the column have made him a popular speaker on the luncheon and banquet circuit. He also uses his tapes there. "At first, I just told Texas jokes and stories," he says. "It was old, boring stuff." Then he incorporated excerpts from his tapes into his speeches. "It was so successful I stopped telling jokes and used the actual voices of the people instead."

Every summer weekend, he performs a stage show in Fort Davis, where he has a second home. He stands with his mike in

Part II—Texas, Our Texas: Some People and Places

front of a rustic front-porch set, with his wife, Susan, working the tapes and sound equipment, and does an hour-long version of his radio show, an audio anthology of Texas folk humor. If his listeners want to take some of it home with them, nine audiocassettes are available for purchase.

Tumbleweed has never tried to turn his show into *Hee Haw West*. His Texans are never presented as corny caricatures or rustic stereotypes. They're people you might meet if you got off the interstate, drove to a town square, and introduced yourself to somebody.

"The small towns are where the real flavor and character of Texas are," he says. "The people are so uninhibited, so *totally* uninhibited. They love to laugh. They have a lot of soul. They're the salt of the earth. And they like to have fun. That's the main deal."

When Hollywood Came to Marfa

The spring of 1955 was one of the hard times in West Texas. Almost no rain had fallen in four years. Great dust storms were turning the sun red and the sky brown and stripping the paint off cars that inched blindly along the narrow highways. On the ranches, the brittle brown grass had been grazed to its roots. Cattlemen who still owned a little money were buying hay and hauling it to their pastures. As they cut the wires on the bales and pushed the hay into the dust, their gaunt Herefords trudged toward their pickups, lowing in desperation. Some ranchers burned the thorns off prickly pear with torches so their cattle could eat it.

People told drought jokes. It was said that a child who had never seen rain fainted from fright when a raindrop hit him on the head. His parents revived him by throwing a bucketful of sand in his face. It was said that Baptists had resorted to baptism by sprinkling, Methodists were using a damp sponge, and Presbyterians were giving rain checks.

The humor eased the pain only a little, for many families were losing their land and animals to creditors. Despite the hopes and prayers of those who were still hanging on, three more years were to pass before the rains would return and put an end to the longest, most severe drought in the region's history.

Part II—Texas, Our Texas: Some People and Places

But in the midst of this dry horror a kind of quirky miracle happened.

Hollywood came to Marfa.

George Stevens, a master director, brought a huge cast and crew to the dusty, worn-out seat of Presidio County, a drought-plagued cow town of some three thousand souls smack in the middle of the Trans-Pecos nowhere, to make a motion picture.

These days, of course, you can hardly walk down a sidewalk in Texas without running into a battalion of actors, grips, best boys, and cinematographers laboring over some epic for the silver screen or TV. Moviemaking is a regular Texas industry now, like Fritos and Corsicana fruitcakes. But in 1955 it was fairly rare for Hollywoodians to venture outside their back lots to make a picture, and much rarer for them to travel to a little town in the Texas outback.

Furthermore, the movie they came to Marfa to make was no B Western. It was *Giant*, based on the best-selling novel by Edna Ferber, one of the most controversial stories ever written about Texas. And the stars Mr. Stevens brought with him were the most glamorous of their time. Elizabeth Taylor, Rock Hudson, and James Dean were the headliners, supported by Sal Mineo, Chill Wills, Dennis Hopper, Jane Withers, Mercedes McCambridge, Earl Holliman, and, in her first film role, Carroll Baker. You had to have stayed away from the Marfa Drive-In and the Palace Theater for a long time not to be familiar with at least some of the players in that lineup.

In May 1995 hundreds of people from throughout the Trans-Pecos ranch country gathered in Marfa for a fortieth anniversary *Giant* reunion, a time of remembrance and celebration of the coming of Hollywood glamor and its two-month-long stay in their drought-stricken country.

At noon they gathered in a pasture on the Clay Evans ranch between Marfa and Valentine, near where the movie's Reata ranch house stood, and ate their barbecue lunch on the very spot where the barbecue scene in the movie was filmed.

When Hollywood Came to Marfa

I remember. Leslie Benedict (Miss Taylor), the tenderfoot Eastern bride of rancher Bick Benedict (Mr. Hudson), faints when a big spoonful of hot roasted cow brains is dumped onto her plate. It was hotter than five kinds of hell the day they shot that scene. Even some of the sun-dried local extras came close to fainting.

The huge Victorian ranch house that stood so starkly on the plain was only a facade, only a part of the Hollywood magic, but for years afterward fans visited it like a shrine, until time and weather destroyed it. "It's just a bunch of poles sticking up there now," said Mr. Evans.

The crowd spent the afternoon at the Paisano Hotel in downtown Marfa, watching a *Giant* star look-alike contest, and examined *Giant* photographs and memorabilia and reminisced about that circusy spring.

I remember. The film crew lived at the Paisano. Several of the prominent ranchers vacated their big houses and rented them to the stars. Every night, almost the whole community gathered at the Palace, just across the street from the Paisano, to see the day's rushes.

The Palace being out of business for many years, the people moved to the Marfa High School auditorium for a showing of *Giant*, the first time the film had been shown in Marfa in twenty years. After the movie, some of the people who participated in its making told of their experiences.

I remember. Julie Nelson, later to be my first wife, twirled two batons in front of the Marfa High School band in the scene where Bob Dace (Mr. Holliman) arrives home from World War II on a train. The band is playing and, for a few seconds, there's Julie, twirling. Mr. Stevens paid the band $200.

Clay Evans, who was eighteen that year, recalled: "James Dean, he was a good fellow. I liked him. We got along fine. And Rock was all right. They all were. We had a good time."

Among the rememberers present were Fran Bennett, who played Julie Benedict, daughter of Bick and Leslie Benedict and twin sister of Jordy (Mr. Hopper). Also, Bob Hinkle, who served as a technical adviser and dialogue coach and taught

167

Part II—Texas, Our Texas: Some People and Places

Jett Rink (Mr. Dean) that little trick he does with the rope in the scene where he refuses to sell Bick the land that Luz Benedict (Miss McCambridge) left him in her will.
 I remember. Bub Evans, Clay's older brother, doubled for Miss McCambridge in the scene where she's bucked off the black stallion and killed. Bub, as tough a cowboy as ever there was, refused to take off the riding skirt he wore in the scene and paraded about the set in drag the rest of the day.

"Just about everybody in Marfa worked on that movie as drivers, as extras, in other jobs," said Kirby Warnock, publisher of the *Big Bend Quarterly* and one of the organizers of the reunion.
 I remember. The undertaker in charge of the funeral of Angel Obregon (Mr. Mineo), the young Mexican-American soldier killed in the war, was Nolan Kelley, Marfa's real funeral director. The priest who performed the wedding ceremony uniting Jordy and the young Mexican-American girl, Juana (Elsa Cardenas), was the real Marfa priest. I can't recall his name. The Anglo baby in the last scene was the child of Dr. and Mrs. Don Gaddis of Fort Davis. Jim Espy of Fort Davis doubled for Mr. Hudson in a horseback riding scene, and his friends called him "Pebble" thereafter.

Miss Ferber's novel, a bestseller nationwide, had been enormously unpopular in Texas because it portrays the Texas cattle and oil barons as crude, greedy, chauvinistic, Mexican-exploiting hicks who are obsessed with bigness and spend their ill-got riches on all the wrong things. Carl Victor, reviewing the book in the old *Houston Press*, called it "a gargantuan hunk of monstrous, ill-informed, hokum-laden hocus-pocus." There was a widely told joke that Miss Ferber had done her research on Texas by flying over the state in a plane.

Although Mr. Stevens' picture includes all Miss Ferber's themes, he softens them and adds the famous fistfight scene in which an aging Bick Benedict goes down battling Sarge (Mickey Simpson), the redneck café proprietor, in defense of his now ethnically mixed family's honor, thus endowing at least a few wealthy Texans with more decency and hope of redemption than Miss Ferber does.

After its premiere at the Palace Theater in 1956, the movie was an enormous success in Texas as well as the rest of the country. It broke the attendance record at the Majestic Theater in Dallas. In 1961 John Connally declared it his favorite movie and used its theme music in his successful gubernatorial campaign. Since its release on videocassette several years ago, it has become the unofficial National Movie of Texas and shares a shelf in many a Lone Star home with John Wayne's equally revered Texas epics, *Red River* and *The Searchers*.

Early in *Giant*, Bick Benedict, asked to explain Texas to the hoity-toity family of his Eastern bride-to-be, tells them simply that it's "almost another country." And Don Graham, Texas motion picture scholar and author of *Cowboys and Cadillacs: How Hollywood Looks at Texas*, writes that Giant has "told millions the world over what Texas looked like and what Texans did that made them, well, different."

What those millions see is West Texas at its worst—weary and depleted by its longest fight against its bitterest enemy, a land made dust by lack of rain—but still, despite it all, magnificent and eternal.

When newlywed Leslie Benedict raises the window shade in her husband's private railroad car for her first look at his sprawling ranch, she sees a dust storm whipping tumbleweeds across a brown plain. "Is that Texas?" she asks.

Yes. On the fortieth anniversary of the terrible, wonderful spring, that old, familiar devil drought was back, too, along with the other visitors.

"1955 was our worst year. Now it's forty years later, and it's drier now than it was then. And this is the fourth year," Mr. Evans said.

"They had their first measurable rainfall in over a year a few weeks ago," said Kirby Warnock. "It made page one of the Marfa paper."

The Last Bell

*I*n the summer of 1880, the U.S. Cavalry chased the Apache Chief Victorio south of the Rio Grande, where the Mexican army killed him.

Later that same year, L.R. Millican built an adobe one-room school for the children who lived on his ranch, not far from where Victorio and his dwindling warrior band crossed the river.

On Friday, May 19, 1995, after one hundred fifteen years of service to the isolated children of the Eagle Mountains and the Sierra Diablo, the door of Mr. Millican's school was shut for the last time. At the end of the day, the last three students who attended Allamoore School, as it came to be called, toted home their belongings in grocery sacks; their teacher and superintendent, Lola Waggoner, locked up; and the last one-room school in Texas was out of business, a tiny victim of the state's new school finance law.

"I never thought I would live to see this," said Maria Mendez, who went to the school to see two of her grandchildren—the third generation of her family to attend Allamoore—pose with their teacher for Polaroid pictures and receive their final report cards. "Closing the school is very, very sad to me," she said, wiping tears from her eyes. "It has always been here for us. But you just can't fight the system. What's going

The Last Bell

to be done is going to be done, and there's nothing I or anybody can do about it."

The school was doomed when the Texas Supreme Court announced in January 1995 that Senate Bill 7, as educators call the new school finance law, is constitutional. The law requires about one hundred of the state's richer public school districts to share their wealth with poorer districts to equalize the educational opportunities of all the state's children. The state's rich districts, including such powerhouses as Plano and Highland Park, fought the law through the courts and lost. Plano and Highland Park will survive, but several small wealthy districts, including Allamoore, will not.

Looking at the Allamoore Independent School District's only school, serving children in kindergarten through sixth grade, probably nobody would call it rich. It is composed of Mr. Millican's little tin-roofed building, the cinder block restrooms that were added in the 1970s, a flagpole, and a playground with two swings, a chinning bar, two seesaws, and a basketball goal. It sits on a Hudspeth County mesquite flat ten miles west of Van Horn beside a dirt road where trucks from two talc mines roar by all day, covering the school with white dust from their cargo and brown dust from the road.

The Allamoore community was established as a railroad section house near Mr. Millican's school and cattle-shipping pens about 1885, and was named for Alla Moore, the wife of an early settler. (Neither the railroads nor the Texas Department of Transportation ever learned to spell the name of the place. Their signs identify it as "Allamore.") Mr. Millican deeded the school to the community in 1912.

When Mrs. Mendez began attending school there around 1940, she was living at a railroad camp called Eagle Flat, eight miles away. "We came down the tracks on a motor car every morning with the railroad work gang," she said. "It was just a flat car with no sides. It was fun, except in the winter, when we had to get up before daylight and sit on that thing in a cold wind."

Part II—Texas, Our Texas: Some People and Places

In those days, Allamoore had a hotel, a grocery store, a gas station, a railroad depot, a Catholic church, and a goodly number of houses. "People built houses wherever they wanted to," Mrs. Mendez said, "and nobody bothered them."

The school had between twenty and seventy students, depending on how many workers the mines and the Southern Pacific and Texas & Pacific railroads were using. But the village slowly withered for lack of water, she said, to three houses, the school, and two talc mills that stand between the railroad tracks and Interstate 10, about a quarter of a mile from the school.

The house where Mrs. Mendez and her large family live used to be the teacherage, a residence provided for the school's lone instructor. She and her husband, Cruz, a retired cowboy, bought it long ago for $300.

Although the village and its school are tiny, the Allamoore ISD is huge. "We have 1,043 square miles of ranch land and the two mines," Ms. Waggoner said. "The tax base is approximately $20 million, taxed at 46 cents per $100 evaluation. It brings in about $93,000 a year."

But under the formula established by the state in the 1993 law, Allamoore had to send $82,000 of that revenue to the neighboring Culberson County ISD, which includes Van Horn, one of the poorer districts in the state. "If we hadn't had a fund balance, we wouldn't have been able to have school for the last couple of years," Ms. Waggoner said. Now the money has run out, and Allamoore will be consolidated into the Culberson County system.

Allamoore's oldest student, Keesey King, a third-generation student of a ranching family who was promoted from the sixth grade on the school's last day, would have attended junior high in Van Horn anyway. One of Mrs. Mendez's granddaughters, Bianca Mendez, will attend second grade in Van Horn. And her cousin, Ruth Ann Del Toro, who will be a third-grader next year, is moving to Dallas, where her mother lives.

Ms. Waggoner will be given an administrative position in the Culberson County system. "Now I'm going to have to sit in an office and wear a three-piece suit and pantyhose," she said.

The old schoolhouse will be refurbished as a community center.

In January the Allamoore school board paid Ms. Waggoner's way to Austin to pick up an award that the school had won. Under the Texas Assessment of Academic Skills (TAAS), in which the state uses student test scores, attendance figures, dropout rates, and other criteria to rate the quality of each public school system, Allamoore was one of only six school districts to receive the highest "exemplary" rating. Just before Governor George W. Bush presented her with the Governor's Certificate for the Texas Successful Schools Award for Allamoore's achievement, the state Supreme Court announced its ruling upholding Senate Bill 7. "The day we got the award for our excellence, we learned that we were going out of business," Ms. Waggoner says.

On the last day, the three students and Ms. Waggoner showed up as usual at 8:30 A.M., but this time they were wearing special T-shirts that Keesey King had made for them. The front of each depicted a map of Texas, with a small picture of the school and the words "Allamoore School, May 19, 1995."

Keesey quietly picked up the furled American and Texas flags. He took them outside and ran them to the top of the pole. Then the teacher and the children walked two brisk laps around the schoolyard, as they have every morning. At the end of their walk, they halted at the flagpole, placed their hands over their hearts, and pledged their allegiance to the flags, then went inside.

The big room, with its two-foot-thick adobe walls, high windows, and beaded ceiling and wainscoting, looks much as it must have when Mr. Millican built it. But it's furnished now with six large cases of library books, a computer, a globe, an art table, four student desks, Mrs. Waggoner's work table, a

Part II—Texas, Our Texas: Some People and Places

rocking chair, a telephone, an ancient upright player piano, and a small trampoline.

Ms. Waggoner immediately gave Bianca and Ruth Ann some arithmetic problems to do, then began instructing Keesey in math at her table. As the girls finished their work, they took their papers to the teacher, who graded them immediately with the child watching, then returned them to their desks with more work to do.

Throughout the morning, she juggled her time and attention among the three children, calling them each to her table for final spelling tests, arithmetic drills, and reading lessons.

About 11 o'clock, the children piled into the bed of Ms. Waggoner's pickup truck and she drove them a quarter-mile to the mill office of Pioneer Talc, where sodas and candy bars are kept in a refrigerator. She bought them each a soda. While they drank them, she showed them the huge piles of talc ore waiting for shipment, told them of its uses in paint, toothpaste, talcum powder and such, and let them pick up a few small pieces to take home.

At 11:30, teacher and children drove back to the school, then walked over to Mrs. Mendez's house, where the grandmother showed them how to make flour tortillas and let them try their hands at kneading the dough and putting it on the hot griddle.

About an hour later, Mrs. Mendez and Linda King, Keesey's mother, came to the school with a lunch of rice, zucchini, beans, salad, and the fresh tortillas.

After lunch, Mrs. King taught the children how to make homemade ice cream. Then they went outside to have their pictures taken with their teacher.

After the photo session, Mrs. King helped the children make frames for the Polaroid snapshots out of Popsicle sticks and letter on them: "Allamoore School, May 19, 1995."

Lacy, the Mendez family dog, wandered in, watched a while, then fell asleep by the bookcase.

Finally, at 3:20 P.M., Keesey, Ruth Ann, and Bianca hauled down the flags and folded them for the last time.

Mrs. Mendez stood on the schoolhouse steps, wiping tears from her eyes. "It's not that there isn't enough money for education in Texas," she said. "It's just not being used properly by our legislature."

Then she followed her dog and her grandchildren home.

Marker Man

*I*n Bell County one time, David Danenfelzer stopped at a cluster of three houses to ask directions to a cemetery. He honked his horn, as is the custom in rural Texas, to let the people know a visitor had come.

The occupants of the houses came out to see what he wanted.

"It was some sort of commune, and nobody was wearing shoes," Mr. Danenfelzer says. "There were twin girls who looked alike and were dressed alike. Both without shoes. The men and women, no shoes. There was also a three-legged dog that kept chasing me."

While he talks, Mr. Danenfelzer is scrubbing an aluminum historical marker with a wire brush. "That's part of the fun of my job," he says. "I get to meet a lot of interesting people."

There are more than twelve thousand aluminum historical markers in Texas. They stand on steel poles beside highways, in cemeteries, in the middle of pastures, up remote canyons, on hilltops, in courthouse squares. They're bolted to the walls of old hotels and stores and Victorian homes. They celebrate past events and people great and small. Mostly small in the cosmic sense, perhaps, but important to the local folks nonetheless.

It's Mr. Danenfelzer's job to repair them.

Marker Man

"I get tired of the First Baptist Church and the First Methodist Church," he says. "Every town has a First Baptist Church and a First Methodist Church. Most of their markers basically tell about the first reverend, how many reverends they've had, stuff like that. One of them had had thirty-seven reverends in the last hundred years. They didn't stick around very long. What must be wrong with that church?"

Mr. Danenfelzer wanders hither and thither over the 266,807 square miles of Texas, searching out those signposts of history that have fallen victim to sun, weather, and gun-toting ignoramuses who can't resist blazing away at them. "If the gun is high enough caliber, the bullets go right through them," he says. "Some of the holes are awfully big. There isn't much I can do. Yesterday I fixed one in a small park here in Waco that had just been mutilated. It still looks pretty bad because people have been throwing rocks at it and several bullets have hit it. Right in the middle of a small community park. It's sad."

The two hundred fifty-four county historical commissions have been erecting the aluminum markers all over the state since the 1960s, with the approval of the Texas Historical Commission in Austin. If the THC agrees with a county historical commission that an event or person is worthy of commemoration, the marker is cast and erected at county expense. Each marker costs between $500 and $1,500, depending on its size.

Now the THC has conducted a survey of them to see how many are in need of repair. On the day he's speaking, seven thousand have been surveyed so far. Of those, about fourteen hundred were found to require the services of Mr. Danenfelzer, the state's only marker repairman. More than five thousand remain to be surveyed. And Mr. Danenfelzer's job is temporary. The grant funding it will expire in less than a year. "I have half of Texas to go," he says. "It's going to be tight."

But he's an energetic young man and is confident he can get the work done. Since he took over the job from a colleague

Part II—Texas, Our Texas: Some People and Places

six months ago, he has repaired more than three hundred markers. "It's remarkable how quickly they can be repaired," he says. "In fifteen or twenty minutes, you have a shiny aluminum sign with a black background that looks like new."

At the moment, Mr. Danenfelzer is about to repair a marker commemorating Pat Neff, twenty-seventh governor of Texas, a big Baptist, and one of the presidents of Baylor University. The marker stands near the flagpole in front of Pat Neff Hall on the Baylor campus. Governor Neff's marker is badly faded and streaked with bird droppings. "A marker is a great place for birds to hang out," Mr. Danenfelzer says.

He climbs over a hedge and attacks the damage with his steel brush. Then he goes over the aluminum plaque with a battery-powered sander, sticks masking tape around its edges, and sprays black paint over the whole marker. He wipes the paint off the raised aluminum words with a lacquer-thinner, leaving the background black. He goes over the surface of the words with the sander again, brushes them with a hair brush, and sprays the entire marker with a clear lacquer to help preserve it. Finally, he takes a picture of the like-new marker, his record to show his bosses back in Austin that he has done the work.

On an average day he repairs ten markers. On extraordinary days he has done as many as seventeen.

But first, he has to find them. That can turn into an adventure.

"It's kind of a treasure hunt," he says. "Many of the markers are in out-of-the-way places, and most of the directions I've got are really bad. Sometimes I can look for three or four hours and still not find it."

So he drives down the lane to some country house and honks.

"I've seen more men in their underwear the last couple of months than I care to remember," he says. "I know it's hot, but it's still surprising when I drive up to someone's house in the middle of the country and I honk my horn and a 300-pound gentleman walks out his front door in his skivvies and stands there just casually talking to me. And I have to watch for dogs. I always look for the tail-wag. If there's no tail-wag, I start to run."

It's the older people who have lived their whole lives in the same community who know where everything is, he says, but even those who can't help him usually are friendly. "I run into a lot of nice people. Some of them invite me into their houses and offer me something to eat or a cup of tea. One lady gave me a bag of kumquats."

Mr. Danenfelzer, a history graduate of the University of Wisconsin, moved to Austin in 1995 with a girlfriend who was enrolling in graduate school at the University of Texas. "I was working as a baker in Minneapolis," he says. "She was worried about moving down here alone. So I said, 'Well, I've got no future here. I'll move with you.'"

He found temporary work at the Texas Historical Commission, stuffing envelopes. When the man who had been repairing the historical markers was moved to other duties, Mr. Danenfelzer applied for his job and got it. His work is a constant revelation about his adopted state, he says. "For one thing, I'm learning how much history Texas has. It's amazing."

He's also discovering that history doesn't always stay the same, and that different people's perceptions of the past don't necessarily agree: "Around Corpus Christi, a lot of the signs involve the Karankawa Indians, who were a major tribe down there. Some of the signs say the Karankawas were cannibals and were fierce fighters and pillaged the settlers' homes. Those markers were erected in the sixties and early seventies. Then I found one erected in 1988. It said the Karankawas were very peaceful and happy people who farmed and hunted in the area. It said they were friendly with the colonists at first and helped them with their crops, but when encroachment on their area became worse, they became confrontational. In twenty or thirty years, people's opinion of the Karankawas had changed.

Part II—Texas, Our Texas: Some People and Places

Or maybe the people of this particular place just didn't share the opinion of the Karankawas that the people at those other places had."

Sometimes people who see Mr. Danenfelzer spray-painting a marker think he's vandalizing them. They call the cops. He encountered a cottonmouth once. One time, he was divebombed by magpies who thought he was working too close to their cornfield. He has almost collapsed from heat exhaustion. He once mistook the whirr of a locust for a rattlesnake and almost scared himself to death.

And sometimes he gets lonely. "The radio is like having a best friend, because it talks to you," he says. "At times, if it's a bad radio station—and there are lots of parts of Texas where there isn't any other kind—it's like having the most annoying person I know sitting next to me. But I don't turn it off. I've got nothing else to listen to."

It's all worthwhile, he says, because not many people write about local history anymore. So when the people who know about these people and events are gone, Mr. Danenfelzer's aluminum markers may be all that remains of the local past.

He finishes with Governor Neff and moves on to the grave of Dr. John Henry Sears, Confederate surgeon and Waco civic leader; then to the Waco State Home "for dependent and neglected children," which operated from 1922 till 1979; then to the site of the 1897 gunfight between James Harris and Judge George Gerald on a street corner in downtown Waco.

In a few days he'll be finished with Waco and move on, westward this time, perhaps. Eventually, to the most remote Texas historical marker of all, at the top of Guadalupe Peak, 8,749 feet above sea level, the highest point in Texas.

"I'll hike up there next fall, when it's cooler," he says.

FDHS Reunion

*I*n the forty years since I graduated from Fort Davis High School, my class had never held a reunion. We were just too small. On graduation night, only eight of us walked across the stage to receive our diplomas. Two of our number—Johnny Granado and Ernest Rivera—had already left school to join the Army. The rest of us—except Frank Higgins—would leave Fort Davis almost immediately to seek our fortunes elsewhere.

Since then, Willie Ridley and Alfred Ramirez have died and nobody knows whatever happened to Sally Mercer. So the best possible attendance for a reunion of the Class of '55 would have been five—Frank, Ernestine Mendoza, Cora Newton, Julie Rodriguez, and me.

Some classes were smaller than ours. Only four graduated in 1953, and only three in 1944 and 1945. In 1942 Mildred Bloys marched down the aisle alone. The cap-and-gown rental companies have never made a lot of money in Fort Davis.

So in the summer of 1994, when Jan Kahl and Ann Espy told me their plan, I was interested but skeptical. Their Class of 1963 was going to organize a reunion of everybody who had ever graduated from old FDHS, from the school's first grads in 1913 through the Class of 1995. I mailed Jan the few addresses I knew and thought, "This is as far as it'll go."

But about a year later, the letter arrived:

Part II—Texas, Our Texas: Some People and Places

"Dear Fort Davis Graduates,
"The Class of 1963 is very excited about the reunion..."
It was going to happen! I marked the "Will Attend" space on the enclosed postcard and mailed it. I made travel arrangements. I found my old yearbooks and pored over them. I bored my wife with tales of yesteryear. I could hardly wait.

But what if nobody came? Forty years is a long time. Some of my old buddies graduated even longer ago. Did they care about the old Green-and-Gold anymore? Did they give a hoot about seeing me again, or anybody else from those long-ago days?

Fort Davis is within sight of the middle of nowhere. For nearly all of us, getting there would be a long journey. How many would take the time and spend the money to trek across the Trans-Pecos to hobnob with old geezers and coots?

One day the light on my answering machine was blinking. "This is Don Turland," the voice said. "About a hundred years ago, you and I lived in Fort Davis..."

I remembered Don as one of the school's wilder lads, a few years older than me. Class of '51, the yearbooks told me. I hadn't heard a word of him since. I didn't know he lives in Dallas. I called him back. We talked for an hour, remembering good and bad stuff that had happened back then, dropping names of kids whose young faces appeared suddenly out of the mists of memory.

"I can hardly wait!" Don said.

Would you believe 247 showed up?

Frank Higgins was ill in a Midland hospital, but Cora Newton and Johnny Granado and I proudly represented the Class of '55. I and Van Kountz ('54), one of my best buddies, remembered songs we used to sing when we were a trio with our other best buddy, Tommy Chapin ('52). We didn't try to sing them again. We wondered together where Tommy is now.

I went alone to the cemetery to visit the graves of my classmate Henry Dutchover, who died in the polio epidemic of

1951, our freshman year, and my pal Albert Fryar, who was crippled by the disease, but lived a difficult and courageous life for twenty-seven years afterward. I told them about our reunion.

Sargie Espy Jones ('19) was the oldest grad there, and her grand-nephew Joe Espy ('94) the youngest. Donna Tarvin ('61) came all the way from Ketchikan, Alaska. Tensie Granado ('58) got a certificate for having more fun than anybody. (Don Turland must have come in second.) Patricia Newton ('54) was voted "Most Looked-For" attendee. For two days we hugged and kissed and exclaimed and laughed and talked. We took snapshots and exchanged old news of friends and family, not all of it happy. Among those absent was my first passionate flame, Virginia Spencer ('54), dead of cancer, Christmas Day 1991. I hadn't known.

We gathered in the old school auditorium and decided we'll do it again at millennium's end, in 2000. I can hardly wait.

Country Cum Laude

John Hartin says to Billy Fairchild, "You gotta get that wrist so it's like it doesn't have a bone in it." Then he plays a dazzling riff on his guitar, showing Billy how.

Billy, who has driven to Levelland from over at Lubbock for his lesson, has been playing only two months, but already he's practicing "Wildwood Flower" and "Folsom Prison Blues" with his teacher. He nods, admiring, and tries again.

"Just relax," Mr. Hartin says. "Only your career is at stake." He laughs. Billy grins.

"I learned to play by the caveman method of trial and error," Mr. Hartin says later. "The only teaching methodology I had when I came here was in my head. There were no workbooks on how to play guitar or bluegrass fiddle or pedal steel."

In 1975 Mr. Hartin was living in Norfolk, Nebraska, and making good money as sales manager of a chain of music stores. It wasn't his dream job, but it was a good one. "I had played in country bands for years, and my heart was still with playing music," he says, "but we had two babies, and I didn't want to be on a bus crisscrossing the country while my kids grew up."

Then one night, "a little bitty ad" in *Country Music* magazine caught his eye. "I was suspicious that it might be a

Country Cum Laude

rip-off," he says, "but I decided to make a phone call and check it out."

Yes, he was told, South Plains College was a legitimate, fully accredited community college in Levelland, Texas. Yes, it really was looking for a professional country guitar picker to join its faculty.

Mr. Hartin caught a plane for Lubbock, where he was met at the airport by Nathan Tubb, the academic dean, who had placed the ad.

Dean Tubb—a second cousin of the great country singer Ernest Tubb—had noticed that enrollment in the traditional music program at South Plains was declining. He had set about finding out why. The students told him they still liked music, all right, they were just tired of the same old band and choir and orchestra stuff they had studied in high school. The music that really interested them was being played by the likes of Joe Ely, Asleep at the Wheel, and Waylon Jennings.

So, reasoned Dean Tubb, why not offer the kids a course of study that appreciated, perpetuated, and promoted the true musical heritage of West Texas?

By the end of his day with Dean Tubb, Mr. Hartin had decided to take a 60 percent pay cut, move to Levelland (the most accurately named town in Texas, with the possible exception of Plainview), and start building the world's only college degree program in country music.

"I had one guitar, one music stand, an amplifier, and a microphone set up in a corner of the women's gymnasium," he says. "That first semester, I had seven students."

More than twenty years later, South Plains College's associate degree program in country and bluegrass music is still unique. "It's the only one in the world," says the school's president, Gary McDaniel. "I've never heard of anything even close."

Now the Creative Arts Department, as Mr. Hartin's program has come to be called, has twenty-six teachers and seven

185

Part II—Texas, Our Texas: Some People and Places

hundred fifty students learning all the skills needed to work in any aspect of the country, bluegrass, or popular music business. And they learn in a multimillion-dollar building full of state-of-the-art recording and video equipment, where professional performing conditions are so perfect that South Plains grads won't be buffaloed by the fancy facilities they might encounter later in Nashville, Branson, Las Vegas, or Disney World.

Many students are enrolled in courses in sound and video technology, the skills needed by recording and video production companies in Nashville and other commercial music centers—skills that can be learned at a number of technical schools and colleges about the country. But one hundred forty-nine of the students are at South Plains to study pickin' and singin', with a major in banjo and a minor in fiddle or some such combination, aiming for an associate of arts degree in country and/or bluegrass music.

Another goodly number are older folk—many of them retired from nonmusical careers—who have had a long hankering to pay the dobro or the pedal steel and now have time to learn. Some come to South Plains for private lessons and ensemble classes just for the heck of it. Some hope eventually to take their newly learned skills on the circuit of folk and bluegrass festivals around the country.

"We've had former airline pilots, a former counselor at the University of Alaska, a former Pentagon cartographer, the former head of the printing division at *The New York Times*, and all kinds of business executives," Mr. Hartin says. "One of Joe Carr's students is a retired farmer in his sixties who started fiddle with him two years ago. From nine to ten every Wednesday, he takes a lesson with Joe, and his wife takes a piano lesson with Rusty Hudelson. One of Alan Munde's banjo students is a practicing neurosurgeon from Lubbock."

Alan Munde is to the banjo what Itzhak Perlman is to the violin. He and his buddy Joe Carr, who's to the guitar what Yo-Yo Ma is to the cello, are the two main reasons would-be bluegrass pickers from all over the world find their way to Levelland (which, as any West Texan knows, is about thirty miles west of Lubbock, on your way to White Face).

"We've had them from everywhere—France, Germany, South Korea, Japan, Australia, Argentina," Mr. Munde says. "This year, I have a student from Denmark and one from Canada."

Both Lisa Fredericson, the Dane, and Shannon Berge, the Canadian, are fiddlers in Mr. Munde's bluegrass ensemble class, practicing a traditional song with several other students.

In the gravel yard, with a number for my name,
Making little rocks out of big rocks all day,
Oh, the work is mighty hard in the gravel yard...

Although they've played together only since the beginning of the semester, and the experience and skill of the players vary widely, the group sounds almost good enough to perform in public.

"They say that what you learn here in two years would take about ten years if you were by yourself on your own," says Ms. Berge, who is in her second semester.

Ippy Greer, a forty-eight-year-old artist who lives in Lubbock, says he signed up after hearing Mr. Munde perform over his local public radio station. "I already played the guitar, and I wanted to play the mandolin," he says. "Eventually, I want to take up the fiddle, too. To be able to come to a place where you have access to guys who play on the level that Alan and Joe do is just fantastic."

Mr. Munde, who grew up in Norman, Oklahoma, spent about fifteen years with Country Gazette, a national touring bluegrass group that recorded several albums. Mr. Carr, who's from Dallas, toured with a group for a while, too. Both have a lot of Nashville experience as well. Sometime in the early eighties, Country Gazette came to South Plains for a concert and workshop. Mr. Hartin was impressed with their teaching skills. In 1984, after Mr. Carr tired of the road, left Country

Part II—Texas, Our Texas: Some People and Places

Gazette, and moved back to Dallas, Mr. Hartin hired him on the faculty. Mr. Munde joined him two years later. On weekends and vacations, they still make recordings and play gigs together.

"We get to tour for nicer situations than we used to when we were slugging it out on the road two hundred days a year," Mr. Carr says. "Now we're on the road about thirty days a year, and they're real nice gigs. You fly over there, you fly back. Years ago, it was get in the van and drive thirty-six hours and play and get back in the van and drive another twenty-four."

While Mr. Munde's bluegrass class practices its prison song, Mr. Carr is next door, teaching his Western swing class a few new licks to the Bob Wills classic "Home in San Antone." Next door to them, Rusty Hudelson's gospel group is practicing "This Old House," and next to them, a rock 'n' roll group is grinding.

"I love teaching," says Mr. Munde. "I love the idea of sharing what I've learned. Most people who want to play the banjo or the guitar are left to their own devices. They just wander around their community and hope to bump into people who know how to do what they want to learn. Here I have a chance to take these kids and say, 'Here's a lot of information people have shared with me over the years and stuff I figured out on my own. Here's the skinny on how this banjo works.' It's sort of passing on the torch, sharing what I've gathered in my life, hoping it has value."

Students typically are in two or three ensemble classes during a semester and take private lessons in two or more instruments. They can join several of sixteen bands, from bluegrass to jazz to rock 'n' roll, although they must audition for the more prestigious ones. The Touring Ensemble travels about West Texas performing for schools, clubs, and conventions and is considered one of the school's best recruiting tools. The TV Ensemble and the Thursday Night Live Band perform shows regularly on local cable, with other students handling the soundboard, the video cameras, and the lighting.

"The potential audience for our shows is just this town," says Mr. Carr. "But still, the red light on that camera goes on and everybody gets nervous. It's a real-life experience, and yet there's a safety net. If you're really bad and things don't go well, you don't have to worry about your reputation being ruined forever."

Even students with years of performing experience find that they can learn a lot at South Plains. Dena Skelly of Lewisville, whose professional name is "just Dena," she says, sings with her partner, Butch Rawlins, every weekend at clubs and oprys around the Dallas-Fort Worth area. The Metroplex Country Music Association named her female entertainer of the year. "But there are so many things I didn't know," she says. "A lot of musicians just don't really know a lot about music. They'll go to an opry and say they want to sing a certain song, and the band will ask, 'In what key?' and they'll say, 'I don't know.'"

So she flies out to Lubbock every Monday morning, lives in an RV in town, showers every morning in the RV park's bathhouse, and studies electric bass with John Reid and voice and keyboard with Mr. Hudelson until Thursday, when she flies back to Dallas and goes to work. "I keep Southwest Airlines in business," she says. "But this school is worth it. It's the only place I can get what I really need. All I want to learn is country music and how to play it and how to sing it and what it takes to get a record deal and what it takes to make a living. I want to work myself to death on a tour bus, traveling all across the country."

Tommy Horton, a land surveyor from Brownwood, has been picking the bass guitar and singing since he was sixteen. "Over the past five years, I've played oprys in Stephenville, Mesquite, Grapevine, and Oklahoma City," he says. "I've played bass professionally for several bands. But I've learned a lot here, boy. I've become a smarter musician. John Hartin spent my first semester breaking me of bad habits. He has taught me to play better. Rusty Hudelson has taught me to sing better."

Mr. Horton will graduate in the spring. "I've always wanted a degree," he says. "It gives me a sense of accomplishment. It's something that can't ever be taken away from me. But I'm going to miss this place.

"School's not supposed to be fun. It's supposed to be something you look forward to getting away from. I dread this year being over. I don't want it to end."

The Death of the Burro

*T*oday it's known as FM 170 or El Camino del Rio or the River Road. In the old days, before it was paved, people called it El Muerte del Burro—The Death of the Burro.

It's still treacherous: two narrow lanes without shoulders, one blind curve after another, roller-coaster-steep hills and dips, sheer cliffs dropping to dizzyingly far canyon floors. It can be full of terror for those who don't like edges and abysses.

Its steep grades keep it still impassable for some of the wide, heavy recreational vehicles that lumber along our highways in such numbers these days. And when it rains in the mountains, flash floods sluice through its canyons and loose rocks tumble down its slopes, sometimes turning it into El Muerte de la Turista.

In 1985 *National Geographic* said it "may be the prettiest drive in all America." But "pretty" is way too tame a word for it. "Awesome" is more accurate. Or "magnificent." Or "humbling." To stand beside the River Road and look down at the Rio Grande flowing through Colorado Canyon, with not a sound but the faraway rippling of the water in all that vastness, it's easy to imagine yourself at the beginning of the world.

But I'm getting ahead of myself.

Part II—Texas, Our Texas: Some People and Places

I joined the River Road at Study Butte, its eastern terminus, having driven the eighty lonesome, empty miles southward from Alpine on State Highway 118. At Study Butte, an old quicksilver-mining ghost town with an ill-looking second growth of shacks, trailers, and a few halfhearted stores and motels, I turned westward.

FM 170 from Study Butte to Lajitas, about fifteen miles, follows the route traveled by the Comanches during the eighteenth and nineteenth centuries for their annual raids into Mexico to steal horses and cattle and to capture slaves. I drove the route in September, the month the Comanches always chose for their long trip down from the High Plains because of the bright moon, which allowed them to ride by night.

In less violent parts of the country, the brilliant September moon is called the Harvest Moon, but in Texas it has always been the dreaded Comanche Moon, a time of death and loss. Even by the light of such a moon, only an incredibly tough people would dare cross these rugged mountains on horseback at night.

A few miles before you get to Lajitas, you reach Terlingua. I arrived about sundown, the best time of day to be there.

The old mining village is famous as the site of the original world-champion chili cook-off, instigated by Texas writer and chili sachem Frank X. Tolbert back in the 1960s. Several years later, a schism occurred in the chili world, and two rival groups stage rival cook-offs in the area now, each naming its own world champion.

Chiliheads get even hotter than usual when they talk of the reasons for the split in their congregation, so that's all I'm going to say about it.

A few settlers live in Terlingua now, but the limestone ruins of the miners' huts and the humble cemetery still give it the aura of a ghost town. Standing among the rotting wooden grave markers at sundown and reflecting on the hard lives of those who lie in the rocky ground is a melancholy experience.

The Death of the Burro

But Terlingua at the hour of sunset and moonrise also offers soul-expanding views of the Chisos Mountains, Mule Ears Peaks, Cerra Castellan, and other mountains of the Big Bend National Park.

When darkness fell, I drove on westward the few miles to Lajitas, a tiny village at the shallow-water crossing where the Comanches used to enter Mexico. Smugglers of cattle, liquor, wax, guns, and drugs also have used the crossing over the years. So have Mexican bandits. During the 1910-20 Mexican Revolution, U.S. Cavalry troops were stationed at Lajitas for a time to try to prevent bandit raids on Texas ranches.

Modern Lajitas was built in the 1970s by Walter Mischer Sr. of Houston as a tourist center and movie set. The block-long boardwalk business area that Mr. Mischer built looks more like old Dodge City than a West Texas town. Indeed, moviemakers looking for a Dodge City setting for *Gunsmoke II*, starring James Arness, chose Lajitas. *Barbarosa*, starring Willie Nelson, and *Streets of Laredo*, starring James Garner, also were shot there.

Several motels—all managed from the same office—and Lajitas' pretty good restaurant make it the best place in the Big Bend area to spend a night. Other businesses offer groceries, liquor and beer, gas, gifts, river trips, and horseback rides. Tennis courts, a golf course, a swimming pool, even an airstrip attest to Mr. Mischer's dream to make his village "the Palm Springs of Texas."

The Barton Warnock Environmental Education Center, on the eastern edge of the village, is a museum and desert garden operated by the Texas Parks and Wildlife Department.

The only remains of the old Lajitas are La Mision de Santa Maria y San Jose—a small adobe chapel built by the village's previous owner, H.W. McGuirk, in 1908—and the Lajitas Trading Post, which stands just a few yards from the river.

The weathered adobe store has been in business since the early days of the century. Citizens of Paso Lajitas, on the

Part II—Texas, Our Texas: Some People and Places

Mexican side of the Rio Grande, like to wade the river in the evening to have a few beers and some quiet conversation on the trading post's shady porch. Clay Henry Jr., a beer-drinking goat, resides in a pen attached to the front of the store. A few yards away, a Mexican operates a row-boat ferry for Paso Lajitas residents who have goods to convey across the river.

I left Lajitas an hour after dawn, the best time of day to experience the rest of El Camino del Rio, with the rising sun at your back and bathing the mountains ahead of you in light and shadow.

Just beyond the village, a highway sign told me I was entering Big Bend Ranch State Park, Texas' largest state-owned wilderness area, which is rich in mountain and river scenery, unique ecosystems, and archaeological sites. Park headquarters are well off the highway, and explorations within the park are severely restricted and closely supervised.

But, for the casual traveler, El Camino along the edge of the ranch is treasure enough. This is where the road becomes El Muerte del Burro. This is the long, narrow stretch of dizzying roller-coaster hills and dips, signs warning of floods and rockslides, and hairpin curves with God-knows-what approaching from the other side. Along this stretch, the wise traveler dares not try to drive and sightsee at the same time. Fortunately, several pullouts offer opportunities to stop and smell the sage and greasewood, watch the sun light up the peaks and canyons, and listen to the ripple of the Rio Grande over the rocks far below.

One of the most glorious views anywhere is from the top of Big Hill. (The origin of the name became more and more obvious as I drove up it.) I looked deep into Dark Canyon and the river and outward to rugged mountain ranges on both the Texas and Mexico sides of the narrow water.

A few miles upriver from Dark Canyon, another pullout offers an equally spectacular view of Colorado Canyon, another of the deep abysses the Rio Grande has carved through the rock. Colorado, about four miles long, is a popular stretch for raft trips. Many floaters continue on downstream through Dark Canyon, which makes a nine-mile day trip.

After leaving Big Bend Ranch, the road flattens and follows the now-sluggish river through the little town of Redford and on to Fort Leaton, the adobe fortress built by one of the Big Bend's first Anglo settlers, rancher and trader Ben Leaton, in 1848.

Because Mr. Leaton traded freely with the marauding Comanches and Apaches, his Mexican neighbors hated him. Some of their descendants still refuse to speak his name, referring to his old fortress simply as *el fortin*.

The state has restored the thick-walled complex and named it Fort Leaton State Historic Park.

I turned northward onto U.S. Highway 67 at Presidio, a thriving farming town across the river from Ojinaga, site of one of Pancho Villa's most important revolutionary victories. Abandoning the river, I headed toward the gentler Davis Mountains.

For beyond Presidio is desolation unimaginable to the city mind.

The Adventure of the Eccentric Sherlockians

*E*very day, Bill Beeson takes up a volume of The Sacred Writings and reads a story or two. "I've been studying them for fifty-five years," he says. "I always find new things. I never tire of them."

Don Hobbs owns editions of The Sacred Writings in thirty-four languages, "not including Braille, pig Latin, and shorthand," he says. They're part of his collection of three thousand books and four thousand newspaper and magazine articles, journals, newsletters, and other ephemera having to do with The Sacred Writings and The Master.

Jim Webb recently returned from a pilgrimage to the Reichenbach Fall in Switzerland, where a century ago The Master and his diabolical archenemy locked in a life-and-death struggle and appeared to have plunged together into the watery abyss.

And when Detective Don Casey is nosing about the city in search of skulduggery, the official Dallas Police Department business card that he gives to his contacts bears not only his name and a picture of his badge, but also, in the lower right-hand corner, a portrait of The Master.

The Master is Sherlock Holmes, of 221B Baker Street, London, the self-styled "world's first consulting detective." He's famous because of the dozens of stage plays, movies, and radio and television shows in which he has been portrayed, and especially because of the stories on which those dramas are based—the adventures recounted by Mr. Holmes' friend and sometime roommate, Dr. John H. Watson.

The British and American magazines that first published the sixty stories a century ago presented them as fiction and attributed them to a British author named A. Conan Doyle. Most of the world goes along with that. Some people, however, chuckle at such a suggestion.

"Every true Sherlockian knows that Holmes and Watson were real!" says Mr. Beeson. "And the accounts of Holmes' cases were really written by Dr. Watson! A. Conan Doyle was merely his literary agent!"

Around the globe at any given moment, thousands of Sherlockians like Mr. Beeson are poring over The Sacred Writings, analyzing them, writing scholarly papers, debating points of fact and chronology, developing Holmesian computer programs, collecting Holmesian documents and artifacts, visiting the scenes of The Master's life, as if it's all supremely important.

"Of course we're serious about it!" says Mr. Beeson. "But it's all in fun." He smiles foxily.

His friend Mr. Hobbs—a seemingly normal clinical systems analyst at Zale Lipshy University Hospital—found himself unable to appease his collecting passion through the garage sales and used-book stores he haunts and the catalogs he studies. He suspected there were Sherlockian books and papers out there that he didn't yet own. So he established the Maniac Collector, the first international Sherlockian collectors society, whose members keep in touch via the Internet.

"They're in France, Spain, India, Japan, Israel, Brazil, all the major places," he says with a chortle. "We trade Sherlockian things. I send them English-language editions of Sherlock Holmes, and they send me whatever I ask for from their countries."

Part II—Texas, Our Texas: Some People and Places

The floor-to-ceiling bookshelves in Mr. Hobbs' home groan under editions of The Sacred Writings in Bengali, Catalan, Chinese, Korean, Icelandic, Dutch, Gaelic, Finnish, French, Malaysian, German, Hebrew, Hungarian, Spanish, Italian, and Japanese, and dozens of English editions, all wrapped neatly in plastic. There are Sherlockian joke books, cookbooks, trivia books, and children's books, even school literature textbooks containing only a single Holmes story. There are shelves of "pastiches"—stories written by later authors, but with Mr. Holmes and Dr. Watson as characters—bearing such titles as *Sherlock Holmes and Dracula* and *Sherlock Holmes and Tarzan*. There are pastiches starring Mr. Holmes' brilliant enemy, Professor James Moriarty, and novelized radio plays and facsimiles of Dr. Watson's handwritten manuscripts. There are Sherlockian salt- and-pepper shakers, Christmas-tree ornaments, nutcrackers, cologne bottles, and nesting dolls.

"I love looking at it all," says Mr. Hobbs. "I love being surrounded by it. If only I could find a Vietnamese edition...."

Mr. Beeson, a retired Texas Instruments technician, also has a goal: To write one thousand verses on the events and characters of The Canon, as The Sacred Writings also are called. "Every story will be represented," he says. "I'm up to verse 328 or 330 so far."

An insomniac, he often awakes in the wee hours with a Sherlockian limerick or dactyl in his head. He jots it down and refines it later at his computer.

'Fore a fire to protect me from winter chills,
I dreamt of The Canon's familiar thrills:
Had a fine time except
Before waking, I stepped
On the tail of the Hound of the Baskervilles.

He first picked up The Sacred Writings when he was eleven, he says, and has seldom ignored them for a day since. "I want to pay back something," he says. "I want to contribute to the Sherlockian literature."

The Adventure of the Eccentric Sherlockians

> As he grappled with doomed Moriarty,
> Holmes remarked, at their Reichenbach party,
> "I'll use my baritsu
> So the waterfall gits you,
> You wicked old villainous smarty!"

Detective Casey, on the other hand, is a latecomer to the Sherlockian world. "Prior to the late 1980s," he says, "my knowledge of Sherlock Holmes probably was that of most normal people." But during nine trips to England to study the investigative techniques of Scotland Yard, he caught the Sherlockian bug. He visited the Holmes museum on Baker Street and the London set where English actor Jeremy Brett filmed forty-one of the tales for television. He wound up a collector of nineteenth-century British nightsticks, police capes, lanterns, and handcuffs, and a student of The Canon.

"I became interested in Sherlock through his connection with the Metropolitan Police in London," he says. "For me, Holmes came along at the right time in history. He didn't have to fool with automobiles and telephones and radios and computers. Nineteenth-century England has a romantic appeal to me. The hansom cabs, the clop of horses' hooves on the cobblestones, gaslight glowing through the fog, hearing Big Ben strike every quarter of the hour...."

During the Christmas season, Detective Casey dresses in the uniform of a London bobby of Queen Victoria's day and patrols Dickens on the Strand in Galveston, the city's yuletide extravaganza.

Sherlockian though he be, he admits that, as a police officer, his sympathies lie with Inspector Lestrade and the other Scotland Yard detectives who often are made to look foolish by Mr. Holmes' unorthodox solutions to cases.

In the story called "The Speckled Band," for instance, Dr. Watson is amazed by "the rapid deductions, as swift as intuitions, and yet always founded on a logical basis, with which he unraveled the problems which were submitted to him."

Part II—Texas, Our Texas: Some People and Places

"Holmes does make intuitive leaps," Detective Casey concedes. "But he doesn't have to do the hard, grinding, nitty-gritty investigative work that Lestrade and the other Scotland Yard men must do. They weren't very well trained, of course. Britain didn't have any formal training for police detectives until 1907. Holmes takes a leap forward in investigative technique, but he's able to do it because he doesn't have the restrictions on him that Lestrade has.

"Besides," Detective Casey mutters unhappily, "in a number of the stories Holmes does some illegal things. And he lets a few bad guys go. Lestrade couldn't do that."

Jim Webb, an international business strategist who consults with corporations around the world, displays the Certificate of Holmesian Studies of the Franco-Midland Hardware Company on his wall.

"I've just submitted my papers—six two-thousand-word essays and one five-thousand-word essay—for the Diploma, the next-to-last level," he says. "I hope someday to make Master, the highest level."

The Franco-Midland Hardware Company is a Sherlockian society in England, one of hundreds of such organizations around the world. Most are "scions" or affiliates, of either the Sherlock Holmes Society of London or the Baker Street Irregulars of New York, both of which held their first meeting on June 5, 1934. On that occasion, they exchanged greetings via the trans-Atlantic cable and have kept in touch with each other since.

Messrs. Beeson, Hobbs, Casey, and Webb are members of the Dallas scion of the Baker Street Irregulars, called the Crew of the Barque Lone Star.

The scion societies take their names from persons, places, or things in The Sacred Writings. The barque *Lone Star* was a sailing ship that figured in the adventure called "The Five Orange Pips."

200

The Adventure of the Eccentric Sherlockians

Mr. Beeson joined the Crew at its first meeting in 1970. He also is an invested member of the Baker Street Irregulars. In Sherlockian circles, this entitles him to place the initials "BSI" after his name.

Many Sherlockians belong to more than one society. Detective Casey is a member of the Crew and a society in Illinois called the Scotland Yarders. Mr. Webb belongs to the Crew and England's Franco-Midland Hardware Company and is an honorary member of a Japanese Sherlockian society called the Black-Headed League.

He, his wife, and two children went with the British group to the Reichenbach Fall, where Mr. Holmes and Professor Moriarty fought. "We followed the train route along which Moriarty pursued Holmes across Europe," Mr. Webb says. "On several occasions, we were required by the rules of the journey to dress in Victorian costumes, as characters in The Canon."

Like all the Sherlockian societies, the Crew of the Barque Lone Star gathers periodically to discuss The Sacred Writings, to inspect Holmesian books and artifacts that its members have acquired, to watch the old movies with Basil Rathbone as Mr. Holmes or the more recent productions starring Mr. Brett.

"Some Sherlockian societies are very scholarly," Mr. Beeson says. "Some are not. The Crew of the Barque Lone Star is not. We're very eccentric. We don't charge any dues. We don't let the super-knowledgeable types take over. We don't tolerate stinkers. Stinkers somehow just don't get notified of the meetings anymore."

"Why are we Sherlockians?" asks Mr. Hobbs rhetorically. "Why do we do the things we do? I think everybody, deep down inside, wants to be like Sherlock Holmes, to be that smart, to be able to work out problems like he did."

"I've had people sneer at me, 'Why don't you get a life?'" adds Mr. Beeson, BSI. "I have a life. There's a big, heavy-duty fantasy component to it, but it's a life." He smiles shrewdly.

Part II—Texas, Our Texas: Some People and Places

"Would you rather live in a world peopled by the likes of Sherlock Holmes and Dr. Watson, or one peopled by the likes of Adolf Hitler and Richard Nixon?"

Remembering the 761st

*J*ohnny Holmes and the other soldiers of the 761st Tank Battalion were in combat for one hundred eighty-three consecutive days in 1944 and 1945, more than any other unit fighting in Europe. They fought their way through six countries, had seventy-one tanks shot from under them and lost thirty-four of their comrades in battle. About three hundred of them—almost half their number—were wounded.

But when Mr. Holmes talks of the horrors of his war years, it isn't his memory of overseas battles that makes his voice tremble with anger and bitterness.

"I was about to get on a train at Temple to go home to Chicago on leave before we were shipped to Europe," he says. "I went into a restaurant to buy some sandwiches to take with me. I was in uniform. There were twenty or thirty people in there. I saw a few black people in the back of the restaurant near some garbage cans and a stack of Coca-Cola crates, but I didn't know why they were there. I had just walked in the front door the way I had back home."

Then the following conversation took place:

Owner: "What you want, boy?"

Soldier: "I'm not a boy. I'm a United States soldier."

Owner: "So what do you want?"

Part II—Texas, Our Texas: Some People and Places

Soldier: "I want a couple of sandwiches to go. What kind have you?"

Owner: "We've got beef, and we've got pork."

Soldier: "Give me one of each, please."

Owner: "All right. But you've got to go around to the back door to get them."

Soldier: "Back there where the garbage cans are? I don't want them then."

Owner: "Well, then, get the hell out of here, nigger."

"As he said that," Mr. Holmes remembers, "every white person in the place grabbed their knives and their forks and raised up like they were coming after me. I backed up to the door and said, 'I'm going.' I hadn't had anything to eat in fourteen hours, and I never got a bite from Temple, Texas, to St. Louis, Missouri. It was damn near two days."

Mr. Holmes and his comrades in the 761st were black soldiers in a segregated U.S. Army. They had just finished their training at Camp Hood (now Fort Hood) in the segregated South. Mr. Holmes' encounter with the restaurant owner wasn't the first racial insult they had suffered while wearing the uniform of their country, nor would it be the last. Many officers in their own army had considered them unworthy of full participation in the war, and only at the urging of first lady Eleanor Roosevelt were they sent to Europe as combat soldiers. Even after they had proved themselves on the battlefield, their deeds would go unnoticed and under-rewarded.

But now, on a hot summer day fifty years later, six members of the battalion had returned to the scene of their most bitter memories to be honored at last for their courage and valor. They had been invited back to Fort Hood by Beverly Taylor, a much younger army veteran who lives in nearby Copperas Cove. She's spearheading an effort to raise between $500,000 and $800,000 in private funds to erect a monument to the men of the 761st. The work is being designed by Eddie Dixon, the sculptor from Lubbock who created the famous monument to the Buffalo Soldiers—black U.S. cavalrymen who helped tame the Western frontier—that now stands at Fort Leavenworth, Kansas.

Mr. Dixon says his design probably will feature a bronze sculpture of three men—a black officer, a white officer, and a black enlisted man—on a polished granite base and will stand near the main entrance to the post where the members of the battalion suffered so much racial prejudice and hatred.

The Army has embraced the project enthusiastically. "The 761st Tank Battalion is an important unit in Army history," says Major General Frank L. Miller Jr., deputy commanding general of III Corps and Fort Hood and the post's senior black officer. "The experience of the 761st as the first all-black unit to see combat in World War II marks a significant milestone in the development of American society. Since the 761st Tank Battalion called Fort Hood its home for a significant part of the time it spent preparing to go overseas, we think it is very appropriate that a monument to the unit is erected at this installation. It will preserve an important part of the history of the Army and Fort Hood."

When the 761st Tank Battalion Planning Committee, headed by Ms. Taylor, sponsored a dinner at the post to help raise funds for the monument, Mr. Holmes and Lawrence Bailey came from Chicago, R.T. Williams and Leonard Rucker from Kansas City, and E.G. McConnell from St. Albans, N.Y., to join another old comrade, James Williams of Killeen—one of only two 761st veterans who live in Texas—for a day of reminiscence and celebration.

Ms. Taylor, who served ten years in the Army, became interested in the battalion a few years earlier when she and her husband, who's also an Army veteran, were watching a TV documentary about black people who served in World War II. "I had never heard anything about that before," she says. Her curiosity piqued, she decided to try to find out more. "I went to the 1st Cavalry and 2nd Armored Division Museum at Fort Hood and found absolutely no evidence that there was any

Part II—Texas, Our Texas: Some People and Places

black participation in World War II. I went to the Fort Hood library and found such a small number of books that mentioned black people in the war that it was almost embarrassing. But I found out that there were twenty-two or so black units in combat."

Because the 761st had battled so long and had compiled such a distinguished record, she decided to focus her research on that unit. It became her passion. "I got real angry when I started," she says, "then I got sad. But beyond those emotions I always ended up being proud. I got angry because I felt cheated out of my education. Every story I had ever heard about black people seemed to be tainted with tales of slavery, and I knew that blacks had contributed more to this country than just being slaves. Then I got sad because I realized that these guys were treated horribly, despite the fact that they were wearing the uniform and were prepared to fight and die for their beloved America. And the majority of historians just chose not to include their accomplishments in their books. But I feel a very strong pride because these guys never gave up, despite all the odds, despite the acts of racism and segregation that were directed at them on a daily basis, both on and off the post."

The 761st had been in training for a year at Fort Knox, Kentucky, and Camp Claiborne, Louisiana, before it was transferred to Camp Hood in September 1943. There, for almost another year, they played the role of the enemy in the training exercises of tank destroyer units. The trouble was, the 761st was so good at its business that the tank destroyers seldom could "destroy" them.

"We were really professionals because we had trained so long," says Mr. McConnell. "Many of our leisure hours we spent down at the motor park, just drilling ourselves. Town wasn't any attraction to us because of the segregation, and that's how we whiled away the time. And we had very high morale."

The officer in charge of keeping up their morale was a young lieutenant named Jackie Robinson, who later would become the first black man to play baseball in the major leagues. As the Brooklyn Dodgers' third baseman he would earn a pedestal in the Hall of Fame.

"Jackie was my platoon leader," says Mr. Holmes. "One day, I was in Temple, and I suffered an attack of pleurisy. I could barely breathe. Jackie got on the bus to the base with me and told me to lie down on the long seat that ran along the wall of the bus, just behind the driver. Another soldier—a buddy of mine—and a white woman were the only other passengers. The driver told us to move to the back of the bus. Jackie said, 'He's where he is, and he's where he's going to stay.' The woman got off the bus. The driver called the military authorities, who told him to bring the bus to camp. When we got to camp, they had a jeep waiting to take me back to my quarters. They arrested Jackie, and they put him up for court-martial. But Colonel Bates stopped that court-martial from taking place, because they were really going to do a job on Jackie."

Instead, Lieutenant Robinson was transferred to another outfit and remained in the United States throughout the war.

Colonel Paul Bates, commander of the 761st, was one of eight white officers who had been assigned to the battalion when it was organized. A number of black officers later joined the unit, and eight of the enlisted men would receive battlefield commissions in Europe, but the colonel and six more of the original officers stayed with the 761st throughout the war. That, says Ms. Taylor, is why a white officer will be included in the memorial.

"It's important that people know that seven white officers treated these men like their own brothers or their own sons," she says. "They really stuck in there with them. And it's time to do something to open up people's eyes and minds. This isn't a black project or a Fort Hood project or a Texas project. This is a national effort to pay tribute to all our World War II veterans, regardless of their ethnic origin, but it will focus on the

Part II—Texas, Our Texas: Some People and Places

contributions of our black veterans, who have never received any real recognition, and the white men who stood with them, despite all the harassment, all the racism, all the segregation. The monument will send the message that although the armed services were segregated back then, there were white men and black men working together and getting the mission accomplished."

The armed forces were desegregated in 1948 by an executive order of President Harry Truman.

During the early years of the war, black units had been used as cooks, officers' servants, engineers, truck drivers, and in other support duties, but none had gone into combat. Despite the fact that black soldiers had served with distinction in every American war including the Revolution, and the Buffalo Soldiers had been the most highly decorated regiments on the frontier, historians say many white generals persisted in believing black men were inferior fighters.

At Fort Hood, the troopers of the 761st were treated as inferior even to the German prisoners of war who were interned there, says Mr. Holmes. "The Germans were allowed to roam the post freely, but we were not. The POWs could go to the PX, but we could not. When POWs were assigned to pick up trash and the like, they didn't have to pick it up in our area. The post commander was even going to have German POWs stand guard over black soldiers who were in the guardhouse, but we let him know that if American soldiers were going to be guarded by the enemy, he was going to have a war on his hands right here at Fort Hood."

"I had lied about my age and joined the army when I was sixteen," says Mr. McConnell. "I did it out of patriotism. But I got so disillusioned with this damn army. I had never experienced this crap, this segregation. I'm telling you, we went through hell."

Mr. McConnell says that when he found out what the army was really like, he could no longer bring himself to say

Remembering the 761st

"sir" to an officer. "But I was no fool," he says. "I always addressed them by their rank: 'Yes, captain. Yes, general.'"

Despite the superb fighting form that the 761st had achieved during its long training, the black panther on the battalion's crest and its motto—"Come Out Fighting"—seemed destined to remain only meaningless ornaments until such black leaders as A. Philip Randolph and Mary McLeod Bethune persuaded Eleanor Roosevelt to intercede with the president. If black people were deprived of the right to fight for their country, they said, they would stand little chance of achieving equality at home.

The first lady, a longtime champion of equal rights, had said earlier in the war, "The nation cannot expect colored people to feel that the United States is worth defending if the Negro continues to be treated as he is now." Her plea to President Roosevelt succeeded, and when General George Patton, commander of the 3rd Army, asked that the best tank battalion remaining in the United States be sent to join him in Europe, the 761st drew the assignment.

The battalion arrived in Europe on October 10, 1944, and entered the war at 6 A.M., November 8, at Athainville, France, fifty miles from the German border. "At that time, the average life of a tank battalion was fifteen days at most," Mr. Holmes says. "When we first went into combat, we were scheduled for elimination. We were not supposed to survive. We are blessed. We are not lucky. We are blessed that we are still here. Believe me."

In their first encounter with the enemy, the 761st recaptured three French towns from the Germans. During the next six months of continuous fighting, they rolled through Belgium, Holland, Luxembourg, Germany, and Austria. They fought in the Battle of the Bulge, were the first unit to break through the Siegfried Line, and linked up with the Soviet army in Austria.

Part II—Texas, Our Texas: Some People and Places

"It was hell," Mr. McConnell says, "but every unit that fought alongside us wanted us back. They had the highest regard for us."
"We had to be better than the whites," Mr. Holmes says. "And we were. Our record proves it."
For their valor, members of the 761st were awarded eleven Silver Stars, seventy Bronze Stars, two hundred ninety-six Purple Hearts, three Certificates of Merit, and four Unit Battle Stars. Although the battalion was recommended for a Presidential Unit Citation, the highest award that a combat unit can receive, Presidents Harry Truman and Dwight Eisenhower —the former commander of all the allied forces in Europe— never presented it. "It lay on Eisenhower's desk throughout his administration," Mr. Holmes says. "He wouldn't sign it."
But in April 1978, two hundred veterans of the 761st and their families gathered at Fort Myer, Virginia, where they were presented the Presidential Unit Citation, signed by President Jimmy Carter. In his letter to the veterans, the president praised them for their "extraordinary gallantry, courage, professionalism, and high esprit de corps," on the battlefield.
"I hope that a white person seeing the monument to the 761st will feel the same pride as a black person will," Ms. Taylor says. "Because, let's face it, all the blood shed on those battlefields was red."

The Red Menace

The Volkswagen people have brought out a new car they say is a Beetle. Yeah. Right. You betcha.

Anyone who knew a Beetle or Super Beetle back in the sixties or seventies knows this is impossible. There can be no 1990s Beetle or 2000s Beetle. The Beetle was a creature of its time. Its time is gone. It doesn't belong in the age of microchips and cellular phones. It had too much soul.

Even now, years after I last knew him, I think of the Red Menace more as a friend than as an automobile. Indeed, the word "automobile" seems too...well, mechanical...to describe him.

The Menace was a 1973 Volkswagen Super Beetle. In 1977, when I was going through the pain of divorce, I turned the family car over to my ex and had to find a replacement—a cheap one—for myself. I found the Menace listed in the newspaper classifieds, and a friend drove me to Mesquite to take a look.

The owner was a teacher who said he used the Menace only to drive back and forth to school. It may have been true. The Menace's red coat, his chrome headlight rims, door handles, and bumpers were pristine and shiny. His interior was immaculate. His mileage was low. I bonded with him at first sight and didn't haggle much over price. The owner wanted $2,000 for

211

Part II—Texas, Our Texas: Some People and Places

him, I offered $1,500, we settled for $1,800. It was the best bargain of my life.

I had never owned a VW before and didn't know that most owners of Beetles and Super Beetles felt compelled to give names to their cars and refer to them as "him" or "her." I thought I was being original, calling my car the Red Menace and designating him a male.

But I wasn't just being cute. From the first, the Menace, unlike any other machine I had ever known, seemed to have an attitude. Despite his small size, his unsleek shape, and tiny, churning engine, he seemed cocky, even aggressive. He seemed to dare the drivers of bigger, fancier cars to treat him as inferior.

And he was the perfect companion for a broke, lonely, divorced guy. He would churn along almost forever on a tank —a small tank—of gas. He required little maintenance. And during the years that I drove him, his little engine didn't require a single major repair.

His body, however, was another matter. Like many small, feisty guys, the Menace seemed to attract trouble.

During the Great New Year's Eve Ice Storm of 1978-79, for example. The Menace was sitting quietly in the driveway of my garage apartment and a tree fell on him. A guy with a chain saw had to uncover him. Miraculously, the Menace suffered only a small dent and a paint chip on his left front fender, too small to bother repairing. It was his first battle scar.

Later that winter I parked the Menace on a street during a snowstorm. I returned to discover that some idiot had skidded into him, badly denting his left rear fender and bending his rear bumper out of shape. It now extended from the Menace's body like a huge hitchhiker's thumb.

The attacker, of course, left no note under the windshield wiper. No phone number. No offer to compensate me for the Menace's injuries. And I, being broke, carried only liability insurance. So these scars, too, remained.

The Red Menace

The following spring, the newspaper where I was employed sent me out of town on an overnight assignment, and I left the Menace in the company parking lot. I returned to discover that some idiot had backed his car into the Menace's left door, leaving a deep dent the size of a washtub. Again, no note under the windshield wiper.

Maybe a month later, the Menace and I were stopped at a red light and a car containing two young men pulled up beside us. "Hey!" one of them yelled. "We'll fix those dents for you real cheap!"

I told the young men to follow me and led them to my driveway. They examined the Menace's wounds and offered to repair his body for $100. I hired them. They pulled some tools from their trunk and went to work. They hammered out the dents in the fenders and filled the big dent in the door with that gray goop that body repair shops use. The young men told me they were from Michigan and were working their way to the Gulf Coast, paying their way by picking up repair jobs like mine. They banged on the rear bumper, but couldn't get it back to its original shape. They fixed the thumb so that it didn't stick out so far, though, and knocked $15 off our agreed fee.

With the big splotch of gray goop on his left door, the Menace seemed more menacing than ever. He resembled an aging, gotch-eared tomcat or a veteran honky-tonk brawler. Driving him on the Dallas North Tollway was one of the cheap pleasures of my bleak life. The Cadillacs, the Mercedes Benzes, the BMWs fled his proximity like the saloon patrons in an old Western movie when the bad guy walks in. I felt like Jesse James, terrifying the snooty nabobs with my faithful sidekick, Red.

The following summer I had custody of my sons, ages eight and five. We loaded the Menace with everything I owned, including the only item of value, a new IBM Selectric typewriter that I had just purchased to write my new novel. We headed for Corpus Christi and Port Aransas for my boys' first

213

Part II—Texas, Our Texas: Some People and Places

experience of beaches, then west on Interstate 10 to spend the rest of the summer at my family home in Fort Davis. I would work on my book and my city-bred boys would enjoy a Tom Sawyer summer in the mountains.

All went well until we reached Fort Stockton, only eighty miles from our destination. While filling the Menace's gas tank, I noticed that a huge chunk of rubber was missing from a rear tire. The station attendant said he had no tires for sale, and, it being Sunday, the only places that sold tires were closed. He put on the spare and assured me that the boys and I surely could make eighty measly miles without more trouble.

But halfway between Fort Stockton and Balmorhea, one of the loneliest fifty-mile stretches of road in Texas, just as the sun was sinking behind the distant mountains, the other rear tire blew out.

I never felt such helpless despair. "Oh, God," I thought. "These little boys are going to have to spend the night in this tiny, overcrowded car out here in the desert. And we have nothing to eat."

At that moment, I heard a chugging in the distance. Coming over the horizon like a miracle was an ancient Mercury, as dented and scarred as the Menace himself. I waved. The Mercury pulled over and stopped.

In the front seat sat two young Mexican cowboys with turkey feathers in their hatbands. They said they were headed to El Paso, and thence home to Mexico. In the back seat were two Anglo hippies wearing shorts and T-shirts. They were hitchhiking from Fort Lauderdale to Los Angeles. All four were smoking pot and were high as kites.

I was nervous, piling my little boys and myself into that car. But as it turned out, we couldn't have been rescued by nicer fellows. They gave us a ride to a service station in Balmorhea. They waited while I phoned to ask my mother if she could come and pick us up. They said that if she couldn't, they would make a detour to Fort Davis and deliver us themselves.

214

My mother said she could come, and our rescuers chugged away, with my everlasting gratitude. The gas station owner towed the Menace into Balmorhea the next day and put four new tires on him.

During his night in the desert, anyone could have stopped, broken into him, and stolen my new typewriter and all our belongings. But no one did. They were afraid, I think. Of the Red Menace.

Later that summer, a guy in Marfa gave him a bright new red paint job, cheap.

And we lived happily ever after.

Until that midnight when the Menace and I got into trouble with the Highland Park cops and I wound up in jail and my bride of a month had to come bail me out.

But that story is better left untold.

Concordia

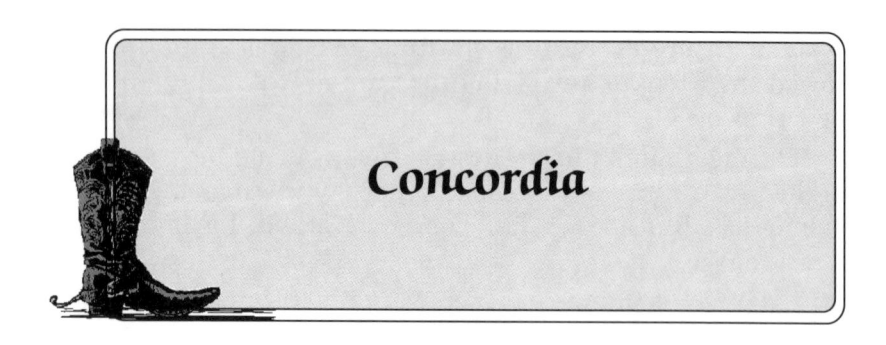

Out in the West Texas town of El Paso, they've been burying folks in Concordia Cemetery since the 1850s. In those days, the graveyard was three miles from a tiny adobe village on the north bank of the Rio Grande. Now it's only a couple of blocks from Interstate 10, El Paso's east-west expressway, and surrounded by the state's fourth-largest city.

Even whizzing by on the highway overpass, you do a double take when you glimpse Concordia, because it looks so much like what it is: a desolate frontier graveyard.

And as you enter the cemetery gate and see tumbleweeds blowing across the barren brown land and cactuses and the few dusty cedars standing among the stark, sun-hot tombstones, you almost can hear that eerie whistle of death that accompanies the Man With No Name in those early Clint Eastwood Westerns.

But El Paso isn't Hollywood. It's as down-to-earth, nononsense, and real as a city can be. The dangerous border village from which it grew was real, too. Its deadly wildness made such legendary hard-case towns as Tombstone, Dodge City, and Deadwood seem orderly and serene by comparison.

El Paso historian Leon Metz thinks the first person buried in Concordia may have been Juana Ascarate, wife of Hugh

Concordia

Stephenson. She died in 1856. "We can't find her grave," Mr. Metz says, "but it has to be here somewhere."

Many of the early graves were never marked and, because of nonchalant or nonexistent record keeping, their locations now are unknown. Others had wooden markers that weather erased or destroyed, and time and vandals have defaced many tombstones.

Even the grave of Concordia's best-known resident, notorious man-killer John Wesley Hardin, shot to death in 1895, wasn't marked until 1965, when a group of citizens got together and bought him a small stone.

Mr. Hardin was the baddest of Western bad men, tougher, meaner, and deadlier than Jesse James, Wild Bill Hickok, Billy the Kid, Wyatt Earp, or any other frontier gunman on either side of the law. Mr. Metz, who wrote his biography, says he killed between twenty and fifty men, "probably closer to fifty," but always claimed he never killed anyone who didn't need killing. One died just for snoring in Mr. Hardin's presence.

But on a hot August night while Mr. Hardin was drinking and rolling dice at the Acme Saloon, El Paso Constable John Selman walked in, shot him in the back of the head, and pumped two more slugs into him as he lay dead.

The killing had nothing to do with Constable Selman's law-enforcement duties. It was a personal matter.

Less than a year later, another sometime lawman named George Scarborough shot Constable Selman dead outside the Wigwam Saloon, only a couple of blocks from where Mr. Selman had killed Mr. Hardin.

Constable Selman was buried in Concordia, too, but nobody bothered to mark his grave. Now nobody knows where it is. Mr. Metz thinks it may be somewhere near Mr. Hardin's because that neighborhood of the cemetery was a sort of boot hill.

Indeed, just two graves from Mr. Hardin's, an outlaw named Martin M'Rose is buried. A few months before his own

217

death, Mr. Hardin had hired Mr. Scarborough and two other law officers to murder Mr. M'Rose, whose wife, Beulah, was Mr. Hardin's mistress. Mrs. M'Rose paid Mr. Hardin's funeral expenses.

So it went in old El Paso.

Although the city does almost nothing to promote its Wild-West past as a tourist attraction, hundreds of visitors manage to find their way to Mr. Hardin every year. Many leave plastic flowers, decks of cards, empty whiskey bottles, and toy six-shooters on the grave, even letters they've written to the killer.

A few years ago, a group of citizens from Gonzales County —including some Hardin descendants—decided a John Wesley Hardin grave would be a nice attraction for their own region. They made a trip to El Paso to dig him up and carry him back to the place where he had once made his home.

When they arrived at Concordia, a posse of El Paso history buffs, news media, and police met them at the grave. No shots were fired, but the Gonzales County people went away without Mr. Hardin.

Since then, El Paso has poured about three inches of concrete over the grave and re-covered it with dirt.

In other parts of Concordia, various ethnic, religious, and fraternal groups—Catholics, Protestants, Jews, African-Americans, Masons, Odd Fellows—have claimed their own sections.

Only a few steps from Mr. Hardin's grave is the Chinese Cemetery, which is walled off from the rest of Concordia because the people buried there were considered heathens and couldn't be lowered into holy ground. Many buried under the flat concrete slabs, which are inscribed in Chinese characters, were descendants of laborers who helped build the railroads through El Paso in the nineteenth century. Others came to El Paso as refugees from across the Rio Grande during the Mexican Revolution of 1910-20.

Concordia

Jake Erlich, who was billed "the tallest man in the world" when he traveled with the Barnum & Bailey Circus, is buried in his family's plot in the Jewish section. Mr. Erlich is said to have been 8-foot-7. Barnum & Bailey exhibited him alongside Tom Thumb, "the smallest man in the world."

Near the entrance to the Masonic section is a large granite vault that used to be the tomb of two prominent figures in the Mexican Revolution. One—Pascual Orozco—eventually was returned to his homeland and given the funeral of a national hero. The other—Victoriano Huerta—was reviled as a traitor to the revolution and moved to an inconspicuous grave in another El Paso cemetery.

In the beginning of the revolution, General Huerta was the highest military confidant of Mexico's revolutionary president, Francisco Madero. But in 1913 he engineered the assassination of President Madero and seized control of the government. Pancho Villa, Venustiano Carranza, and other revolutionary leaders then rebelled against General Huerta and marched on Mexico City, eventually driving the dictator into exile in Spain.

In 1914, after General Carranza became president, another disenchanted revolutionary, General Orozco, persuaded General Huerta to return to North America and lead another revolt against the government. But a few months later, U.S. troops arrested the pair at the tiny town of Newman, Texas, north of El Paso, where they were getting off a train and about to try to sneak into Mexico. They were placed under house arrest in El Paso.

General Orozco jumped bond and was killed near Sierra Blanca, Texas, by Texas Rangers and others, supposedly for resisting arrest. His body was placed in the borrowed tomb at Concordia.

A few months later, General Huerta, a heavy drinker, died of cirrhosis of the liver. He joined General Orozco in the tomb.

219

Part II—Texas, Our Texas: Some People and Places

In the 1930s, the Mexican government declared General Orozco a hero of the revolution and returned his body to his hometown for burial. But Mexico didn't want the villainous General Huerta. He remained in the tomb until his family decided to move him to nearby Evergreen Cemetery, where he still lies.

Concordia caretakers now use the warriors' old tomb as a tool shed.

The High Frontier

Joel is telling in horrible detail of his stepfather's abuse of his mother, of his choking her and beating her with a baseball bat. He tells of his mother's heroin habit and her death from AIDS, and of his stepfather sexually molesting his sister.

He tells of his stepfather catching AIDS from his mother, and his sentencing to prison, where Joel saw him last. Joel thinks he may be dead by now.

Joel wonders if he did the right thing, not killing him when he had the chance.

He's new here. His face is tight with tension. "I've never talked about this," he says. "I never really wanted to talk about it, because it hurts a lot."

"I understand where you're coming from, man," Roy replies. "I'm sure you're hurting, man. You were trying to protect your mom. But you're doing good, bringing it out here. You've got to look for the positive side of the situation."

"Just learn from this," urges another boy, Andrew. "When you get older and you get a wife and you get kids, just think back how it made you feel when he was beating up your mom. If you can just think like that, maybe you won't go down the pathway he went down."

Joel, Roy, and Andrew (the names are made up to protect the privacy of the real boys) are in one of their regular formal

Part II—Texas, Our Texas: Some People and Places

therapy sessions at High Frontier, a treatment center and school for emotionally disturbed teenagers in the remote Davis Mountains of Trans-Pecos Texas.

There are eight in the group, all boys, their chairs in a circle, filling the small, dim room. Outside the only window, the morning glares and birds are singing in the eaves.

Joel and the others are among sixty-eight adolescent boys and girls who have been sent to this place by social service and juvenile justice agencies in the big cities of Texas and several other states, and by the tribal authorities of American Indian reservations in South Carolina, Mississippi, and New Mexico.

The other boys aren't shocked by Joel's story. They've heard it all before, from one another. Despite the differences in their backgrounds, a depressing sameness runs through nearly all their stories: neglect, physical abuse, sexual molestation, abandonment, rage, drugs, violence, gangs.

Roy, who is seventeen, says he considered killing his stepfather, too. "I had easy access to guns and stuff," he says. "It would have been easy to go in there and just shoot him. I started thinking about the stuff that could happen to me. I started thinking, 'I'm still young. I could be out of prison by the time I'm forty-something.' I could have talked myself into it. I decided not to, because where would my kid be? My kid would be without a dad. This is why I'm at this place here. It has taught me to talk myself out of a lot of negative stuff. It has taught me to think ahead."

The emotional troubles of some of the teenagers at High Frontier were discovered when they ran afoul of the law, says Barry Blevins, the center's administrator. Other children were taken out of their parents' custody by social service agencies because of abuse, neglect, or abandonment.

"At times, eighty percent of the kids here have been sexually abused, some as the result of neglect," Mr. Blevins says. "There was nobody around to care for them. Almost all of them have had all parental rights taken away."

The center was founded in 1976 by a group of men and women—both professionals and lay people—who were concerned at the low success rate in the treatment of emotionally disturbed teenagers by traditional means. The agencies that send the children pay a per-day fee per child.

"I was adopted when I was a little kid," says Bill McKay, one of the founders. The now-retired Fort Worth businessman is president of the nonprofit corporation that operates High Frontier. "Sometimes, when you're adopted and you see a kid in trouble, you say, 'There but for the grace of God go I.'"

Years ago, when he was a deputy U.S. marshal, Mr. McKay escorted a Dallas boy to Houston for sentencing in federal court. "The kid had never been in trouble with the law before, but he was sentenced to thirty years in prison," he says. "As I brought him back, he lay in the back seat of my car, all chained up and handcuffed, and cried all the way back to Dallas. I could hardly hold myself together. I felt it was such a tragedy. That got me started."

After brief efforts at two other sites in the Davis Mountains, High Frontier moved in 1982 to a former youth summer camp on the Weston Ranch, four miles from Fort Davis. The corporation renovated existing buildings and added new ones until the campus now includes dormitories for up to seventy-six residents, a dining hall, gymnasium, recreation building, stables, swimming pool, art center, and administration building, most of which sit around a large, open square. Surrounded by a vast countryside rugged with rocks and brush, the campus resembles a cavalry fort of the frontier days.

Just over the hill is the High Frontier School, where the kids study with eleven special education teachers and five instructional aides. Although no local students go there, the school is accredited and operated as part of the Fort Davis Independent School District.

During its first two years, rebellious youngsters troubled High Frontier with vandalism and violence against staff members and one another. Then in 1978 the center adopted a treatment program called "Positive Peer Culture," first described in a book by the same name by Harry H. Vorrath and Larry K. Brendtro, two Midwestern specialists in the education and treatment of troubled youth.

The program is now used by a number of social service agencies, courts, and schools around the country, and the High Frontier staff has made Positive Peer Culture its bible.

"We all know that kids are strongly influenced by their peers," says Mr. Blevins. "With some kids, that peer influence is negative. It leads kids to use drugs, to join gangs, to shoot each other. What we're doing is redirecting that peer influence into something positive. We're not asking them for a superficial behavior change. We're asking for a change in values. We're trying to turn the negative energy and toughness that so many of these kids have into a positive energy and toughness."

The aim, Mr. Blevins says, is to turn the young human time bombs into productive and responsible citizens by helping each child build a system of values based on caring for himself and others.

So from the mean streets of their cities and their nightmare homes, the children are brought to High Frontier's isolated campus for a dose of fresh air, sunshine, spectacular scenery, and a chance to rebuild their lives away from the influences that were destroying them.

Each newcomer immediately becomes a member of a tiny society of eight people—all members of his own sex, from twelve to eighteen years old—with which he must learn to live. There are eight such groups, each with its own name and own cabin dormitory. The Blackfoot, the Tigua, and the Falcons are the boys; the Cheyenne, the Cherokee, the Seminole, and the Tejas are the girls. The eighth group, called Challenge, comprises both boys and girls who significantly progressed in their treatment and have emerged as leaders in helping others. Membership in Challenge is a coveted honor, carrying a number of privileges and responsibilities. Its members are expected to help the members of all the other groups. Advancement to

Challenge is only with the approval of the candidate's own group. And if he doesn't live up to the new position's responsibilities, the other members of Challenge can send him back to his old group.

Each group lives in its own cabin, two or three children to a room, with two counselors who are with them 24 hours a day. Furniture is Spartan, just a bed and a desk per child, and a little wall space for posters or photographs. A small common room provides a TV and VCR and sofas. There are no doors on the bedrooms and only swinging half doors on the bathrooms. The windows are plexiglass. Each counselor—and every other staff member—carries a walkie-talkie to call for help.

The group lives together, eats together, plays together, and goes to class and its formal group therapy sessions together. If one member wants to lend another a T-shirt or a pair of sneakers, the group must give its permission and records the transaction so there can be no misunderstanding or accusation of theft. If a member wants to leave the campus for some reason, he must have the group's permission as well as the staff's. If a member's behavior is unacceptable or someone is having a problem, the group calls a spontaneous therapy session on the spot to deal with it. These can be brief and simple, or long and full of pain and tears. "The problem may be as trivial as a kid using inappropriate language," Mr. Blevins says, "or as serious as a kid disclosing for the first time that he was a victim of sexual abuse."

The kids rise at 6 A.M., clean themselves up, clean their dorms, and go to breakfast at 7:30. After their meal, each group has an assigned chore, such as cleaning the dining room or recreation hall or picking up trash on the grounds. At 8:30 they walk over the hill to school, which, with a break for lunch, lasts until 3:30 P.M.

After school hours, one group might study horticulture, another wildlife management or auto mechanics. Another may learn how to take care of the horses that are kept on the place. Another might go to art, one of the more popular activities.

"It's one of the ways the kids go public with their thoughts and feelings," says Jim Maris, the art program director. "The verbal ability of a lot of these kids is severely limited, but they're able to express themselves through images. Art isn't a luxury here, and it's not just an activity. It's part of the treatment."

The students have exhibited their paintings at Sul Ross State University in nearby Alpine and the North Texas Health Science Atrium Gallery in Fort Worth, where CNN reported on their work. Some Davis Mountains residents now collect High Frontier art.

In their spare time, a group may play volleyball in the sandpit or basketball in the gym, ride horseback or go hiking. But whatever they do, group members must do it together and in their counselors' company.

At 9 P.M., the children go to their dorms, and at 10 the lights go off—unless somebody calls for a "group."

"The kids' treatment takes precedence over everything," Mr. Blevins says. "Sometimes an eruption of anger in a dorm can be the catalyst for the best work, if it's channeled right. Sometimes such an eruption is a last-ditch effort to resist change. A group session can last late into the night."

If a child becomes violent, the group has been taught how to restrain him safely.

Although a group may include kids of different ages and abilities, they also study together at the school. Each student progresses at his own pace under nearly tutorial attention, and every teacher is trained in the Positive Peer Culture program.

"We know how to hold a group session when the children need that help," says Ann Fitzgerald, their language arts teacher. "There can't be teaching going on if the kids have problems and are unable to get help from their group."

Mrs. Fitzgerald, who taught in New York state, New Mexico, and several West Texas public school systems before coming to High Frontier, says she enjoys her present job more than any other she has had. "There are days when I can hardly keep up with the kids, they're so excited about doing their work and wanting to move ahead. We've had some real success cases. Several of our kids have gone on to college."

Melinda Hinajos, the kids' English teacher, says that despite the violent histories of some of the children, discipline is never a problem. "People from outside think teaching here is hard because a lot of the kids have been in trouble with the law," she says. "But they have more respect for the teachers than a lot of high school students do. Here you don't have the problem of having to deal one-on-one with the kids because they take care of each other. The teacher never has to be the mean one who says you have to do this or that. The group takes care of that. They handle their own discipline."

"You can see miracles happen in these kids' minds," says Mrs. Fitzgerald. "But when some of these kids leave, I wish I could hang onto them just a little bit longer. It bothers me that so many of them have to go back to the same situations they came from. These are good kids. They just haven't had a fair chance."

How long a child stays at High Frontier is up to the social service or juvenile justice agency that sent him there. Some leave after only nine months. Some remain as long as two years. Some leave because they've turned eighteen and are no longer juveniles. Ready or not, they go into the world as adults, to college, to the military, to job training. Some of the younger ones go into foster homes. Others return to the streets and homes they knew before.

"The horrible thing is that the family is in such trouble these days," says Mr. McKay. "I'm afraid that when this generation of kids starts having kids themselves... It's just going to be a monster. Somebody's got to do something about it.

"We feel that if we've saved one Charles Manson, we've done a pretty good job."

227

Morris Neal's Handy Hamburgers

Sometimes somebody phones Morris Neal's Handy Hamburgers and asks for Morris Neal. "Is Mr. Neal there?" they say.

Benny Earl Johnson always replies: "I hope not. He's been dead for eight years."

Mr. Johnson owns Morris Neal's Handy Hamburgers now, but Mr. Neal's name is still on the sign. Mr. Johnson says he wouldn't dream of changing it. In Cleburne, "Morris Neal" means "hamburgers."

Mr. Neal built the little brick joint at 200 South Mill Street, a couple of blocks from the Johnson County Courthouse, after the original Morris Neal's Handy Hamburgers burned down. About thirty years ago.

"Morris was doing something else on the side, a little part-time deal, and he left his grill on one day while he was gone," says Mr. Johnson. "Something went amok and Morris wasn't in there to stop it."

The original place was a wooden lean-to Mr. Neal built in the late thirties or early forties against the back wall of a brick building in an alley off Main Street. It was just big enough for him and his grill. He sold his burgers out the window.

Some of his old customers believe Mr. Neal's window may have been the first burger drive-through window in the world or the United States or Texas, but Mr. Johnson shakes his head. "The way that alley worked, you was lucky if you could drive through it," he says. "You'd have to get out of your car and walk over there and get your burger. Then you could stand in the alley and eat it."

When Mr. Johnson was a boy, he and almost everybody who lived in Cleburne or came there on business showed up at Morris Neal's window from time to time. "He sold them for fifteen cents a piece or seven for a dollar," Mr. Johnson says. "I was a big old tall kid, hollow plumb to the ground. I would go over there and buy me a dollar's worth and gulp them down like somebody was trying to take them from me. I got about three bites to the burger. Old Morris, he was a good fellow. He was better at cutting corners than I am. His burger was small, about a three-inch bun, probably. He put mustard, meat, pickles, and onions on them, and that's it. You could order anything you wanted to on them, and he would say, 'Well, OK, but here's the way I'm going to fix them.' If you wanted something left off, he would leave it off, but he wouldn't put anything extra on."

Mr. Neal built his new place on land he had inherited, next to the old shed where for many years his father had bought and sold chickens, eggs, pecans, and such. The shed still stands, leaning slightly.

He put a walk-up window in the new building, too. A customer can call up and tell Mr. Johnson what he wants, pick up his burgers at the window, and take them home. "On an average day, probably forty percent of my business is done over that phone," Mr. Johnson says. Or a customer can stand outside and give an order to Mr. Johnson through the window and sit at one of the two picnic tables on the sidewalk to eat it.

But most open the door with the big SMOKING ALLOWED sign on it.

The room is the size of a master bedroom. Half of it is the kitchen, separated from the customers by a low counter. The cash register sits on a glass counter by the door, near the

Part II—Texas, Our Texas: Some People and Places

outdoor order window. Three booths line the back wall, two more stand along the wall where the door is. Two or three small shoved-together tables form a long one down the center.

The walls are covered with photographs of rodeo riders, clowns, and announcers (Mr. Johnson is an announcer himself, working most weekends at the Kowbell Indoor Rodeo in Mansfield, "Bull-Riding Capital of Texas"), and a few Western movie singers and movie actors, including Roy Rogers' old sidekick, Gabby Hayes. Mr. Hayes' picture has hung there since Morris Neal's time.

There are several hand-lettered signs:

OUR HAMBURGERS COME HIGHLY RECOMMENDED
(BY THE OWNER);

YES! TIPPING ALLOWED!;

WE WILL EXTEND CREDIT TO ANY PERSON 90
YEARS OF AGE OR OLDER. MUST BE ACCOMPANIED
BY BOTH PARENTS;

SOME DAYS I WAKE UP GROUCHY.
SOME DAYS I JUST LET HER SLEEP.

During the noon rush, customers sit anywhere they can find a seat. They spot friends and join them, joking with Mr. Johnson and with each other.

Mr. Johnson is wearing a gimme cap advertising the Flying 'O' Ranch (featuring a picture of a fully equipped bull), a blue-and-white Western shirt, jeans, and boots. A wad of keys dangles from his belt. A towel hangs from a hip pocket.

He moves like a broken-field runner, taking orders at the cash register, moving food from the grill to the tables, hopping from booth to table to booth, greeting customers, joking.

"Keep your eyes on Leo Williams, will you?" he tells a customer who's sitting with Leo in a booth.

"His eyes don't move fast enough to keep up with me," Leo says.

Mr. Johnson and Leo went to school together. "The hallowed halls of CHS," Mr. Johnson says. "I was probably one of the nicer young men that ever went across that stage."

"When was that?" Leo says. "Three or four years ago? I got a letter the other day saying I've been out of school for forty years. They're lying. They've got me mixed up with somebody else, Benny."

"Believe them. They're telling the truth."

Mr. Johnson treats strangers with the same easy camaraderie as the regulars. "If I don't know them when they come in the door, they think I do by the time they leave," he says. "Everybody, I don't care who it is, likes a little recognition."

He's sixty-one. Like most of his customers, he has lived in Cleburne nearly all his life. Just out of high school he worked for a railroad for six months, then as a sheetrock hanger, commuting to Dallas every day, then as a clerk in the Holliday & Anderson Shoe Store in Cleburne, then as an insurance salesman, commuting to Fort Worth. For thirteen years he had a construction job at the Comanche Peak nuclear power plant, commuting to Glen Rose. Then he bought Morris Neal's Handy Hamburgers.

"Mrs. Neal and one of her nieces ran it for two years after Morris died," he says. "Then she sold it to Leon Burgess. Leon kept it for about three years. In January of '95 he talked me into buying it off of him. I don't know why he picked on me. I thought he liked me."

Mr. Johnson didn't change a thing in the joint, he says. "The only thing that's changed since Morris had it is the prices."

When Mr. Neal built his bigger place, he started selling bigger burgers. Sizes range from "small" to "small double

Part II—Texas, Our Texas: Some People and Places

meat" to "jumbo" to "jumbo double meat," with or without cheese. Fries can be had, and chili. Prices range from $1 for a small hamburger to $2.65 for a jumbo double-meat cheeseburger. All burgers include lettuce, tomato, onion, pickle, and mustard and come wrapped in paper. The fries arrive in a little cardboard tray, the Cokes and Dr. Peppers in plastic cups still decorated with Christmas bells five months after the holiday.

"You're not going to go somewhere else and get a burger like we cook," Mr. Johnson says. "I buy fifty-five to fifty-eight pounds of fresh meat every morning. This meat has never been frozen. It's not in pre-made patties. I go to the H.E.B. store and they've got it ready. I bring it down here and Bettie rolls it up in balls."

Bettie is Bettie Malone. She's one of the cooks. The other is Essie Huneycutt. The cooks are one of the things Mr. Johnson didn't change when he bought the place. "These ladies are solid," he says. "Bettie has been here fourteen years. Essie has been here twenty-two."

"I've buried one boss and retired two," says Ms. Huneycutt, who wears her gimme cap backward. "I don't know what I'm going to do with this one," she says, waving her spatula at Mr. Johnson.

The first day after she went to work for Morris Neal, she nearly didn't come back, Ms. Huneycutt says. "It was awful, but I learned to like it. I fit in. We see everybody in town and everybody from miles around, from Dallas, Fort Worth, everywhere. They even come in here from Canada, California, overseas, and New Jersey. Everywhere."

Another thing Mr. Johnson never changed is the grill. It's still the one Morris Neal installed in 1970. "I really need a new grill," Mr. Johnson says. "This one's cracked. It has lots of grease underneath it. But I'm afraid to buy a new one. That grill to me is like a cast-iron skillet is with some cooks. The more you cook on it, the better it gets."

And the meat that Ms. Huneycutt and Ms. Malone flip onto the cracked grill for six and a half hours a day, six days a week, is still plain old ground beef, purveyed with no apologies for the fat.

"I don't use ground chuck or sirloin because you don't need too lean a meat for a burger," Mr. Johnson says. "It's got to have some fat on it or it'll stick to the grill. It'll be burned on the outside and still red in the middle. Ours is the cheapest ground beef they sell over the counter. I got one guy that lives up around Godley somewhere. He comes down here about once a month. He says, 'Ooh, I checked and my cholesterol is down. I've got to fill it up.'"

Mr. Johnson makes a wry face. "The funniest thing is, a lot of people come in here and order up a big old jumbo double-meat cheeseburger—that's a biiiiig burger with lots of goodies on it—and some good old greasy fries, and they'll drink a diet Coke! I don't understand that. I get plumb tickled at that."

Getting It Wrong: A Memory

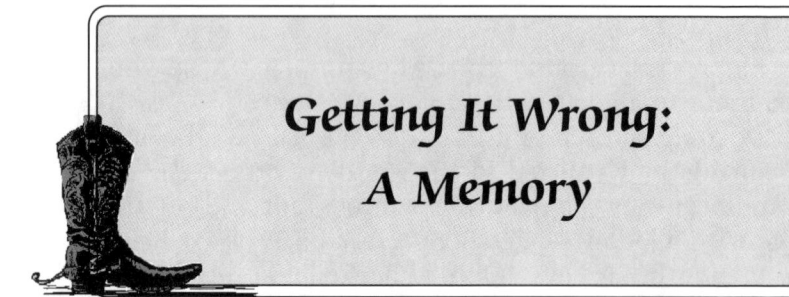

*I*f you don't do a high school ritual correctly, it will scar you for life, like a criminal record or an IRS audit. Your family, your friends, your neighbors may never know about the shadow on your past, but it sticks in your own mind always, ready to jump up and remind you what a hopeless idiot you were.

My life-tainting failure was the very first high school ritual I attempted to perform.

I was fourteen, a freshman and a second-string end on tiny Fort Davis High School's six-man football squad. At the end of our season, we were to have a team banquet in the band room. The folding tables would have white tablecloths on them. The coach of the Texas Western College Miners in faraway El Paso would come to speak to us. We were to bring dates and wear our flannel sports coats and neckties. The girls were to wear what we called "formals," which were long, stiff dresses covered with net.

I didn't have a regular girlfriend. In fact, I hadn't yet had a real date. I decided to ask Patricia to accompany me.

Patricia was a pretty brunette, a year older than I, a sophomore. She had gone steady with Billy Ray, one of our football stars, but he had graduated the previous spring and joined the Air Force. She still wrote letters to him, but he was far away. Patricia had been showing signs of restlessness. And there I was, unattached and available. I entertained secret hopes that I might replace Billy Ray.

After ratcheting up my courage for several days, I approached Patricia in the hallway between classes and managed to utter my invitation. To my surprise, she accepted!

During the few days between her acceptance and the banquet, I began to think of Patricia as my girlfriend and enjoyed many sorts of romantic fantasies. So by the time I drove my mother's car to her house to pick her up, I was pretty much in love.

Patricia was gorgeous in her stiff, netted formal. I was nervous, pinning on the carnation corsage I had brought her. She was calm, pinning the carnation boutonniere on my lapel.

For some reason that I have never known, the banquet was to begin at 5 o'clock. The early November sun still was shining brightly as I helped Patricia stuff her netting into the front seat and drove the two blocks to the school.

I proudly squired her into the band room. I could tell that the older football players were surprised and impressed that I was with her. I must have glowed, sitting at the table beside Patricia while we listened to the jokes the Texas Western coach told, ate our chicken, and accepted the little gold footballs that our coach gave us for winning district.

When the banquet ended, I helped Patricia stuff her netting back into the car, drove her home, escorted her to the door, gave her a peck on the cheek, got back into the car, and went home. The sun was just disappearing behind Blue Mountain.

"Back already?" my mother asked.

What a fool I was! I didn't know the banquet was only the first part of the end-of-football-season ritual. After the chicken and the speech and the awards, we were supposed to go home, change clothes, and take our dates to a movie in Marfa or Alpine, buy them hamburgers and Cokes afterward, then drive back to park in Limpia Canyon and pet a little.

Part II—Texas, Our Texas: Some People and Places

To add to the humiliation, someone had observed my premature dumping of the popular Patricia, and the gossip columnist noted it in the next edition of the school newspaper:

"What perky sophomore was escorted home from the football banquet in the daylight last Friday?"

None of my friends or classmates ever mentioned my hideous fiasco in my presence. Neither did Patricia. But I never mustered the nerve to ask her for another date. And to this day, whenever that awful evening pops into my consciousness, I feel my face get red.

After Patricia graduated, I didn't see her again for more than forty years. Then we both showed up at a high school reunion.

She smiled at me. I kissed her on the cheek. I wondered if she remembered. She didn't say.

Preacher Men

The Wallace children didn't have a choice. Whenever the doors of Mt. Pisgah Baptist Church were open, they were there. Archie and Ola Wallace, their parents, saw to it.

"We were at the church in the morning for Sunday school and worship, which lasted till 12:30 or 1 o'clock," says Curtis Wallace, the ninth of Archie and Ola's eleven children. "We were back at the church at five in the evening for discipleship training. Every week. It wasn't optional."

It was a long time ago. Archie and Ola are dead now. So are all their daughters, Viola and Theodora and Gladys Fay, and their eldest son, C.B.

But on the third Sunday of every March, the surviving Wallace children return to Paris, the town where they grew up. There they celebrate in song the faith they learned during all those Sundays in Mt. Pisgah's pews, and they pay tribute to the love that kept them there and eventually led all eight brothers into the ministry.

"It was just the Lord's will that we all be preachers," Curtis says. "We came up in that kind of atmosphere."

"Mother taught us, Daddy taught us. They kept us before the Lord," says his brother, Harvey.

Part II—Texas, Our Texas: Some People and Places

"It goes along with that scripture that says, 'Train up a child in the way he should go, and when he is old he will not depart from it,'" says another brother, Scotty.

So today Curtis, fifty-one, is pastor of Pilgrim Rest Baptist Church in Dallas; Harvey, fifty-four, is pastor of Mt. Rose Missionary Baptist Church in Oklahoma City; and Scotty, forty-one, is pastor of youth and young adults at Shiloh Church in Flower Mound.

Their eldest surviving brother, Willie, sixty-five, is pastor of Jehovah Missionary Baptist Church in Milo, Oklahoma; Johnny, fifty-eight, is pastor of Praise of Zion Missionary Baptist Church in Oklahoma City; Gerald, forty-nine, is pastor of Bread of Life Baptist Church Ministry in Oklahoma City; and Don, sixty, is pastor of Greater New Faith Baptist Church in Paris.

Before he died at sixty-five in 1997, C.B. was pastor of New Salem Baptist Church in Paris. The annual celebration was his idea.

"When it first got started, it was just the brothers and sisters singing," Willie says. "We called it the Wallace Children's Sing. Now it's the Wallace Family Sing, and it's growing every year."

Ola and Archie's sons and daughters had forty-six children of their own. There are many grandchildren, cousins and in-laws, and several great-grandchildren. At today's sing, some forty Wallaces are in the choir and several more are playing instruments. Still others are in the audience.

"We're just Archie and Ola Wallace's children, and we've grown to this," Wallace tells the crowd, sweeping his arm toward the choir behind him.

In its early years, the sing was held in New Salem Church, where its organizer, C.B., was the pastor. But as the family grew, so did the crowds that came to hear. "We got so big we couldn't accommodate all the people," says Don, this year's emcee. "The Lord kept blessing us, and different churches opened their doors to us. And here we are again. Our sixteenth year."

There's standing room only in the Mt. Pisgah sanctuary. Five hundred people or more, dressed in their Sunday best, have come to listen, clap their hands, sway with the choir, and shout amen. "It's just good to be here," Don tells them. "The Lord is good, isn't he? Let's give him the praise."

The Wallaces sing "Hallelujah!" They sing "It Meant It for My Good" and "I Will Let Nothing Separate Me from the Lord God" and "So Good I Just Can't Tell It All." The old stone church seems to tremble with the sound.

Don improvises on a psalm, alternating narrative and song. Curtis, who once was offered a recording contract before he entered the ministry, heeds the request of an aunt and sings "I Won't Complain." In another setting, it would be called a showstopper. The listeners rise, raise their hands in praise, shout. "Mother, Dad, C.B. and all of them are smiling on us today," Curtis tells them.

It began generations ago. The Wallace brothers' maternal grandfather was a circuit preacher, serving two or three churches at the same time. Then he moved from Longview to Paris, organized a congregation there, and stopped traveling.

"He died before I was born," Curtis says, "but I learned about him from my mother. She and I would have these fireside chats. I have his picture at home. He liked to wear black coats with tails. My father's father was a singer. My father was a deacon and a singer. His two brothers were ministers. My mother was a local church missionary."

But each of the brothers had to find his own way into his vocation, and none was short or easy. Late in the day, they gather away from the departing crowd and remember.

"It was a Saturday, June 26, 1965, was when I was called to preach," says Willie, the first after C.B. to become a pastor. "I really didn't want to preach. But my daughter got hurt that day, and she was unconscious. I went home, I never shall

Part II—Texas, Our Texas: Some People and Places

forget, and laid with my head in the West, and I prayed to the Lord: 'Lord, if this is my calling, let my child know me in the morning.' So I went back to the hospital the next morning. A nurse was standing beside my daughter, and she said, 'Evelyn, who is this?' And Evelyn said, 'That's my dad.' I started preaching in the hospital that day."

Curtis, on the other hand, knew when he was seven that he was going to be a minister. "I knew there was a calling on my life to preach," he says. "I knew for sure at thirteen. There wasn't any doubt about it. I don't know how I knew. Something just happened."

But years passed before he responded to his call. He graduated from Paul Quinn College. He worked as a manager for Westinghouse in Paris. He sang in clubs and was offered a recording contract and a trip to New York to make a demo.

"I didn't want to preach," he says, "but I couldn't get it out of my mind. Finally, I said, 'If this is what you want me to do, Lord, then I'm ready.' I was twenty-five at the time."

His first pastorate was at Mt. Pisgah, the church where he had grown up. His father was one of the deacons. "He was a good deacon," Curtis says. "He would come into the sanctuary with the other deacons, and I would look at him, and he would be crying. I don't know if he was proud or happy, but he cried a lot."

Harvey was thirty-four years old and a captain in the Oklahoma City Fire Department when he heeded the call. "Years earlier, I had heard God's voice," he says. "It was not an audible voice, but I felt him talking to me. He told me to pick up the Bible and turn to I Timothy, the second chapter and the seventh verse: '...I am ordained a preacher and an apostle,...a teacher of the Gentiles in faith and verity.' That verse told me to go preach. My oldest brother, C.B., who has gone on now, he had said to me, 'You know, when you pray, you talk to God. But when you read his Word, he talks to you.' I didn't obey at that time, but he wouldn't let me rest until I gave in. It was 1971, right here in Mt. Pisgah Church. My sister Viola, who has now gone on, was singing 'The Lord Will Make a Way Somehow' when the Lord touched me."

"You just can't be satisfied until you accept the call," says Johnny. "I did some drinking, trying to fill a void in my life, but eventually it all went back to the way I was raised up. I had to go back to the old root, and I had to say, 'Yes, Lord.' After I gave in, I felt light. I felt like a feather."

"I had a continuous burning desire to preach the word," says Don. "In 1975 the Lord brought all of that to push. It was on a Wednesday night. The Lord said, 'I called you when you were thirteen years old, and now it's time to do it.' I was forty-four. I surrendered to preach the gospel of Jesus Christ. I've been doing it ever since, and it has been a blessing."

"My situation was totally different," says Scotty, the youngest. "I didn't know at nine, I didn't know at ten. As a matter of fact, I didn't want to be a preacher from what I saw going on in the churches. I thought they were all hypocrites. But in 1987 I was out on the disco floor, dancing to 'You Can Ring My Bell,' and all of a sudden I get a vision of the Lord saying, 'I'm ringing my bell for you.' Then I became uncomfortable living the lifestyle I was living. The Lord impressed upon me that, imperfect as it is, the Body of Christ is all we've got. He said he was calling me to do his work. So I said, 'Yes, Lord.' You can't be peaceful until you do what you're called to do. Well, now I'm at peace."

Gerald was minister of music and Sunday school superintendent in his brother Johnny's church. "I was playing the organ and the piano and directing the choir and teaching the songs," he says. "I thought that was all I was going to do. But the Lord had more in store for me. He began to work in me. He let me know that I had to preach the gospel."

"So much prayer has gone into this family," Willie had told the crowd during the sing. "It's got to be prayer."

Near sundown, after two and a half hours of music and praise, Harvey had risen to lead the final petition:

Part II—Texas, Our Texas: Some People and Places

"Thank you, Lord, for the preachers whom you called out of the world, fixed them up, and sent them back into the world. Thank you, Lord, for the Wallaces. And thank you for everybody that's connected with the Wallaces. Hallelujah! Amen!"

"You all go home praying for us for another year," Willie then told the departing crowd.

And all the people said, "Amen!"

Rattler Roundup

A herpetophobe's meanest nightmare: hundreds of Western diamondback rattlesnakes, all coiled, poised to strike, their rattles blurred in motion, sending their unified, whirring warning.

Among them stands a man in a red Jaycees vest and black cowboy hat, nursing a pinch of snuff between cheek and gum. He's holding a serpent aloft with bare hands, displaying its fangs to a bunch of tots sitting on their daddies' shoulders around the wall of the pit, while the snake's comrades strike and strike at his booted ankles.

In our crowded calendar of small-town doings, Texans celebrate almost everything under the sun. On any given weekend, we might be throwing a fandango in honor of black-eyed peas or onions, peaches or peanuts, rice or roses, strawberries or watermelons, turkeys or mules or longhorn cows.

In Taft, they celebrate boll weevils; in Clute, mosquitoes; in Marshall, fire ants.

In Sweetwater, it's rattlesnakes.

Ever since the drought-stricken 1950s, when too many rattlesnakes were nipping at the hocks of too many cows on the ranches surrounding the town, Sweetwater has devoted the second weekend in March to what's now billed as the World's Largest Rattlesnake Roundup.

Part II—Texas, Our Texas: Some People and Places

The event sends dozens of hunters into the rugged, rolling-plains countryside to poke among the bluffs and rocks. They capture the snakes live and haul them during the festival to the Nolan County Coliseum, where they're milked of their venom, weighed and measured, and put on display for the populace to goggle at. A festival queen called Miss Snake Charmer is crowned with the traditional rhinestone tiara; the hunters who bring in the longest snake and the most pounds of live rattler are presented with cash prizes and trophies; and the Sweetwater Jaycees—the event's sponsors—pay $6 a pound for all the snakes that the hunters catch.

The Jaycees estimate that the roundup—with its ancillary chili and brisket cook-offs; its gun, knife, and coin show; its arts-and-crafts vendors' booths; its fried rattlesnake concession stand; its carnival rides; and its two dances—adds from 20,000 to 30,000 temporary residents to their town of 12,000 annually.

When the roundup is over, the Jaycees sell the collected venom for $1.50 per cubic centimeter for use in medical products and research and ship the gall bladders of the snakes butchered for the concession stand to Japan, where they will be dried, ground up into powder, and used to spike sake as a popular aphrodisiac. The Jaycees resell the live snakes to George Wills, a Farmers Branch businessman, who sends them to his processing plant in Grady. He eventually will fashion belts, wallets, purses, hatbands, earrings, and other articles from their hides, heads, and rattles to sell at his Maverick Trading Post store in Farmers Branch, at weekend festivals and shows, and through his mail-order catalog. He will sell the snakes' flesh to a meat broker, who will ship it to restaurants around the world, which will feature it on their menus as a delicacy.

Mr. Wills, whose business began as a hobby in 1965, is the biggest buyer of rattlesnakes in the United States. He goes to roundups from coast to coast, but the Sweetwater affair is still what it's advertised to be, he says—the world's largest.

Rattler Roundup

The unofficial snake hunting season begins soon after deer season ends, while the rattlers are still hibernating, and continues until about April 1, when they're coming out of their dens. "After that, they become so active you don't want to be messing with them," says Mr. Wills.

The hunters save up their catch until the roundup, then turn it in for cash and to compete for the prizes. The Jaycees estimate that 229,000 snakes have been corralled in their pits since the first roundup in 1958. Annual yields have ranged from 2,340 pounds in 1964 to 16,086 in 1985.

From time to time, animal rights activists have shown up to protest, claiming that the rattlesnake hunters are destroying the species. But despite the heavy hunting, there's no sign that the snake supply has diminished, Mr. Wills says. "Nolan County is the most hunted county in the country for snakes. Everybody who comes from Sweetwater hunts snakes. And you can see how many they still get."

Laverl Stephens, one of the Jaycees running the festival, says no protesters have shown up for several years now. "I guess they've decided it wasn't worth their time and effort," he says. "What they were saying just wasn't true. We're doing no harm here. The way these snakes are used, it's just like butchering cows. Everything in the snake is used except the intestines."

A mother rattlesnake gives birth to eight to sixteen babies per litter. When weather conditions are right, she might produce two litters in a year. So it's unlikely, the Jaycees say, that the snake population of Nolan County will ever be disastrously affected by their roundup.

"When this thing started," says Rick Wilkinson, who's manning the safety-and-handling demonstration pit at the coliseum, "the idea was to eradicate the snake. Get rid of him. But things have changed through the years. We feel like he's part of our heritage, with his own niche in the scheme of things. We don't want to see him go."

Part II—Texas, Our Texas: Some People and Places

Nor, he says, does the snake hunt upset the ecological balance among the wildlife of the region. "The mouse and rat population isn't much affected by the rattlesnake one way or the other. The owls and roadrunners take care of them. A rattlesnake can go for a whole year without eating and never eats more than four or five times a year. He's lazy. He doesn't hunt. He just lies there and waits for his meals to come to him. He might lie beside a mouse trail for three or four weeks, just waiting for something to come by that he can eat."

But the roundup's purpose isn't only to harvest a peculiar resource with which Mother Nature has seen fit to, uh, bless West Texas. It's also to raise money for the Jaycees' charity projects and provide a buzz, so to speak, for thrill-seekers. "It's a macho deal," Mr. Stephens says. "The adrenalin rush you get from hunting snakes and walking around in that pit is just unreal."

Mr. Wilkinson agrees. He has worked the safety-and-handling pit for twelve years, standing amid a score of buzzing, coiled rattlers, scooping them onto a table with a snake hook, waving an inflated balloon before them, coaxing them to strike at it, lecturing the crowd on how to avoid getting bitten. "Never pick up a rattlesnake with your bare hands," he says, while picking them up and handling them as casually as kittens.

A few snakebites have happened at the roundup through the years, he says, but they're rare. He doesn't remember one in the last ten or twelve years. He has never been bitten.

The twenty or so snakes in his pit seem unusually docile, lying coiled and rattling, but rarely striking at him. "A rattlesnake has a little bitty brain," Mr. Wilkinson says. "They know I was in this pit yesterday, and their noses are getting sore from striking at these old boots. And they know I keep coming back. After a while, they learn that they're not in any kind of danger, and they'll just put up with me. Now, you get a snake shook up and he thinks he's got a problem, well, he'll go right back to striking at me."

Rattlesnakes have fascinated Mr. Wilkinson since he did a science fair project about them in high school. "I lived close to the fellow who used to do this every year and watched him and learned from him," he says. Twelve years ago, Mr. Wilkinson climbed into the pit himself. He likes the work so much, he has done it every year since and works three other roundups every year as well. "Any man likes that adrenalin," he says. "Adrenalin is the perfect legal drug. It's the reason so many guys climb them mountains and put theirselves in a little bit of danger. The adrenalin rush. I like it."

For $60 each, dudes who drive out from the cities for a taste of life in the West Texas wilds can sign up for their chance to experience that rush. During the roundup weekend, several snake-savvy Jaycees lead caravans of paying novices into the countryside for an afternoon, teach them the rudiments of snake hunting, and try to keep them from getting hurt. The money paid to the guides goes into the Jaycee coffers.

One of the guides, Wayne Wilson, has been a hunter since 1962, when he was still in high school. "There's not much entertainment in Sweetwater to spend your money on," he says, "so we hunt snakes." He has been guiding beginners for about ten years. "A lot of people from the city just want to get out in the country and walk around," he says. "I'd say that maybe five to ten of the twenty-five or so people I take out each day are really serious and want to learn how it's done. What they're doing is paying us $60 to show them how to hunt snakes. The rest just want to be outdoors, or they're coming along to party."

About noon, his caravan of twenty vehicles stops at the foot of a rocky hill that's hyperbolically called a "mountain" in these parts. He gathers his pupils about him and shows them how to use a mirror to reflect the sun into the crannies between the rocks to reveal any serpents that may be resting there. He shows them how to spray a thin mist of gasoline into the hole to irritate the snakes and force them into the open.

He shows them how to pick up a snake with a pair of tongs and place him in a sack.

"Look for a hole where the dirt is smooth in front," he says, "where the trash has been cleared away. Sometimes there are even crawl marks at the entrance."

He issues the standard warnings about watching where you step, not poking your arm into a hole, not picking up snakes. He repeats the caveat he gave them at the coliseum before they began: There's no guarantee that they'll catch anything. Although the day is clear and the sun bright, the temperature is in the unseasonable forties this afternoon, and the snakes, if they're found, may be deep in their dens and hard to coax outside.

Some of the beginning hunters are decked out in brand new canvas snake leggings and carrying shiny new snake hooks and tongs, just purchased at the coliseum. They listen intently to Mr. Wilson's lecture. Others gaze absently about the rough countryside. One or two already are popping open beers. As Mr. Wilson concludes his brief lecture, the novice hunters and several Jaycees who have come along to help shepherd them scatter across the rocky slope of the hill like children hunting Easter eggs. They attack the hillside's holes and crevices with a will, but the mirrors reveal nothing.

Thirty minutes into the hunt, some of the hunters are sitting on the rocks sunning themselves. By 1:15 P.M., about an hour after their arrival, several are trudging down the hill for a beer and sandwich. Most don't climb the hill again, but stand about the vehicles telling snake stories they've heard. At 2 P.M. Mr. Wilson gives up on the hill and moves his flock to another a few hundred yards away. About half the hunters don't make the short hike to the new hunting ground, but stay close to the beer coolers and pose for photos with their new snake-hunting gear.

In the next hour, seven snakes are captured on the second hill, and the hunters are ready to declare victory. They troop back to the vehicles for more beer and sandwiches. Then

Mr. Wilson brings forth a wooden box he has brought along from town. It contains a large rattler. Experienced Jaycees hold the snake at each end, while the hunters take turns posing for snapshots touching it. Then the troop caravans back to Sweetwater.

"Not as many snakes as I had hoped," Mr. Wilson says, "but they got a taste of what it's like."

A total of 2,228 pounds of rattlesnake are captured during the roundup, the lowest total in the event's history. Bill Westerman of Sweetwater wins the prize money and the trophy for the most pounds delivered: 414. Bill Stinson of Colorado City wins the longest-snake contest: 73½ inches, the second longest in the history of the roundup.

As he's heading for the exit, Mr. Stinson is accosted by a TV reporter who thrusts a microphone into his face. "Where did you find such a long snake?" the reporter asks.

Mr. Stinson stares at him in disbelief. "Under a rock," he says.

Three Little Towns

Rowlett

Nanci Dominguez got really steamed when construction forced her to sit in traffic for twenty-five minutes just to go to her supermarket. When she got home, she did what a lot of people do when they get steamed. She wrote a letter to the editor.

"I have lived in Rowlett almost seventeen years. I resent the way my small town is being made into another Plano," her letter to *The Dallas Morning News* began. "Stop the building of houses and businesses. We have enough," she concluded after five paragraphs of anger and grief. "Leave us alone and move elsewhere. Find another town to spoil. You've done enough to our town already."

Now, about a year after she mailed her letter, Mrs. Dominguez sounds resigned. "People have decided that change is inevitable," she says. "They say it's like a steamroller. You go with it, or you get run over."

Inevitable or not, Rowlett certainly is changing. When Mrs. Dominguez and her family moved there, the population was 7,200. Now, less than twenty years later, it's 41,000. Its mayor, H.K. "Buddy" Wall, predicts that by the year 2006, more than 50,000 people will live in the town.

"Growth is going to happen," says Mr. Wall, who sells real estate. "I think we've managed it quite well."

Settlers first came to the area more than one hundred fifty years ago, but the tiny cotton-farming town wasn't named Rowlett until 1889, three years after the Greenville & Dallas Railroad came through. Now sprawling from northeastern Dallas County into Rockwall County, it's quickly becoming another suburban bedroom community. Developers are building houses and shopping centers identical to those they've built over the past two decades in Plano, Wylie, Frisco, and Rockwall. Jack in the Box and Dickey's Barbecue have opened for business on Rowlett Road.

"I love Rowlett, and I just hate what it's changing to," says Mrs. Dominguez. "It's losing its identity. There's no sense of community left. It's just not Rowlett anymore."

She speaks of neighbors who used to meet on narrow two-lane roads and wave to each other as they drove past; of cows that broke out of their pastures and wandered through front yards; of stopping at the old Dalrock general store and, without hassle, picking up whatever she needed for dinner; of children roaming the town without worry of gangs or drugs or crime.

"Back then," she says, "you came into Rowlett and there was a Safeway and a little old convenience store called Mr. M, and cows all over the place. And I liked it. I wish somebody would say, 'Stop. This is enough. We've got enough banks, enough gas stations, enough barbecue places and hamburger places, enough grocery stores. Let's leave Rowlett small, instead of growing it into another Garland or Plano.'"

Vernon Schrade, who has lived in Rowlett all his seventy-five years, remembers when its population was about two hundred and "Dallas was a long way off." Change isn't new to the place, he says. When he was young, the lands that Mrs.

251

Part II—Texas, Our Texas: Some People and Places

Dominguez remembers as cow pastures were cotton fields. Ginning the cotton, and the railroad that hauled it away, were the biggest business activities around. His family owned one of the gins. "Rowlett stayed agricultural until the 1960s," he says. "But around 1970, when Lake Ray Hubbard went in, it started growing big-time."

As late as the 1960s, parts of Rowlett still used cisterns for their water supply, and outdoor toilets. "It was quite a luxury when we got our water system in l954. That old water tower over there is the most precious thing in this town," he says, waving toward the steel structure, the tallest landmark in Rowlett, a couple of blocks from his office.

That also was the year Mr. Schrade opened his plumbing business in the little building on Main Street that had been the town barbershop. Near his office, in front of the tiny Rowlett Historical Society building, a collection of farm machinery—a plow, a disc, a mower, a planter, the chassis of a rotted wagon—sit rusting, relics of a vanished lifestyle.

"When they built Lake Ray Hubbard, the water covered most of the land that had been our tax base," Mr. Schrade says. "We thought we were going to be ruined. But the lake triggered a building boom and made us what we are."

That boom was interrupted by the economic bust that crippled all of Texas in the mid-1980s. Developers who already had built streets and sewer systems for new subdivisions went bankrupt. Ironically, the builders' misfortune is partly responsible for Rowlett's current building boom. The federal Resolution Trust Commission (RTC) that took over the foreclosed property later sold it cheap to new developers. "Today, the price is considerably lower in Rowlett for the same house that's being built in North Dallas," says Mr. Wall. "We're about twenty percent cheaper than Frisco or Plano."

Despite the prosperity that the building boom is bringing, Mr. Schrade and other longtime Rowlett residents fear that the concrete covering the farm land may bury the town's past as well.

"All the people who sweated blood to build this community, very few people ever think about them," he says. "The newcomers don't know anything about the heritage of the place, or care. They come in, they make a lot of changes, they pass a lot of restrictions—things that sometimes hurt us and our way of thinking. They come in, and they bring their ideas with them, and that don't suit us too good. But my parents taught me that progress has got to go on, and we have to prepare for the future and accept reality. So I learned to live with it myself, and I invite people to come on into Rowlett. People are coming in here like blackbirds now, and I can see why. I've been in a lot of directions, and I've never seen a better place to live in than Rowlett, Texas."

Meanwhile, Mrs. Dominguez is thinking of leaving as soon as her children graduate from Rowlett's new high school.

"There are places where there are still small towns and lots of space," she says. "I've even thought of going someplace like Idaho."

Granbury

One busy Sunday in 1971, a stranger walked into the Nutt House Dining Room in Granbury and introduced himself to the owner, Mary Lou Watkins. He said he wanted to talk about the old buildings on the town square.

"I was tired," Mrs. Watkins says. "I didn't want to talk to him. But Mama had always brought me up to be polite." She told the stranger she would visit with him if he would wait until closing time. He said he would and gave her his business card.

The name on the card wasn't familiar to Mrs. Watkins, but it was a famous one. The stranger was O'Neil Ford, the great architect from San Antonio. He had driven through town and had noticed the 1891 Hood County Courthouse and its clock

Part II—Texas, Our Texas: Some People and Places

tower and the Victorian business buildings around its square. He had sensed a possibility.

"After I finished my work, we sat down and talked about the buildings and which ones should be designated as historic," says Mrs. Watkins. "Finally, Mr. Ford said, 'Oh, hell. Just do the whole damn square.'

"The name O'Neil Ford didn't mean anything to me. I didn't know who that man was until much later. But he inspired me."

His visit with Mrs. Watkins changed the destiny of Granbury. Before long, what had been a declining agricultural town was reinventing itself as a popular tourist destination. And the town square is what makes it popular.

Mrs. Watkins is a member of the Nutt family, who in 1866 donated part of the land on which downtown Granbury was built. She had moved back to her hometown after years in Dallas and had opened her restaurant in the old Nutt House hotel, which her grandmother had founded. After Mr. Ford's visit, she recruited a few allies and told the city council she wanted to turn the square into a historic district. The council said, "Fine. What's that?" Three years later, after many legislative and bureaucratic hoops had been jumped through, the National Register of Historic Places listed the entire square as a historic district.

The century-old brick and limestone buildings that once housed a garage, a tractor company, a barbershop, a drugstore, and other enterprises of a farm town have been carefully restored and converted to antique shops, restaurants, bookstores, and boutiques. Many old houses have become bed-and-breakfasts. The ruin of the old Opera House, where hay had been stored, was renovated, and a repertory company of actors now performs there year round in such productions as *Driving Miss Daisy*, *Singing in the Rain*, and *Steel Magnolias*.

Almost every month, a festival of some sort is going on. In March the town celebrates the birthday of Confederate General Hiram Bronson Granbury, for whom the town was named. There's a Fourth of July parade, a Civil War reenactment in September, the Harvest Moon Festival in October, a lighted Christmas parade the day after Thanksgiving, and a candlelight tour of historic homes in December. "The reason for all those events is to give people a reason to come to Granbury," says Lisa Johnson, a city councilwoman and Visitors Center board member. "We want people to come here and feel like they're stepping back in time. We want people to feel something that they're not going to feel in Dallas and Fort Worth. And we want people to spend their money."

It works so well that tourists have become the basis of the economy in Granbury, a town that used to depend on peanuts, cattle, and cotton. Mrs. Johnson says the city collected $2.4 million in sales taxes in 1998, compared to just over $1 million in city property taxes.

And an increasing number are like Mrs. Johnson. "I came to the Fourth of July parade about fourteen years ago," she says. "After then, I worked every way I could to figure out a way to move here and make a living." Mrs. Johnson, an insurance agent, left Dallas and made Granbury her home in 1988.

Many other "newcomers" commute to the Comanche Peak nuclear power plant in nearby Glen Rose. Others make a longer commute to Fort Worth and Dallas. New subdivisions are going up, including those symbols of upscale snobbery, gated communities with security guards, just like North Dallas and Plano. "We don't mind," Mrs. Johnson says. "Granbury can grow all over, except in the historic district."

The idea that even the downtown square is an authentic throwback to some romantic Granbury past is largely an illusion, says Mary Downs, eighty-two, who owns Log Cabin Books just off the square and has known the town since she was young. "I remember coming through Granbury with my father one evening when I was a child," she says. "We stopped at a filling station on the square so my father could fill his radiator. An old hen and five chickens, very nearly frying size and all blistered and sunburned like chickens got in the hot

Part II—Texas, Our Texas: Some People and Places

summertime, came out of the dark, walked through the filling station, and disappeared down Pearl Street. That was sort of typical of the way things really used to be in Granbury."

It never was a quaint Victorian town, she says. "There were big houses, but they were big because they housed big families. Gingerbread wasn't expensive, so they would nail some of it on the front porch. Granbury was just a little country town. Now we have to constantly fight Victorian blight. People think anything that's a hundred years old is fine old Victorian. We've got more beveled glass front doors in this town than you can shake a stick at."

Keeping Granbury a real Texas town is an ongoing fight for Mrs. Watkins, who's in her eighties now, and the other preservationists—most of them women—who helped save the square.

"Every year, we get at least five people coming in here from New York, California, or Dallas who want to tell us what we ought to do with our town," says Jeannine Macon, founder of two businesses on the square and one of Mrs. Watkins' longtime allies. "They see the potential, and they want to add something to it that is entirely wrong."

"They want to make the buildings look like New Orleans," Mrs. Watkins says. "But we're not New Orleans. We never were New Orleans. And we don't want to be. We just want to be ourselves. Keeping this honest is our real struggle."

"We don't want to become a Disneyland or a Fredericksburg, either," adds Mrs. Macon.

"And we have to keep our eye on the Chamber of Commerce, which always wants to attract industry," says Mrs. Watkins. "We don't want that. We don't need it."

Almost three decades after the Granbury town square became a historic district, it's still the only one of its kind in Texas. Progress has ruined most of the others. "You can't buy old; you have to grow your own," says Mrs. Johnson. "But in most town squares in Texas, something old has been torn down and replaced with something new."

It almost happened in Granbury, back in the early seventies, when Cordova Dam was built on the Brazos River, creating Lake Granbury. The city council hired a consultant to advise what it should do with its town, now that it had a lake. He recommended that the town tear down the south side of the square, level it off, and build a park between the square and the lake.

"But in those days, there wasn't enough money here to tear anything down or build anything new," says Mrs. Watkins. "Sometimes a little poverty can be a wonderful thing."

Cranfills Gap

The city limit sign at the edge of town says the population of Cranfills Gap is two hundred sixty-nine, but it could be wrong. It's probably wrong.

"That figure is from the 1980 census," says Curt Haley, principal of the only school in town. "Cranfills Gap didn't get counted in 1990. Wires were crossed. The figures didn't get turned in to the right person. We're going to make sure we get an accurate count next year."

The count in 2000 isn't likely to be more than a handful lower or higher than it was in 1980 or might have been in 1990. But in Cranfills Gap, an individual counts for far more than in the big cities. A person's presence—or absence—is noticed.

"Every person who lives here is involved in the life of the community," says Mr. Haley. "Two or three families moving in or out make a big difference to the town."

Overall, during the past several decades, there has been more moving out of Cranfills Gap than moving in.

Part II—Texas, Our Texas: Some People and Places

Kenneth Reierson, who builds gorgeously chromed and painted custom cars and trucks for out-of-towners at his Kountry Klassics garage, remembers when the population was twice what it is now, and he's only forty-eight years old. "When I was growing up here in the sixties, you couldn't find a parking spot on Main Street," he says. "There was two or three cafes, two or three gas stations, two garages, a lumber yard, two grocery stores."

Now, at 3 o'clock on a Friday afternoon, not a car is parked on Main Street, and none is moving on the road.

"I've got the only garage and body shop in town," Mr. Reierson says. "We're down to one gas station. We've got a convenience store, but no grocery store. We've still got a bank and a hardware store, but we've lost a lot of small businesses, like the five-and-dime stores. The pool hall is gone. The domino hall is gone. Well, there's still a domino hall, but it's real small compared to what it was."

Also gone is the community newspaper, *The Gap Index,* which Mr. Reierson's parents ran.

"Cranfills Gap has just *changed*," he says.

It has changed because the countryside around it has changed. When it was founded in the nineteenth century, Cranfills Gap, like most Texas small towns, existed for the people who lived outside it. It supplied the needs of the Norwegian and German families who had settled western Bosque County and lived on small cotton farms. At its peak, around 1940, some six hundred people lived in the town and hundreds more on the farms. But as cotton wore out the land, the farmers switched to cattle. Not so many hands were needed to run the places. So as the farmers' children grew up, they moved away to find jobs in larger places.

Later, a second change began.

"In the early to mid-1970s, people around here started selling off their land," says Mr. Reierson. "A lot of big ranchers came in and bought out the small farmers and ranchers. The big ranchers don't live in Cranfills Gap. They live where they made their money. North of town, there were fifteen or twenty small farms, and one person bought them all. All those people moved off. The families are gone. The kids are gone. South of here, the same way. Pretty much all around us, the same way. Cranfills Gap has died out slowly. It hasn't done it overnight. There's nobody out in the country now to come in and spend money here, so there's nobody here to spend money with."

Larry Cox, who moved from Grand Prairie thirty years ago, says Cranfills Gap was a town of four hundred then, and had three small industries. A factory that made Western shirts employed fifteen to twenty seamstresses. It closed in the early 1980s. Another company made cinches for saddles. It employed three salespersons and ten workers in the shop, but closed in the early nineties. "The only industry we have left is Gap Tractor," says Mr. Cox. "It salvages used tractor parts—it calls them 'experienced' parts—and ships them all over the world."

For twenty years, Mr. Cox has worked for the town's biggest employer, the Cranfills Gap Independent School District. He teaches six classes a day of economics, government, and Texas, American, and world history. He also drives one of the system's three school buses at the end of the day. "It's a long day," he says. "But I'm not chopping cedar."

From time to time, he also has coached boys' basketball. "In 1989 the team I coached won district for the first time in fifty-five years," he says. "Cranfills Gap hasn't won district since."

Parents of some of the school system's one hundred fifty-or-so students work as foremen and ranch hands on the land their families used to own. Others operate the town's remaining businesses. Most of the rest work for the school.

The school is crucial. So long as it lives, the town is likely to survive, too, says Mr. Haley. "When other little communities around here—Carlton, Fairy, many others—lost their schools, the towns died, too," he says. "When the school isn't

Part II—Texas, Our Texas: Some People and Places

there, the people who are the core of the community have to go someplace else to work. That really pulls the plug on a town."

As the high-tech age and the Internet enable more people to do their work wherever they want to be, Mr. Haley hopes at least a few will make their way to Cranfills Gap.

"A couple of people have moved in here from the city and work at home in computer-related fields," he says. "I hope that's a trend. That would be great. But the majority of people here now are retirees. A lot of them grew up here, went away, and moved back after they retired. Most of the kids who graduate from Cranfills Gap move away. They want to go off and make their way in the world. They say, 'I'm getting out of this little town.' I would like to see young people say, 'I like the values here. I like the strong churches. I like the fact that the individual is important. I want to raise my family here.' I would like for there to be some job opportunity, so that if some kid made that choice, he could stay. That doesn't exist now."

La Vida del Charro

Sure, his senior prom was important. He was graduating, wasn't he? Farewell, dear alma mater, dear Fort Worth North Side High. He had done all the right things, rented the tux and the shiny new car, bought the corsage. He liked the girl he was with. He was having a good time.

But at 10 o'clock, Jose Piña bugged out.

"I was at the airport by 11," he says. "My plane left at 11:30. I was in San Antonio, ready to compete, the next morning. The prom was important, but the *charreada* was more important."

Defined simply, a *charreada* is a Mexican rodeo. Its events are similar to the events in an American rodeo, focusing on the riding and roping skills of cowboys. A Mexican rodeo cowboy is called a *charro*.

But, like most simple definitions, those are too simple. In the minds of those who compete in it, a *charreada* is much more than a series of athletic contests involving men and animals. And a *charro* is more than a rodeo contestant.

Becoming a *charro* and competing in a *charreada* are expressions of a way of life called *charrería*, peculiar to Mexico. And for many North Texas families, *charrería* is a proud expression of their Mexican-ness, whether they've been Texas citizens for

Part II—Texas, Our Texas: Some People and Places

generations or have arrived so recently that they don't yet speak English.

"*Charrería* is tradition," says Mr. Piña. "It has kept us in our roots."

As he speaks, he's standing in a remote pasture on a ranch near the small town of Kemp in Kaufman County, about thirty-five miles southeast of Dallas. He's wearing boots and spurs, pants and shirt decorated with fancy braid work, and a butterfly-shaped necktie. He's about to put on leather chaps and a wide-brimmed straw *sombrero*, also decorated with braid, that will complete the rigidly traditional costume that a *charro* is required to wear while competing in a *charreada*.

His horse's gear is as traditional as his own: a rawhide-covered Mexican saddle with a horn as big as a saucer, a rolled *sarape* tied behind it, a braided leather quirt hanging on the left side, a braided bridle with a Mexican bit.

It all must be just so.

Because of photographs of Mexican revolutionary hero Emiliano Zapata, who dressed in such costumes, and Mexican movies and TV shows starring *charro* characters, and thousands of travel posters and brochures decorated with his image, the *charro* has become a national symbol of Mexico, as his cowboy counterpart is to Texas. He's the embodiment of Mexican history and pride.

A few yards from Mr. Piña stands a makeshift arena, shaped like a keyhole, called a *lienzo*. There, for the next two days, five or six teams of *charros*, all members of the Charros Association of the Northern Zone of Texas, will compete in a practice *charreada* to prepare for the state championship competition in San Antonio.

Winners in the San Antonio event qualify for the fifteen-day Mexican national championship *charreada*, which will be in Morelia, west of Mexico City.

"All the top dogs in Mexico will be at Morelia," says Mr. Piña. He expects to be among the contestants there. At twenty-two, he has been a *charro* for seven years, and he's one of the best in North Texas.

He says he and his nineteen-year-old brother, Fidel, and their father, Jose Sr., will shut down their construction business to make the long trip together.

"Fifteen days of nothing but *charrería*," he says. "God, it's beautiful!"

✻

The beginnings of *charrería* arrived in Mexico with Spanish conqueror Hernán Cortés and the first horses on April 21, 1519. The events of *charreada* competition grew out of the skills required for working with cattle and horses on the big *haciendas* that the Spanish established.

"Ever since it was brought over from Spain, the *charro* tradition has been carried on year after year after year," says Juan De Leon, forty-nine, an investigator for the Tarrant County district attorney's office during the week, but a *charro* on weekends. "It was a tradition of the nobility. It was the way aristocrats entertained themselves."

Charrería also celebrates the close bonds of family and community. And, because of the roles *charros* have played in their history, it sustains strong patriotic feelings in Mexicans wherever they live.

"*Charrería* was in Texas way before the Pilgrims came to this country," says Mr. De Leon. "It's passed on from generation to generation."

Because aristocratic *charros* were prominent in Mexico's war of independence from Spain in the early nineteenth century, the big-hatted rider became a patriotic symbol. But it was a foreign usurper, the emperor Maximilian, who's largely responsible for the costume that *charros* still wear today.

"He saw the prosperous Mexican landlords dressed in a certain way," says Mr. De Leon. "He liked their style. He took it up and made it popular throughout Mexico."

Part II—Texas, Our Texas: Some People and Places

Maximilian's clothes were more popular than he was. In 1867, three years after the emperor Napoleon III sent him to Mexico City to establish a monarchy and bring Mexico into the French empire, rebels led by Benito Juárez overthrew and executed him. The Mexican holiday Cinco de Mayo celebrates the demise of his reign.

In the 1910 revolution against another dictator, Porfirio Díaz, *charros* again played a prominent role, especially Zapata, who before the rebellion was a famous horse trainer, *charreada* competitor, and village dandy. Because of his skill as a military leader, Zapata is still the most revered figure of *charrería*. And because of the deeds of their kind in the revolution, *charros* give a military salute to the Mexican flag at the beginning of every *charreada* as they ride into the *lienzo* to the music of the Mexican national anthem.

In Mexico, the *charros* still are considered part of the army reserve and are authorized by law to carry guns.

"Of course, in Texas, none of that applies," says Mr. De Leon.

C⋲ ★ ⋺Ↄ

According to the *Encyclopedia of Mexico,* there are about 700,000 *charros* in Mexico, Texas, California, New Mexico, and Arizona who compete in *charreadas* sanctioned by the Federación de Charros in Mexico City. Of those, not many are in North Texas. Over the past ten years, the number of *charro* teams in the area has grown from three to six, each with fifteen members or more, including wives and children. The largest is the Fort Worth team, with about thirty members. There are sixteen teams in the whole state.

The Dallas-Fort Worth area teams compete against each other in half a dozen *lienzos* built on land owned or leased by *charro* families in the area. Most of the contests are casual affairs, organized with little advance notice, almost like pickup softball games at a city park.

La Vida del Charro

Sometimes members of five or six teams participate, other times maybe only two. The *charros* show up one or two at a time, bouncing along rough ranch roads in pickups, pulling trailers loaded with horses or steers.

The *charreada* begins whenever enough people and animals are present. The Kemp competition, scheduled to begin at 10:30 A.M., doesn't get under way until 1 P.M. A number of the contestants have had trouble finding the remote pasture where the *lienzo* is. But nobody cares.

The trucks are filled with whole families. Many women and children are performers, too, in the larger *charreadas*. At the smaller competitions, the women serve as cooks and helpers for their men. They're often the only spectators, as well.

Joe Gomez, forty-seven, is the fifth generation of his family to roam the *charreada* circuit. He has followed it for more than twenty years.

"My family were into *charrería* long before we left Mexico and came to Texas," he says. "Being a *charro* is part of our pride. It's going back to the old ways. You know, like owning an old '57 Chevy gets you to thinking about the 1950s? Well, *charrería* is getting on a good horse and thinking back on what our fathers and forefathers did. For them, it was their living. For us, it's a sport. I learned it from my grandfather. Most boys learn it from their grandfathers. Their fathers are too busy to teach them, so the grandfathers do it. It's typical. Some of these families have a hard time getting the money together to buy and feed horses and buy costumes and equipment and travel. But they still try."

Juan De Leon estimates that eighty percent of the *charros* in North Texas work as ranch hands. "The rest come from all walks of life," he says, "but *charrería* is their passion. It's what they live for."

For Jose Piña Jr., the passion began when he was eleven and, like many boys his age, was pestering his father unsuccessfully for a horse. Then, when he was fifteen, he learned

Part II—Texas, Our Texas: Some People and Places

that a *charro* named Gastulo was working on a ranch owned by Mr. Gomez.

"Gastulo told my father he would teach *charrería* to me and my brother, Fidel, who was eleven," Mr. Piña says. "My dad thought it was something we would try for a while and get tired of. My dad and Gastulo agreed on a fee, and Gastulo loaned us a horse. Fidel and I went out to that ranch every day, every day, every day. Fidel and I were born in Texas. Our parents spoke English at home. When we first started with Gastulo, our Spanish was poor. But Gastulo would say, 'Hey, I don't want you speaking English around the *lienzo*.' So we had to pick up Spanish. It got us back to our roots. Since then, we haven't stopped. We built our own *lienzo* with our own hands. My dad sponsors our team. He pays for our trips. And every *charreada* we go to, our mother is there, too. We've always been a very tight family. We move as a pack, always."

The Piñas own a ranch near Alvarado where they stable their horses and practice in their own *lienzo*. They travel to *charreadas* all over the Southwest and Mexico and provide the livestock for many of the *charreadas* in North Texas. "It's our family obsession," says Mr. Piña. "No telling how many thousands of dollars a year we spend on it."

Even for families not quite as obsessed as the Piñas, *charrería* is expensive. "It's like golf," says Mr. De Leon. "Once you get into it, you spend more and more money. You've got to buy all the clothing and your saddle and horse. You've got to feed that horse and stable it and carry it in a trailer. You've got to have something to pull the trailer with."

A *charro sombrero* costs $400 to $500, chaps about $250, a saddle anywhere from $200 to $1,800. A fancy *charro* suit —pants, shirt, vest, necktie—can cost $1,000.

"It's got to be a real family thing," says Mr. De Leon. "You can't do it by yourself."

La Vida del Charro

It's hard, says Caty Ochoa. She's the *capitana* of the Fort Worth Charro Association's eight-member women's team, which competes in a precision riding event called *escaramuza*. The women perform intricate drill patterns on horseback, wearing long dresses and riding sidesaddle at a full gallop.

Mrs. Ochoa, thirty, spent her childhood on a ranch in the Mexican state of Durango, but she and her husband, Reuben, didn't become involved in *charrería* until three years ago.

"Reuben started first," she says. "Then the ladies asked me if I wanted to go with them. I said, 'Well, let me see.' Then I started riding my horse real slow. I was holding on for my life. But I'm still doing it. I love it now. We spend a lot of money on *charrería*. We have three horses to feed. We keep them in Alvarado and have to drive from Arlington every day to take care of them. It isn't easy for us. I work in a school cafeteria in Arlington. My husband is a cook at On the Border. He has worked there for seventeen years. But he's from Mexico, too, like me."

Mrs. Ochoa's nine-year-old daughter, Berenice, wears a dress identical to her mother's and rides with her in the *escaramuza*. The Ochoas' eleven-year-old son, Reuben Jr., is a miniature version of his father in *sombrero* and chaps and boots. In time, the youngest Ochoa, four-year-old Chably, will become a *charra*, too.

"Our kids were born here," Mrs. Ochoa says. "They're U.S. citizens. But they're still Mexican. So this is important to us."

267

Fort Davis Christmas

I'm worried to hear that the community Christmas service is going to be in the high school auditorium this year.

I remember how it's supposed to be:

The choirs of all the churches in Fort Davis are supposed to wear white robes and file down the aisle of the Presbyterian church at the foot of Sleeping Lion Mountain, singing "O come, O come, Emmanuel."

All the town's ministers are supposed to deliver meditations and say prayers, and the people of the town, jam-packed into the beautiful old church, are supposed to sing carols along with the choirs.

Alternating with the meditations and prayers and carols, a kid is supposed to read the verses of the Christmas story from the gospels of Matthew and Luke.

And it came to pass in those days that there went out a decree from Caesar Augustus...

As he reads, two kids dressed as Mary and Joseph are supposed to come into the chancel and kneel before a makeshift cradle.

And she brought forth her firstborn son and wrapped him in swaddling clothes and laid him in a manger...

Fort Davis Christmas

As the kid reads each part of the story, angels in bed sheets and shepherds in bathrobes and tinsel-crowned wise men are supposed to join Mary and Joseph in adoration of the Christ Child.

Then a lighted candle is supposed to be passed among the congregation, and each of us is supposed to light a candle from its flame. We're supposed to sing "Silent Night" and go out into the cold mountain moonlight, rejoicing.

That was the way the community Christmas service was in 1949, when I was twelve and stood before the congregation and read the ancient story from the King James Bible that was my grandmother's gift to me that year.

I remember the aroma of the pinon pine Christmas tree that stood in the church that evening, and the aroma of the new leather and India paper of my new Bible. I remember my nervousness as I read.

And the angel said unto them, Fear not, for behold, I bring you good tidings of great joy...

After the service, I lingered so the members of the congregation could compliment me on the way I read.

After nearly everyone was gone, I stepped onto the church porch with my Bible under my arm. The light of the full moon was gleaming on the snow-covered pasture across the street. The mesquite trees were casting shadows. A dog over toward Dolores Mountain was barking, the only sound. It was like the song we had sung:

Silent night, holy night,
All is calm, all is bright.

As the quiet, cold air touched my face, I thought, "This is the way it must have been. It must have happened on a night just like this."

Ever since, that's how a Christmas worship service is supposed to be.

Part II—Texas, Our Texas: Some People and Places

When I call to inquire about it, Lanna Duncan, who runs the Hotel Limpia with her husband, Joe, tells me the Christmas service is held at the Catholic church now, because the town is bigger and St. Joseph's is the biggest church in town.

That's all right. St. Joseph's, like First Presbyterian, is a beautiful old adobe church built back in the frontier days, a good place for the annual appearance of angels, shepherds, and wise men.

When I was growing up there in the 1940s and '50s, Fort Davis was still a tiny ranch community tucked into a mountainous corner of Far West Texas, isolated from nearly all the rest of the world.

The history of the place, with its Apaches and Buffalo Soldiers and cowboys and ranchers, was so recent that it wasn't even considered history. It was just interesting stories about things that had happened within the lifetimes of many people who were still living.

But even a place as isolated as Fort Davis isn't protected from the changes that are wrought by such phenomena as interstate highways, cable television, and computers.

People from far away have discovered the beauty of the Davis Mountains and have moved there to raise their children away from the dangers and temptations of the cities or to retire to a peaceful place.

The huge frontier ranches are being split among heirs. Some have been sold to outsiders. Some have even been cut into subdivisions. The ranches no longer are the backbone of the little town's economy. Many of the old stone buildings where ranchers and cowboys used to buy horseshoes, ropes, rifles, ammunition, groceries, and jeans now house gift shops, art galleries, and restaurants catering to the tourist trade. The old military post, which was a sheep pasture the first time I climbed a fence to play among its ruins, is a national historic site. The tourists go to Fort Davis for all the things we took for granted back then—the mountains, the history, the clean, clear air—and the visitors' pleasure and comfort have replaced the cattle trade as the reason for the town's being.

So in recent years, Christmas there has taken on the air of a festival, designed to persuade the merchants to go beyond the simple wreath in the window in the way of decorations and to entice residents of the countryside and such neighboring towns as Marfa and Alpine to come take a look and maybe leave behind a few yuletide dollars.

This year's festival is billed as a Fort Davis Western Frontier Christmas, and the list of events in the *Jeff Davis County Mountain Dispatch* indicates that at least a few people in the community have put a great deal of work into it.

There's going to be a Christmas parade, with Santa Claus arriving in a wagon, escorted by a detail of Buffalo Soldiers. The gift shops will stay open until 9 P.M. and offer refreshments. Shoppers of all ages may participate in a treasure hunt game and possibly win prizes. A Victorian tea is to be served in the Hotel Limpia lobby, and the bed-and-breakfast places that now occupy three of the town's historic houses will be open for touring. A horse-drawn wagon filled with hay will haul people around town to view the festively lighted homes and businesses. Several times during the festival weekend and the following week, Fort Davis children will perform a Christmas play called *The Best Christmas Pageant Ever* in the high school auditorium.

When I arrive on the day the festival begins, I learn to my alarm that a performance of the play also has been incorporated into the annual community Christmas service. The service will be at the high school Sunday night, I'm told, and not at St. Joseph's church as previously announced.

That doesn't seem right.

⌲ ★ ⌱

Thursday just before sundown, cars pull up along Main Street. Little children jump out and run about, yelling, excited.

Part II—Texas, Our Texas: Some People and Places

Old folks, in sweaters and jackets despite the unseasonably warm evening, set up lawn chairs along the sidewalks and sit, talking quietly.

Suddenly the sirens of the community's only fire truck and the sheriff's car scream. Fathers and mothers lift toddlers to their shoulders. "OK," they say. "Here it comes."

Sheriff Harvey Adams leads the parade, clearing traffic with his siren. He waves and waves. He's retiring at the end of the year.

Then come Santa and Mrs. Claus in the wagon. "Ho, ho, ho." Two big Clydesdales pull the Clauses along.

Cowboys, one big, one little, march behind the wagon. They're draped in Christmas lights, waving. Their lights wave with them.

Then come a trailer full of angels blowing bubbles; four Buffalo Soldiers marching; floats featuring a bare-shouldered girl in an old-fashioned bathtub full of balloons, a Victorian family sitting in their parlor, waiting for Santa's visit, waving, waving; and a pickup loaded with kids and balloons.

It's a short procession, but a boisterous one. As the fire truck brings up the end of the parade, cars and pickups fall in behind it, horns honking, loud Mexican music blasting from tape decks.

Santa and Mrs. Claus alight in front of the Colonel's Lady, a gift shop on the square, and sit in rocking chairs on the porch and take children into their laps to hear their Christmas wishes.

Two little girls, among the first to whisper into Santa's ear, afterward dance across the square, hand in hand. "That was fun!" says one.

"Think it'll do any good?" asks the other.

For an hour or more, Santa and his wife listen, until the last child jumps from his lap and runs to her mother. "Merry Christmas to you, dear!" Santa calls after her. "See you later!"

Soon the square is empty and quiet. The lights that cover the old cedar tree in the little Jeff Davis memorial garden shine all night. So does the red Christmas star high above the town on Sleeping Lion Mountain.

⁂

Saturday, the turnout for the Victorian tea and the bed-and-breakfast tour are disappointing. Everybody, it seems, is at the high school gym, where teams from Alpine, Wink, Van Horn, Presidio, Marathon, El Paso, and Juarez and the home boys and girls are playing in the seventeenth annual Fort Davis Basketball Tournament.

"We thought scheduling the festival on the same weekend as the tournament was a good idea," says Lanna Duncan, who heads up the Western Frontier Christmas this year. "We thought a lot of out-of-town people would be here. Well, they're here, but they're all at the basketball games. I guess most of the local people are at the gym, too. In Fort Davis, it's hard for anything to compete with sports. We're new at this. We're still learning."

Later, I go into the Presbyterian church to sit for a while, to remember. The greenery is in place along the deep adobe windowsills and the chancel rail. Its aroma fills the sanctuary.

Pansy Espy, who for many years decorated the church for Christmas, comes in with her daughter-in-law, Sally, to whom she has passed on that responsibility. They're here to check on the poinsettias, which seem to be either too wet or too dry.

"Remember when you all used to dress up in bathrobes with towels on your heads?" Pansy says to me. "We had a lot of plaid shepherds in those days. Remember the year we borrowed the robes from the Masonic Lodge? No? That was after your time, I guess. The pageant was so beautiful that year."

Sunday night, the high school auditorium seems big and cold and austere compared to the warm intimacy of the little church. But while the crowd gathers, a pianist and a fiddler

Part II—Texas, Our Texas: Some People and Places

play "What Child is This?" and "O Little Town of Bethlehem," and the Christmas spirit begins to move.

Malisa Hargrove and Nancy Davis and nearly forty school kids have worked for weeks on *The Best Christmas Pageant Ever*, a play based on a classic story by Barbara Robinson. It's about the efforts of a woman to put on a church Christmas pageant despite having to cast the seven Herdman children—the dirtiest, meanest, most irreverent, most feared kids in town—in all the important roles.

It's funny, and the kids seem to enjoy doing it. Between scenes, the congregation sings "The First Noel" and "Joy to the World" and all the great old carols, the ministers say their prayers, and a couple of cowboys pass their hats for an offering to help those who find themselves in Fort Davis and in trouble, as Mary and Joseph were in Bethlehem.

During the final scene, when all the children are on stage together—the angels in their bed sheets and cardboard wings, the wise men in their tinsel crowns, the shepherds in their bathrobes and towels, and Tori Prude and Tate Dillard kneeling before the manger, the most vulnerable, poignant Mary and Joseph that I've ever seen—and the Herdman delinquents and the self-righteous church people in the play all are redeemed by the wonder of Christmas...

I admit it. I choke up. I get teary-eyed.

Hey! cry the little dirty-faced Herdman angels. *Unto you a child is born! Go see him! He's in the barn!*

It's all just perfect.

Index

761st Tank Battalion, 203-210

A

Abilene Blues, 105-107
Absher, Truett, 159-160
Affirmative action, 123
Alamo, 60-64
Allamoore school, 170-175
Allison, Clay, 8
Amigo Yates, 15-16
Arnold, Bill, 126, 128
Arnold, Pat, 126-129
astronomers, 101
Austin, Stephen F., 62

B

Barrow, Buck, 141
Barrow, Clyde, 139-147
Barrow, Henry, 141-142
Barrow, Marie, 139-147
Bates, Colonel Paul, 207
Bean, Judge Roy, 13
Beeson, Bill, 195-198
Big Bend Ranch State Park, 194
Blevins, Barry, 222
Bohanan, Walter, 11
Brittingham, Bob, 45
Broken Spoke, 74
Brooks, Edna, 12
Butler, Glenn, 89

Byrd, Peck, 50

C

Carr, Joe, 186-188
Casey, Don, 196, 199-201
Cauble, Bill, 43
Centennial Exposition, 29
Charles Goodnight, 6
charreada, 262-263
charrería, 262-268
charro, 262-263
chicken dance, 148-152
Chinese Cemetery, 218
Christmas, Fort Davis, 269-275
Church of Weeping Mary, 82, 85, 87-88
Cinco do Mayo, 265
civil rights movement, 117
Clark, Dave, 102
Clayton, Lawrence, 40
Coats Saddlery, 35, 37
Comanches, 192
Conan the Barbarian, 95-96
Concordia Cemetery, 216-220
Congress of Racial Equality (CORE), 117-118, 122
court battle with New Mexico, 10
Cowboy Ramsey, 73-74
Cox, Larry, 260

Index

Craft, Jerry, 104-108
Cranfills Gap, 258-261
crew of the barque *Lone Star*, 200-201
Crockett, Davy, 64

D
Danenfelzer, David, 176-180
Daughters of the Republic of Texas, 61
de Leon, Juan, 264, 266
Dearen, Patrick, 4-5
Dixon, Eddie, 204-205
Dominguez, Nanci, 251-252
Downs, Mary, 256
Duncan, Dave, 24

E
Emo's, 75
Erlich, Jake, 219
Evans, Clay, 166-167

F
Fairchild, Billy, 184
Farmer, Dr. James Leonard, 116
Farmer, James, 115-124
Farmer, Pearl, 116
Ferguson, Miriam "Ma," 29
Ferro, Dickie Dell, 13
Fitzgerald, Ann, 227
Ford, O'Neil, 254-255
Fort Davis High School reunion, 181-183
Freedom Ride, 117
Frontier Battalion, 28

G
Garcia, Marie, 32
Gastulo, 267
Gates, John W. "Bet a Million," 19
Geissler, Heinz, 74-75
Girvin Social Club, 11-12
Gomez, Joe, 266
Gonzaullas, M.T. "Lone Wolf," 25, 30
Goodrich, Lloyd, 9-11
Graham, Don, 53-59
Granbury, 254-258
Grant, Donald M., 97
Green, Bob, 40, 46-47
Greer, Ippy, 187
Guffey, Stan, 27

H
Haley, Curt, 258
Hamill, Al, 50
Hamill, Curt, 50
Hardin, John Wesley, 217-218
Hartin, John, 184-187
Heard, Charles, 145
Hearn, Rob, 149
Higgins, Patillo, 49
High Frontier School, 223
High Frontier, 221-228
High Pockets Duncan, 71
Hinajos, Melinda, 227
Hobbs, Don, 196-198
Hockman, Brent H., 145
Hodge, Bill, 84
Holley, Mary Austin, 62
Holmes, Johnny, 201-205
Holmes, Sherlock, 196-199

Index

Horton, Tommy, 189-190
Howard, Robert E., 93-98
Huerta, Victoriano, 219-220
Huneycutt, Essie, 232-233

I

Interwoven, 42
Iraan, 12

J

J.A. Matthews Ranch Co., 45
Jackson, Joaquin, 30
Jenkins, Cherry, 86
Jersey Lilly Saloon, 14
Johnson, Benny Earl, 229-234
Johnson, Byron, 24
Johnson, Lyndon, 122-123
Jones, Elgin "Punk," 4
Jones, Mary Belle, 4
Jones, Skeet, 7
Juneteenth, 82-83

K

Karankawa Indians, 179
Kelton, Elmer, 9
Keovilay, Leck, 153, 156
King, Keesey, 172-175
King, Linda, 174-175
Krauss, J.R., 148
Ku Klux Klan, 118

L

Lajitas, 193
Lake Amistad dam, 14
Lambshead Ranch, 39-46
Lambshead, Thomas, 41
Langtry, 13
leather throne, 34
Leaton, Ben, 195
LeNeveu, Carolynne, 63-64
Lewis, Bob, 161
Limpia Creek Hat Company, 134-137
Lockhart, Nancy Ross, 84
longhorn, 15-22
Lord, Glenn, 94
Lorette, Lineaus, 77-81
Loving County, 9-10
Loving, Billie Ruth, 94
Lucas, Anthony F., 50

M

M'Rose, Martin, 217-218
Macon, Jeannine, 257
Malone, Bettie, 233
Marfa, 163-169
Maris, Jim, 226
Martin, Gregg, 146
Martin, Janice, 82-84
Matthews Land and Cattle Co., 44
Matthews, B.E., 109, 112
Matthews, Sallie Reynolds, 39, 41-42
Matthews, Watt, 39, 42-44
Maximilian, 264
McConnell, E.G., 205
McCoy, Joseph, 18
McDonald, W.J., 28
McKay, Bill, 223
Meador, Catherine, 76
medicine ball, 77-80
Mendez, Maria, 170-175

277

Index

Mentone, 9
Metz, Leon, 216-217
Middle Concho River, 6
Miller, Major General Frank L. Jr., 205
Millican, L.R., 170-171
Mills, Buster, 134-137
Mills, Stanley, 150-152
Mischer, Walter Jr., 193
Mitchell, Larry, 103
Moberley, Terry, 46
Moore, Barbara, 114
Morris Neal's Handy Hamburgers, 229-234
movies about Texas, 53-58
   Blood Simple, 57
   Bonnie and Clyde, 56
   Dancer, Texas Pop. 81, 54, 58
   Deep in the Heart of Texas, 54
   Giant, 53, 166-169
   Hope Floats, 54, 58
   Horseman, Pass By, 56
   Hud, 56
   Lone Star, 57
   Red River, 54
   Still Breathing, 54
   The Border, 57
   The Getaway, 57
   The Last Picture Show, 56
   The Searchers, 54
   The Wind, 53
   Urban Cowboy, 58
Munde, Alan, 186-188

N
Navarro, Jose Antonio, 63
Nix, Christine, 23, 32
Noelke, Fred, 76

O
Ochoa, Caty, 268
oil well derricks, 48-52
Oliver Loving, 6
Orozco, Pascual, 219-220

P
Paine, Albert Bigelow, 28
Parker, Bessie Mae, 82-84, 86
Parker, Bonnie, 139
Parker, Oliver Wendell, 13
Patterson, Paul, 6-9
Pecos Bill, 6
Pecos movies, 7
Pecos River, 3-14
Peña-Lopez, Mary Alice, 60-62
Piña, Jose, 262-263
Positive Peer Culture, 224
Powell, Gaylon, 110, 112-113
Pringle, Burl, 12
Pringle, Frankie, 12
Project Pride, 94

R
R.E. Donaho Concho Saddle Shop, 33-34
Ratcliffe, Sylvia, 148
Red Bluff, 10
Red Menace, 211-215
Redding, Gid, 8
Reierson, Kenneth, 259

Index

Rigler, Lewis, 30
River Road, 191-192
Roberts Jr., Robert Jenkins, 78-79
Robinson, Jackie, 207
Rogers, Al, 114
Rogers, Jerry, 158
Rowlett, 251-254
Rubin, Mark, 75
Ruiz, Francisco, 63

S

Sacred Harp, The, 109-114
Sacred Writings, The, 196-198, 201
saddles, 33-38
salt cedar, 10,
San Jacinto Monument, 65
Santa Anna, Antonio Lopez de, 61, 63
Schell, Patty, 152
Schoonmaker, Sandra, 99-100
Schreiner, Walter, 17
Scott, Jack, 93
Sedberry, Carl, 105-108
Seguin, Juan, 62, 65
Selman, John, 217
Shank, Keith, 100-102
Shivers, Dub, 48
Shivers, William Gilbert, 51
Schrade, Vernon, 251-253
Skelly, Dena, 189
Skinner, Elijah, 85
Skinner, Emily Ross, 84
Skinner, Minnie Ross, 86-88
Smith, David, 35
Soukhoumrath, Inpeng, 154

Southwest Texas Sacred Harp Singing Convention, 110
Spasic, Larry, 63-66
Special Force, 28
Special Rangers, 29
Spindletop, 49
State Police, 28
Stephens, Laverl, 246
Story, Rector, 33-38
Sweetwater Jaycees, 245
Sweetwater, 244

T

Taylor, Beverly, 204-205
Tejanos, 65
Terlingua, 192
Texas Emancipation Day, 83
Texas Historical Commission, 177
Texas Longhorn Breeders Association of America (TLBAA), 16, 20-21
Texas longhorn, 17
Texas National Guard, 71
Texas Ranger Hall of Fame and Museum, 25
Texas Rangers, 23-32
Texas Revolution, 60-66
Texas Star Party, 99-103
The Stars Fell on Henrietta, 48
Tolson, Melvin B., 120-121
Travis, William Barret, 61
Tubb, Nathan, 185
Tumbleweed Smith, 161-164
Tumlinson, John, 27

Index

V
Villalobos, Gerry, 24
Vongxone, Lucy, 155-156
Vongxone, Sam, 155-158
Vongxone, Sekmouk, 157

W
Waggoner, Lola, 170-174
Wall, H.K. "Buddy," 252
Wallace, Archie, 238
Wallace, C.B., 239
Wallace, Curtis, 238-241
Wallace, Don, 239, 242
Wallace, Gerald, 239, 242
Wallace, Harvey, 239, 241
Wallace, Johnny, 239, 242
Wallace, Ola, 238
Wallace, Scotty, 239, 242
Wallace, Willie, 239-240
Walser, Don, 69-76
Walser, Pat, 72
Watermelon Records, 70, 74
Watkins, Mary Lou, 254-258
Webb, Jim, 200
Webb, Walter Prescott, 29
Weeping Mary, 82-88
Weird Tales, 96

West Texas Colored League, 104, 107
Whiskey Pete's, 144
White, Major Benjamin Franklin, 111
Whitmer, Charles, 111
Wichita Falls Stars, 104-108
Wilcox, Sarah, 150
Wilcox, Walter, 150
Wilkinson, Rick, 246
Williams, James, 205
Williams, Leo, 232
Wills, George, 245-246
Wilson, Wayne, 248-250
Wichita Mountains longhorns, 20
World's Largest Rattlesnake Roundup, 244
Wurstfest, 148

Y
Yates Oil Field, 12
Yates, Fayette, 16
YO Ranch, 18
Young, Lee, 26, 31

Z
Zapata, Emiliano, 263, 265
Zavala, Lorenzo de, 63